REVIEWS OF UNITED KINGDOM STATISTICAL SOURCES

Edited by W. F. MAUNDER

Professor of Economic and Social Statistics
University of Exeter

VOLUME VIII

LAND USE

by

J. T. COPPOCK

Ogilvie Professor of Geography
University of Edinburgh

and

TOWN AND COUNTRY PLANNING

by

L. F. GEBBETT

Department of Planning and Transportation
Greater London Council

Published for

The Royal Statistical Society and
the Social Science Research Council

by

PERGAMON PRESS

OXFORD · NEW YORK · TORONTO · SYDNEY
PARIS · FRANKFURT

U.K.	Pergamon Press Ltd., Headington Hill Hall, Oxford OX3 0BW, England
U.S.A.	Pergamon Press Inc., Maxwell House, Fairview Park, Elmsford, New York 10523, U.S.A.
CANADA	Pergamon of Canada Ltd., 75 The East Mall, Toronto, Ontario, Canada
AUSTRALIA	Pergamon Press (Aust.) Pty. Ltd., 19a Boundary Street, Rushcutters Bay, N.S.W. 2011, Australia
FRANCE	Pergamon Press SARL, 24 rue des Ecoles, 75240 Paris, Cedex 05, France
FEDERAL REPUBLIC OF GERMANY	Pergamon Press GmbH, 6242 Kronberg-Taunus, Pferdstrasse 1, Federal Republic of Germany

First published 1978

British Library Cataloguing in Publication Data

Reviews of United Kingdom statistical sources.
Vol 8: Land Use and Town and Country Planning.
1. Great Britain – Statistical services.
I. Maunder, Wynne Frederick.
II. Coppock, John Terence. III. Gebbett,
Leonard Frank. IV. Royal Statistical Society.
V. Social Science Research Council,
Great Britain
314.1   HA37.G7   77–30349
ISBN 0–08–022451–2

For bibliographical purposes this volume should be cited as:
Coppock, J. T. and Gebbett, L. F., *Land Use and Town and Country Planning*,
Pergamon Press Ltd. on behalf of The Royal Statistical Society
and the Social Science Research Council, 1978

Printed Offset Litho in Great Britain by Cox & Wyman Ltd, Fakenham, Norfolk

VOLUME CONTENTS

FOREWORD

The Sources and Nature of the Statistics of the United Kingdom produced under the auspices of the Royal Statistical Society and edited by Maurice Kendall, filled a notable gap on the library shelves when it made its appearance in the early post-war years. Through a series of critical reviews by many of the foremost national experts, it constituted a valuable contemporary guide to statisticians working in many fields as well as a benchmark to which historians of the development of Statistics in this country are likely to return again and again. The Social Science Research Council and the Society were both delighted when Professor Maunder came forward with the proposal that a revised version should be produced, indicating as well his willingness to take on the onerous task of editor. The two bodies were more than happy to act as co-sponsors of the project and to help in its planning through a joint steering committee. The result, we are confident, will be adjudged a worthy successor to the previous volumes by the very much larger 'statistics public' that has come into being in the intervening years.

Dr C. S. Smith

Secretary
Social Science Research Council

February 1978

R. F. A. Hopes

Honorary Secretary
Royal Statistical Society

February 1978

MEMBERSHIP OF THE JOINT STEERING COMMITTEE
(February 1978)

Chairman: Miss S. V. Cunliffe

Representing the Royal Statistical Society:
Dr W. R. Buckland
Mr M. C. Fessey
Dr S. Rosenbaum

Representing the Social Research Council:
Mr A. S. Noble
Mrs J. Peretz
Dr W. Taylor

Secretary: Mr D. E. Allen

INTRODUCTION

The two reviews which constitute Volume VIII have a common concern in tracing statistical sources relating to that most fundamental resource, the national land surface area. The first of the pair deals with the topic in its extensive aspect and does not present more than the usual difficulties in determining the boundaries of its proper coverage. (Incidental to this issue, it may be worth commenting that the review of sources of agricultural statistics will continue from the main boundary reached by Coppock.) The second review is more specific and is essentially concerned with statistics bearing on the control of the intensive use of land by man. Since virtually any human activity requires the occupation of space, the determination of boundaries of coverage becomes particularly difficult; to mention only a few obvious instances, housing, industry, commerce, transport and recreation have immediate and competing demands which generate direct interactions with planning procedures. There is the inevitable consequence that the statistics *of* town planning tend to become statistics *about* town planning.

The obvious answer to the problem of overlapping coverage, which is a system of cross-referencing to the appropriate review where the subject at issue is dealt with in detail, is not entirely satisfactory in this instance for two main reasons. In the first place, the aspect of a particular topic which is relevant in the present context is clearly specialised and it may not coincide at all closely with the manner of its treatment as a central theme. Secondly, it is assumed that this volume will be of especial interest to workers in the general field of planning and where a specific type of user is concerned it is possible to anticipate some of the related sources which are likely to be sought. Hence, there appears to be a case for some modification of normal policy with respect to the planning review and, at least at a certain level of use, to aim at being more self-contained. However, it cannot be otherwise than that the more serious user will reach the point at some stage where it is necessary to consult other reviews in the series in order to obtain more detailed information on particular topics; the required references are noted both with respect to reviews already in print and those in process of production.

The primary aim of this series is to act as a work of reference to the sources of statistical material of all kinds, both official and unofficial. It seeks to enable the user to discover what data are available on the subject in which he is interested, from where they may be obtained, and what the limitations are to their use. Data are regarded as available not only if published in the normal printed format but also if they are likely to be released to a *bona fide* inquirer in any other form, such as duplicated documents, computer print-out or even magnetic tape. On the other hand, no reference is made to material which, even if it is known to exist, is not accessible to the general run of potential users. The distinction, of course, is not clear-cut and mention of a source is not to be regarded as a guarantee that data will be released; in particular cases it may very well be a matter for negotiation. The latter caution applies with particular force to the question of obtaining computer print-outs of custom specified tabulations. Where original records are held on magnetic tape it might appear that there should be no insuperable problem, apart from confidentiality, in obtaining any feasible analysis at a cost; in practice, it may well turn out that there are capacity restraints which override any simple cost calculation. Thus, what is requested might make demands on computer and programming resources to the extent that the routine work of the agency concerned would be intolerably affected.

The intention is that the sources for each topic should be reviewed in detail, and the brief supplied to authors has called for comprehensive coverage at the level of 'national interest'. This term does not denote any necessary restriction to statistics collected on a national basis (still less, of course, to national aggregates) but it means that sources of a purely local character, without wider interest in either content or methodology, are excluded. Indeed, the mere task of identifying all material of this latter kind is an impossibility. The interpretation of the brief has obviously involved discretion and it is up to the users of these reviews to say what unreasonable gaps become apparent to them. They are cordially invited to do so by communicating with me.

To facilitate the use of the series as a work of reference, certain features have been incorporated which are worth a word or two of explanation.

First, the text of each review is designed, in so far as varying subject matter permits, to follow a standard form of arrangement so that users may expect a similar pattern to be followed throughout the series. The starting point is a brief summary of the activity concerned and its organisation, in order to give a clear background understanding of how data are collected, what is being measured, the stage at which measurements are made, what the reporting units are, the channels through which returns are routed and where they are processed. As a further part of this introductory material, there is a discussion of the specific problems of definition and measurement to which the topic gives rise. The core sections on available sources which follow are arranged at the author's discretion—by origin, by subject subdivision, or by type of data; there is too much heterogeneity between topics to permit any imposition of complete uniformity on all authors. The final section is devoted to a discussion of general shortcomings and possibly desirable improvements. In case a contrary expectation should be aroused, it should be said that authors have not been asked to produce a comprehensive plan for the reform of statistical reporting in the whole of their field. However, a review of existing sources is a natural opportunity to make some suggestions for future policy on the collection and publication of statistics within the scope concerned.

Secondly, detailed factual information about statistical series and other data are given in a Quick Reference List (QRL). The exact nature of the entries is best seen by glancing at the list and accordingly they are not described here. Again, the ordering is not prescribed except that entries are not classified by publication source since it is presumed that it is this which is unknown to the reader. In general, the routine type of information which is given in the QRL is not repeated verbally in the text; the former, however, serves as a search route to the latter in that a reference (by section number) is shown against a QRL entry when there is a related discussion in the text.

Third, a subject index to each review acts as a more or less conventional line of enquiry on textual references; however, it is a computerised system and, for an individual review, the only peculiarity which it introduces is the possibility of easily permuting entries. Thus an entry in the index to the first review in this volume is:

East Sussex small settlements survey

which is shown also as:

Settlements survey, East Sussex small

as well as:

Survey, East Sussex small settlements

The object at this level is merely to facilitate search by giving as many variants as possible. In addition, individual review subject indexes are merged into a cumulative index which is held on magnetic tape and may possibly be used to produce a printed version from time to time if that seems desirable. Computer print-outs of the cumulative index to date are available on application to me at the Department of Economics, University of Exeter. In addition, selective searches of this index may be made by the input of key-words; the result is a print-out of all entries in which the key-word appears in the initial position in the subject index of any review. Like the cumulative index itself, this is a facility which may be of increasing help as the number of reviews in print grows.

Fourth, each review contains two listings of publications. The QRL key gives full details of the publications shown as sources and text references to them are made in the form [QRL serial number]; this list is confined essentially to data publications. The other listing is a general bibliography of works discussing wider aspects; text references in this case are made in the form [B serial number].

Finally, an attempt is made to reproduce the more important returns or forms used in data collection so that it may be seen what tabulations it is possible to make as well as helping to clarify the basis of those actually available. Unfortunately, there are severe practical limitations on the number of such forms that it is possible to append to a review and authors perforce have to be highly selective.

If all or any of these features succeed in their intention of increasing the value of the series in its basic function as a work of reference it will be gratifying; the extent to which the purpose is achieved, however, will be difficult to assess without 'feedback' from the readership. Users, therefore, will be rendering an essential service if they will send me a note of specific instances where, in consulting a review, they have failed to find the information sought.

As editor, I must express my very grateful thanks to all the members of the Joint Steering Committee of the Royal Statistical Society and the Social Science Research Council. It would be unfair to saddle them with any responsibility for shortcomings in execution but they have directed the overall strategy with as admirable a mixture of guidance and forbearance as any editor of such a series could desire. Especial thanks are due to the Secretary of the Committee who is an unfailing source of help even when sorely pressed by the more urgent demands of his other offices.

The authors join me in thanking all those who gave up their time to attend the seminar held to discuss the first drafts of their reviews and which contributed materially to improving the final versions. The subject index entries for both reviews were compiled by Mrs Marion Reed, and Mrs Juliet Horwood has been responsible for many other aspects of the work. Our thanks go also to Mrs Gill Skinner, of the Social Studies Data Processing Unit at the University of Exeter, who has written the computer programs for the production of the subject indexes. Finally, we also wish to record our appreciation of the permission granted to us by the Controller of Her Majesty's Stationery Office to reproduce Crown copyright material.

University of Exeter   W. F. MAUNDER
February
   1978

14: LAND USE

J. T. Coppock

University of Edinburgh

REFERENCE DATE OF SOURCES REVIEWED

This review is believed to represent the position, broadly speaking, as it obtained in July 1974. Later revisions have been inserted up to the proof-reading stage October 1977 taking account, as far as possible, of any major changes in the situation.

INDEX TO INITIALS USED IN THE TEXT

CSO	Central Statistical Office
DAFS	Department of Agriculture and Fisheries for Scotland
DANI	Department of Agriculture for Northern Ireland
DOE	Department of the Environment
FC	Forestry Commission
HWMOT	High Water Mark of Ordinary Tides
HWMST	High Water Mark of Spring Tides
MAF	Ministry of Agriculture and Fisheries
MAFF	Ministry of Agriculture, Fisheries and Food
NCC	Nature Conservancy Council
ptp	per thousand population
SDD	Scottish Development Department
SSSI	Site of Special Scientific Interest

CONTENTS OF REVIEW 14

5

CHAPTER 1

INTRODUCTION

Despite the fact that all human activities require some portion of the earth's surface for their performance, there are very few statistics regularly and systematically collected about the way in which it is used. Such a situation is characteristic of both developing and developed countries, even those such as the United Kingdom which have been long settled and where most land is used and land-use planning has long been accepted and practised. There are, it is true, many statistics which appear to serve this end, but most of these are obtained incidentally as a by-product of the collection of statistics for some other purpose and consequently have deficiencies when employed to describe how the land is used which would not be tolerated if this was their prime justification. The approach to be adopted in this discussion of land-use statistics will therefore differ from that adopted in previous contributions in this series, in that some attention will first be paid to the nature of land use and to the desirable characteristics of land-use statistics, and that the main discussion of the sources of material will stress the inadequacy of many of them. In one sense, these criticisms are unfair in that the deficiencies of these sources as land-use records do not necessarily affect their validity for the purposes for which they are primarily collected; moreover, most statistics have improved in accuracy and consistency over the years. Nevertheless, they have been misunderstood in the past and have been asked to serve purposes for which they were not intended; it is therefore important that their limitations be understood. Attention will also be directed to sources which are publicly available for the whole of the United Kingdom or substantial parts of it; the wealth of information in private hands or available to a particular local authority will not be discussed [B 5, 41] although the total amount of such information may well be larger than that for the United Kingdom as a whole or for its constituent countries.

Though regrettable, the present situation is understandable. The pattern of land use is extremely complex and, while the activities, whether economic or otherwise, which are the concern of individual ministries and agencies all have a land-using aspect, its importance, both in objective terms and as perceived by those responsible for policy relating to it, varies greatly; for example, land use appears to play a much less prominent role in the thinking of officials of the Department of Education and Science (despite the significance of educational land in the composition of the urban area) than in that of officials of the Ministry of Agriculture, Fisheries and Food. The Department of the Environment, the Department of Housing, Local Government and Development (formerly Ministry of Health and Local Government) in Northern Ireland and the Scottish Development Department clearly have considerable interest in land use in connection with their duties and powers in land-use planning; but, in practice at least, land-use planning has not been equally concerned with all land uses, but rather with those land-use changes which are statutorily subject to planning control. Furthermore, the three departments are not line departments with direct responsibilities for collecting data, which is undertaken on a piecemeal basis by local planning authorities. Indeed, there has been only one successful and complete attempt to collect data on the use of land for the whole of the United Kingdom, the first Land Utilisation Survey of Great Britain, undertaken in the 1930s under the direction of Professor Dudley Stamp, and its counterpart for Northern Ireland, which was under the direction of Mr. A. H. Hill, the results of which were published in *The Land of Britain—its Use and Misuse* [QRL 11] and *Land Use in Northern Ireland* [B 48].

CHAPTER 2

THE NATURE OF LAND USE

2.1. Collection and classification of statistics

Many of the problems of securing adequate statistics on the use of land spring from the multiplicity of responsibilities (or, in some instances, from the absence of any body with such responsibilities) and also from ambiguities over what is meant by land use. A working party of the Department of the Environment, the Scottish Development Department and the local planning authorities has struggled manfully with these difficulties in attempting to devise a National Land-use Classification and has not been able to reach unanimous agreement [B 81]. The consensus of opinion was that land use should be defined by activity and that classifications should not be confused by considerations of appearance, ownership or other aspects not directly related to activities; but, while the intention is praiseworthy and there would probably be general agreement that activity was *the* distinguishing characteristic, it cannot so readily be divorced from other considerations. It is implicit in the concept of land use that there should be decision-makers and units of decision-making, and these will generally be property units of some kind. The working party recommended that the fundamental unit for the collection of data on land use in urban areas should be the hereditament (or rateable subject in Scotland), though in rural areas it proposed that the fundamental unit should be the parcel as shown on the Ordnance Survey maps; it also recommended that both hereditament and parcel should be subdivided where they contained two or more activities. In practice, most land-use statistics or other statistics which serve this purpose are collected from decision-making units—estates, farms, factories, firms and the like—and little is known, at least to those who collect the data, about activities within the component parcels. Even in a planning context, where detailed information is often required G. C. Dickinson and M. G. Shaw have argued that land use is best defined in terms of the main activity within a functional unit [B 116]. At present, no universally accepted definition of land use can be given, and practices vary with different government departments and agencies.

2.2. Requirements of Land-use Statistics ✓

There is also much confusion about land-use terminology, and this affects both the nature and the interpretation of statistics bearing on the use of land. In the first place, a great deal depends on the scale at which the information is required. Although all activities require some space, these requirements differ greatly; at most operational scales there are activities which can be considered to occupy points, e.g., the emission of micro-waves carrying telephone messages from a radio mast, others which, for all practical purposes, can be considered linear, e.g., the transport of North Sea gas along pipe lines, while others have areal characteristics (though flows of information, men and materials between the component areas may play an important part in such activities). Yet, even where land requirements are small their significance, as expressed in land values, may be considerable; a square foot of land in the City of London may command a higher rent than an acre in the Highlands. Location and activity are thus closely connected, and information on both is essential for good land-use statistics. It also follows that there can be no universal prescription of desirable scales or detail, for these will depend largely on the purpose for which the information is required. Thus, where information is needed for urban redevelopment, it may be essential to have detailed information on the alloca-tion of land uses, and to subdivide an area classified as, say, industrial among its compo-nent uses, viz., land for manufacturing processes, administration, storage and car parking. For a view of a city as a whole, however, it may be sufficient to have generalised data showing the broad zonation of land uses throughout the city, though these zones will contain a variety of 'impurities' or non-conforming uses.

2.3. Concepts of Land and Land Use ✓

2.3.1. Although it will be generally agreed that an approach through activity is the most promising one, land-use statistics are often confused by the employment of terms defining status, appearance or structure. In many instances, these terms represent a short-hand reference to the activity; in others, they are a legacy from the past, when there was a considerable emphasis on appearance or what was directly observable. Thus, woodland or forest are often employed as surrogates for forestry, while moorland and heathland, not themselves uses of land, are widely used to describe rough land mainly used for grazing. While it is difficult to break long-established habits, it is desirable that vegetative cover or legal status should not be used as synonyms for land use, although the legal status in particular may well affect the way in which the land is used. It is to be hoped that the initiative of the working party which has compiled the National Land Use Classification will be widely followed by those responsible for the collection of statistics relating to the use of land. It must, however, be recognised that the multiplicity of purposes for which data on land use are required cannot be satisfied by a single classification; consistency and compatibility are the most that can be expected.

2.3.2. A further source of confusion is the meaning of land. Over most of the countryside, this presents no problem; land is the point of contact between soil mantle and atmosphere. Yet even this situation presents difficulties; a proportion of the national territory is covered by inland water bodies, whether natural or man-made, and the concept of land could be extended to include water surfaces, while also recognising that these differ from the underlying land surface, a contrast that is very apparent in a newly flooded reservoir, as at Cow Green in Upper Teesdale. In urban areas a large part of the land surface is covered by man-made structures which are often divided into two or more levels, so that there is in effect a series of superimposed land-use patterns, with, for example, retailing on the ground level, administrative activities on the first floor and residential uses on the second and higher floors. It would be illogical to confine the term 'land use' only to those activities which occupy the ground floor, but it is arguable how far this extension of meaning should apply to activities beneath the ground, such as mining, or in the air above, such as domestic air services. The legal concept of land, formulated before either deep mining or flying were possible, envisaged rights in land as extending both upwards to the skies and downwards to the centre of the earth; the working party therefore argued that both subterranean and aerial dimensions should be added to the concept of land, even though this has not been the practice in the past [B 81].

2.3.3. Similar problems arise in areas of low-intensity uses, particularly in respect of the concept of multiple use. This term is often employed very loosely, and in a strict sense it should be confined to concurrent uses, i.e., those which take place at the same time on the same area of land, as when land is used for both water collection and the grazing of sheep; but it is sometimes employed to describe situations where different activities take place on the same land but at different times, e.g., because they occur in different seasons, as with corn-growing and fox hunting, or because one or more activity occurs only occasionally, as with the use of large tracts of farm land for military manoeuvres. Furthermore, although such activities may take place on the same land, at least in part, the units of decision-making may be different in nature and in areal extent, as is the case with the management of hill sheep farms and of grouse moors. A further problem in such low-intensity uses is that while the maximum limits of any activity may be defined by the decision-making unit in which they occur, distributions may be very uneven and little is known about where the activity actually occurs, e.g., which areas classified as rough grazings are in fact grazed by sheep. Just as land uses in the city may be viewed as multi-dimensional, so rural land uses may be conceived as comprising one or more super-imposed patterns, though these will not normally have a vertical component.

CHAPTER 3

LAND

3.1. Land Measurement in Great Britain

Nearly all land-use data are expressed, for comparative purposes, as proportions of the total area of the country or of its administrative subdivisions; some data have also been computed as residual figures after deduction of the area occupied by other uses. It is, therefore, desirable to consider briefly the information available on total area. The principal source in Great Britain is the Ordnance Survey, although there is no known authority or statutory requirement for area measurement [B 106, QRL 20]. Areas are computed from measurements made of individual parcels of land shown on the 1:2500 plans; these parcels are selected in such a way that the total extent of administrative areas can be calculated. For those parts of the country at which there is no cover at the 1:2500 scale, measurements of administrative areas are made on the 1:10,000 scale maps. The smallest parcel measured is 0.040 ha. (0.1 acre). The last complete revision of the large-scale maps was made between 1891 and 1914; since parts of the country are still covered by the county series on which measurements have not been updated, some areas were last measured in the late nineteenth century. Measurements on county series are updated only when national grid maps are produced; measurements in the latter series are automatically revised whenever a revised edition of maps at scales of 1:2500 or 1:10,000 is produced. Measurements do not therefore refer to a specific date since large-scale mapping is revised on a continuous programme which is related to the amount of change in the area rather than the age of the map; in rural areas the period of revision will be approximately every 20-25 years [B 106]. The areas of counties and other administrative units are also computed from these parcels and reflect the latest data available for the area in question; the same is true in respect of statutory changes in administrative areas, which are computed as soon as they occur.

3.2. Limits of Area Measured

There are, of course, small annual changes in the total area as a result of coastal erosion and accretion, and land reclamation, but the net change is probably less than 0.01 per cent per annum. The limits of the area measured can also affect the result. The Ordnance Survey recognises three categories, viz. land, inland water, and tidal water and foreshore; the boundary of the land is High-water Mark of Ordinary Tides (HWMOT) in England and Wales, but High-water Mark of Spring Tides (HWMST) in Scotland. The administrative areas supplied to the Registrar General of England and Wales and published in the volumes of the population census includes both land and inland water, but those supplied to the Registrar General of Scotland exclude inland water; the figures are thus not strictly comparable though they could be made so [QLR 27, 28]. Areas of counties are also given in the published volumes of agricultural statistics [QRL 13, 14].

3.3. Land Measurement in Northern Ireland

In Northern Ireland the measurement of land is the responsibility of a separate Ordnance Survey under the Department of Finance. The method of computing was changed in 1972. Previously, as in Great Britain, the area of each parcel was computed planimetrically on the 1:2500 maps, which cover most of the country; for those mountainous areas which are not covered by this series, measurements were made on the 1:10,560 or 1:10,000 series. Measurements of land include water and are made to High-water Mark of Spring Tides (HWMST). Areas were measured when maps were resurveyed, but to speed up production in 1972 it was decided to discontinue the measurement and publication of the areas of parcels. Before that date the areas of administrative units were computed by totalling the areas of all including townlands (which are not themselves administrative units); these figures were updated at each revision and supplied to the Registrar General, Northern Ireland, as required by him. On the reorganisation of local government in 1972, the areas of the new administrative units were computed directly by direct measurement on the 6 inch maps [B 107].

CHAPTER 4

METRICATION

4.1. Adoption of the Metric System

A further complication in the computation of areas is metrication. The Ordnance Survey has already adopted the metric system, although older maps provide areas and scales in Imperial measures. The Ministry of Agriculture, Fisheries and Food (MAFF), the Department of Agriculture and Fisheries for Scotland (DAFS) and the Department (formerly Ministry) of Agriculture in Northern Ireland (DANI), adopted metric measures for the agricultural census in 1976 [B 104], but the Forestry Commission has used metric units since 1971 [B 102]. References to acreages in the following text should also, where appropriate, be read as referring to areas measured in hectares (for which no convenient general term exists).

CHAPTER 5

AGRICULTURE

5.1. Rural Land Use

5.1.1. In the very broadest analysis, land uses can be divided into four groups, viz., urban activities, farming, forestry and other rural activities. For largely historical reasons, very much more is known about rural land uses than about urban, although the latter are economically far more important and in fact account for three-quarters of the categories suggested for the National Land Use Classification [B 81]; this analysis will therefore be strongly biased in favour of rural land uses, though there is some logical justification for such bias in that rural land uses account for probably nine-tenths of the total land surface of the country. Measured in areal terms, farming is overwhelmingly the most important of these rural uses, as it occupies some four fifths of the total land surface of the United Kingdom; it is also the activity for which statistics have been collected for the longest time on a systematic and continuing basis, for this was begun in Ireland in 1847 and in Great Britain in 1866, and has been undertaken in every subsequent year [QRL 3]. Their collection, originally the responsibility of the constabulary in Ireland and of the Board of Inland Revenue in Great Britain, is now undertaken by the three agricultural departments, MAFF in England and Wales, DAFS in Scotland and DANI in Northern Ireland, though the basis of collection is very similar. It is undertaken under the authority of the Agriculture Act, 1947, as amended by subsequent legislation, and the Agricultural Returns Act (Northern Ireland), 1939, and there is a statutory obligation on occupiers of agricultural land, as defined for census purposes, to supply information when required to do so by the responsible ministry [B 104]. The agricultural returns will be considered at some length, not only because of their intrinsic importance as the most comprehensive body of statistical data relating to the use of land in the United Kingdom, in both a temporal and a spatial sense, but also because they illustrate many of the problems associated with the collection and interpretation of land-use statistics.

5.1.2. Although the censuses provide information about the acreages devoted to crops, grass and rough grazing, and so can justifiably be regarded as land-use statistics, this is not their main purpose. Their collection was instituted to provide an indication of trends in agricultural production and as an aid to the formulation of policies and the monitoring of their effects [B 104]; and while their value as statistics of land use is increasingly recognised, this is still an incidental feature of their collection and a minor aspect of the use to which such statistics are put.

15

5.2. Agricultural Census

5.2.1. The first regular collection of agricultural statistics in Great Britain was undertaken on 25th June 1866 and in Ireland in 1847, although censuses in Scotland were also undertaken annually between 1854 and 1857 [QRL 3]. An annual census in June remains the principal source of information about the agricultural use of land in all parts of the United Kingdom, but there is now a variety of censuses and the practices of the three ministries often differ in detail. In England and Wales the June census is now the only complete census. A December census was introduced in 1935 and there have been quarterly censuses in September, December and March since 1940 [QRL 3]. Between 1953 and 1972 these were collected from only a third of the holdings, the list of holdings being divided into approximately three equal groups on a random basis, a different third being sampled at each quarter. The method of sampling was changed in 1958, when all the holdings in one-third of the parishes was sampled on each occasion; from 1972 much smaller stratified random samples have been used. No land-use data from these quarterly censuses is published. In Northern Ireland and Scotland, on the other hand, the June census is complemented by a second census in December, in which information is sought from all eligible holdings (though there are quarterly censuses of pigs and poultry in April and August). County figures from the December censuses for certain land uses in Scotland are published annually with the June census in *Agricultural Statistics Scotland* [QRL 14]. Nevertheless, while these other censuses do contain some information on the use of land, they are primarily concerned with livestock, and attention will therefore be focused on the main census in June.

5.2.2. In England and Wales this main census is conducted on 4th June or the preceding Friday when this date falls on a Saturday or Sunday, by means of a postal questionnaire sent to every known occupier of an agricultural holding producing significant output, a method which dates from the time when agricultural statistics were first collected, although the schedule to be completed then was much shorter and simpler; the Scottish census is very similar, but in Northern Ireland, census day is 1st June [B 100]. Both the interpretation of agricultural land and the minimum size of holding from which data are collected have changed over the course of time; data were collected in 1866 from all holdings of 5 acres and over, in 1867 and 1868 from all occupiers of land while from 1869 till 1892 the minimum size of eligible holdings was a quarter of an acre and from 1892 to 1968 more than 1 acre [QRL 3]. In Northern Ireland, a minimum acreage was adopted in 1954 when postal enumeration was instituted for the first time; previously when the census was collected by the police, the minimum was one-quarter of an acre [B 100]. But here, too, collection is now from those holdings producing significant output (see below). The method of letting land in conacre, or seasonal leases for eleven months, is an additional complication. About 20 per cent of the land in crops and grass in Northern Ireland is let in this way and many of the smaller holdings are entirely let in conacre, so that in practice they form part of larger holdings [QRL 56]. Occupiers are required to provide details of all the land they take and let in conacre [B 100].

5.2.3. Decisions on what constitutes agricultural land clearly pose difficulties and a sample survey in Hertfordshire in 1931 showed that only 53 per cent of the holdings recorded were strictly agricultural, the remainder comprising grounds of large estates, recreation fields, golf courses, holding paddocks and the like [B 67]. The dividing line is particularly difficult around large cities, especially London, where there are many semi-agricultural uses and large numbers of occupiers who have other occupations and whose holdings are only part-time [B 24, 26]. Although land of this kind may serve some agricultural purpose, by providing limited grazing, its significance for total agricultural production is often small and the problems posed by attempting to collect data from numerous small holdings are out of all proportion to their contribution to agricultural production. Since 1968, therefore, MAFF has attempted a more rational approach by excluding from the census those holdings which, though exceeding 1 acre in extent, have fewer than 10 acres of crops and grass, no regular full-time worker and standard labour requirements of less than 26 standard man days, a figure which was raised to 40 in 1972 [B 104]. It is also recognised that there may be agricultural units, producing such commodities as broilers and glasshouse crops, which occupy less than 1 acre, and while these have been included in the past to the extent of obtaining an estimate of numbers of livestock on them, from 1973 statistically significant holdings of less than one acre have been brought fully into the census. In Scotland, where the existence of large numbers of crofts (only 3% of which provide enough work for a full-time occupier [QRL 43]) presents particular difficulties, statistically insignificant holdings with fewer than 26 standard man days have been excluded from the main census since 1970, although a special census of such holdings is made every three years [QRL 14]. The practice in Northern Ireland is similar, and in both countries the man-day threshold has now been raised to 40 [B 99, 100].

5.2.4. Changes in the minimum size of holding may have only a small effect upon the total acreage of agricultural land in the country; thus, the increase in the minimum size in Great Britain in 1892 was estimated to have reduced the area returned by only one-tenth of 1 per cent or less [QRL 3]. Nevertheless, such changes may be locally significant, especially around large towns, and they do affect the comparability of data from year to year. The value of the resulting statistics as a record of land use also depends on the completeness of official lists of agricultural holdings. At first, there were many omissions and the apparent increase in the extent of agricultural land between 1866 and 1891 must have been largely due to more complete enumeration; in reality, the area devoted to agriculture was almost certainly declining, as land was transferred to urban uses. Even as late as 1936 a survey of Buckinghamshire revealed a total of 349 holdings, occupying 13,332 acres, which were not on the official list of holdings, including twenty-eight farms of 100 acres and over [B 51], and the National Farm Survey 1941-3 [B 80] (see below) revealed many other omissions. The introduction of livestock rationing during the Second World War led to the 'discovery' of some 250,000 acres of land in England and Wales which had not previously been enumerated because their occupiers were not known to those responsible for the agricultural census [B 78]. It is probable that the greater involvement of the agricultural departments in all aspects of agricultural affairs in the post-war period, and in particular the wide range of commodities with guaranteed prices and of different grants and subsidies, some of which require field inspection, has ensured that most occupiers of agricultural land do now receive census forms. Even so, the large number of changes in the extent of individual holdings, estimated in the 1950s at some 80,000 per year in England and Wales alone, makes it difficult to keep track of all the land so recorded, especially when land is brought into agricultural use through the clearance of woodlands or the restoration of derelict land [B 89].

5.2.5. A further problem is the inability or unwillingness of occupiers to provide accurate information. In the early years of the census areal measures other than statute acres were sometimes used and, as is shown below, farmers may not, in any case, know the areas of their fields accurately [QRL 3]. There is some evidence that farmers copy information relating to the previous year's census and DAFS has found that, when returns of areas have had to be checked for administrative purposes, they have often been in error [B 99]. The difficulty of keeping track of individual holdings is aggravated by the absence of any cadastral records of the ownership and occupation of land, such as are common in other European countries. An attempt was made during the Second World War to record the boundaries of all agricultural holdings larger than 5 acres in the course of the National Farm Survey of England and Wales, some of the results of which are in *The National Farm Survey—a summary report* [B 80]. Their boundaries were marked on maps at a scale of either 6 inches or $12\frac{1}{2}$ inches to the mile and these have now been deposited in the Public Record Office; they are, however, regarded as confidential, were probably never very accurate and are now substantially out of date. Similar maps were prepared in Scotland in the 1940s and remain in the possession of DAFS; they have been updated in places. None of these sources is used as a basis for monitoring returns; instead, the agricultural departments rely primarily upon the knowledge of their local staff. In Northern Ireland, the Agricultural Inspectorate has land-use maps for internal use for each holding and these are up-dated annually [B 100].

5.3. Areas Under Different Crops

5.3.1. The agricultural census provides considerable detail about the use to which land nominally in agricultural use is put. The fullest information is obtained about the acreages under the various crops; in England and Wales the acreages under 34 kinds of vegetables, 16 kinds of fruit crops, 8 other horticultural crops and 21 of other crops are enumerated, as well as the acreages under different kinds of grass [QRL 13]. More strictly, the acreage under each crop or prepared for that crop on the holding on 4th June or other census day is recorded rather than the maximum acreage under that crop during the crop year. At the date chosen for the main census most crops are in the ground, though some early potatoes may have been lifted in late May in west Cornwall and several vegetables, such as turnips and swedes, are underestimated because planting continues after the census. Some of these omissions are made good by other censuses, such as the vegetable census conducted in October in England and Wales. Unfortunately, this information is not brought together at the level of the individual holding, though estimates of the cropped acreages of the various horticultural crops in England and Wales are provided in the published statistics; for example, the cropped acreage of turnips and swedes for human consumption in the crop year 1969–70 was some 9900 acres, compared with an acreage of some 7300 recorded in the June census [QRL 13]. Crops are not as important in Scotland and Northern Ireland and less information is therefore collected about them in the June censuses in those countries, although the approach adopted is very similar

[QRL 14, 49, 56]. However, it should be noted that the acreage under orchards in Scotland is enumerated only in the December census [QRL 14].

5.3.2. The acreages under the different crops are probably the most accurate of the land-use data recorded in the agricultural census. The acreage which he devotes to each crop is important to the individual farmer, who plans his rotations with the various crops in mind, and they are generally grown in fields of known size since their areas are recorded on the large-scale plans of the Ordnance Survey. Difficulties do arise where fields are subdivided for cropping, especially where field boundaries have been removed as part of the process of rationalising farm layout; and while occupiers are asked to provide information correct to the nearest quarter acre, many of these figures can only be estimates. Fields may also be known by an approximate area (e.g., 'the 10-acre field') or farmers may not have access to Ordnance Survey maps; formerly there were also difficulties arising from the use of local measures [QRL 3]. In any case, the acreage recorded in Great Britain is not strictly that under the crop in question, for occupiers are instructed to include the area of any associated headlands, ditches and hedges, i.e., the acreage as given on the Ordnance Survey maps, although these may be considerably larger than the area under the crop, especially where fields are small and boundaries wide, as in Devon. No such instruction is given to occupiers in Northern Ireland, but officers of DANI are confident that farmers do, in fact, give the total acreage of fields [B 100]. Other problems arise over intercropping, especially of orchards, and over the definition of orchards themselves, which may range from a few neglected trees in what is primarily a field used for grazing to a well-tended commercial orchard. Since 1964 in England and Wales the acreages under commercial and non-commercial orchards have been separately enumerated [QRL 13]; since 1969 only commercial orchards have been enumerated in Scotland [QRL 14].

5.4. Grassland and Rough Grazing

5.4.1. The acreage under grass is probably less accurately recorded and it is possible that many occupiers may deduct the acreage under the various crops from the total farm acreage in arriving at this figure and that of rough grazing. It is also probable that much of the land which escapes enumeration is under grass of some kind. Traditionally, a distinction has been made between permanent grass, that which is infrequently, if ever ploughed, and temporary grass, which plays a part in arable rotations, especially in systems of alternate husbandry or ley farming, in which grass leys alternate with periods of arable cropping. Both permanent and temporary grass are divided into that intended for mowing in the year of the Census and that not so intended. The practice of ley farming has long been established in Scotland but has become common in lowland England only since the Second World War; in western areas, too, permanent grass is often ploughed at fairly long intervals and reseeded to maintain the quality of the grass. The distinction between permanent and temporary grass is becoming increasingly arbitrary and is no longer made in the agricultural censuses in Northern Ireland and Scotland. In Northern Ireland grass is divided into that which has been down for less than 4 years and that which has been under grass for 4 years and over, though figures before 1961, when the maximum age of temporary grass was 6 years, are not strictly comparable with those from 1961 onwards [QRL 49]. In Scotland, a division is made into grass which was laid down for less than 7 years and other grass, categories which are broadly equivalent to those of temporary and permanent grass recognised elsewhere in the United Kingdom. This latter distinction also illustrates how changes in definition or in terminology can affect results, because this change in the Scottish census in 1960 was followed by an increase of some 80,000 acres in the acreage formerly returned under temporary grass, presumably because some farmers had previously regarded such grass as permanent [QRL 14]. There was a similar increase in England and Wales when farmers were asked to subdivide their temporary grass according to the date at which it was sown. Historically, too, there have been many fluctuations in the acreage of temporary and permanent grass as a result of changes in the definitions used or in farmers' interpretations of them [QRL 3]. In any case, it is not easy to produce definitions which are equally applicable in all parts of the country.

5.4.2. The distinction between permanent (or older) grassland and the third principal category of agricultural land, rough grazing, is important for at least two reasons. First, it determines the boundary between improved and unimproved land, to which reference is frequently made in discussions of agricultural land use; and secondly, it illustrates how interpretations of land use can vary throughout the country. In principle, there is a clear distinction between permanent grassland, which is generally enclosed and receives some treatment, such as liming and harrowing, and rough grazing, which is unimproved and is mainly unenclosed or divided into large enclosures. In practice, there is a continuum between land that is grazed intensively, supporting more than one livestock unit to the acre, and extensively grazed land with perhaps a fiftieth of that carrying capacity. The boundary between them is thus an arbitrary line which is likely to be drawn at different points on that continuum throughout the country, for it will be seen in a different context; an East Anglian farmer may well classify a field as rough grazing which a Welsh hill farmer, against his local background, would regard as permanent pasture.

5.4.3. The extent of rough grazing, which has been recorded since 1891 in Great Britain, is the least well known of all the categories of agricultural land and its measurement epitomises the difficulties of making any reliable record of extensive land uses. In Northern Ireland, data on rough grazing have been published since 1930; while up to 1929 the term 'Mountain Land-grazed' was used. Between 1891 and 1921, such rough land in Great Britain was recorded as Mountain and Heath Land, and the replacement of this term by Rough Grazing led to a considerable transfer of land previously returned as permanent pasture [QRL 3]. In the main, the acreage of such land is much less important to the individual farmer than its carrying capacity and he may well not know the acreage on his farm with any degree of accuracy, for most upland areas have not been mapped at the 1:2500 scale. Even the ownership of such land may be uncertain, and J. Fraser Hart records that in one area he studied in Scotland, $1\frac{1}{4}$ square miles of hill was unclaimed by any of the farmers whose fields surrounded it [B 27]. In any case, the use of such land is likely to be highly variable, with most of the grazing concentrated in a relatively small part of the area. Even where the use of such land changes, farmers are likely to continue to return it as rough grazing, deriving the figure as a residual from the total area of their farm, so that the agricultural census can throw no light on the extent to which there has

been any withdrawal of hill land from effective agricultural use, although such changes
are said to be widespread in the Scottish Highlands [QRL 43].

5.5. Common Land

5.5.1. Further complications arise from the uncertain legal status of much agricultural
land classified as rough grazing. In England and Wales about 1.5 million acres are thought
to be common land, over which those occupiers with common rights can pasture livestock [QRL 13]. Common land was first recorded in the agricultural census in 1921,
though there is evidence that some occupiers previously included such land as their own
[QRL 3]. Such land, though not the stock that graze on it, is excluded from the agricultural returns made by the individual farmers; instead, estimates are made at infrequent
intervals by MAFF officials, the last being in 1952, though minor adjustments have been
made since [B 104]. The basis of such estimates is not at all clear, and in any case, considerable uncertainty has existed in the past about what land is in fact common. In
Breconshire, for example, more land was returned in 1938 than the total acreage of the
county because many farmers had included such land in their returns [B 104], while
some areas returned as common, notably in the Northern Pennines, are thought in fact
to be private land held in undivided shares. In Merionethshire, where only 26,544 acres
of common rough grazings were recorded in the census in 1969 some 50,000 acres had
already been provisionally registered under the Commons Registration Act by 1968
and the Crown Estates Commissioners alone claimed to own 17,469 acres [B 40]. It is
hoped that registration will in due course clarify this issue. Hill land held in undivided
shares presents similar problems in Northern Ireland and is excluded from the returns; it
was last estimated in 1953 [B 100]. In Scotland, where there is little or no remaining
common land in the English sense, similar problems of definition exist in the $1\frac{1}{4}$ million
acres of common pasture, particularly in the seven crofting counties, where crofters have
the right to pasture stock on such land [B 38]. Estimates of common pasture are made by
the secretaries of the grazing committees in each crofting township, but although the
existence of the Crofters Commission, which has the duty of safeguarding the interests
of crofting communities, suggests that the extent of common pastures is likely to be better
known than that of common grazings or land in multiple occupation in other parts of the
United Kingdom, there are discrepancies between the acreages recorded by the Crofters
Commission and DAFS, and no comprehensive maps exist to show the extent and
location of such common pastures other than those prepared by H. A. Moisley [QRL 22,
B 38, 76].

5.5.2. It follows from these comments on the low level of accuracy of the data on rough
grazing in the agricultural census that changes in their extent cannot be monitored very
reliably and that any trends shown, even in the national figures, must be treated with
caution; it cannot be established with any certainty from the census how far the
apparent increase in the acreage of rough grazing in the 1920s and 1930s represents an
actual change in land use or simply a reclassification of land or changes resulting from
differences of interpretation. Other complications arise from changes in administrative
procedures, especially in Scotland and Northern Ireland. Between 1922 and 1932 the
acreage of rough grazing as recorded in the Scottish census included any parts of deer

forests that were grazed by sheep, but in 1932 this instruction was amended to include any parts of deer forests which were thought to be capable of being grazed by sheep; in 1959 the instructions were altered again so that the total acreage of deer forests on farms, irrespective of whether it is grazed or is capable of being grazed, is now included in the acreages of rough grazing [QRL 14]. The acreage returned increased by 1,447,717 acres, and it is clearly impossible to compare the acreages of rough grazing before and after these dates. A change in 1964 in the definition of rough grazing used in Northern Ireland from 'mountain grazing or grass of very poor quality on land which is not generally suitable for cropping' to 'mountain grazing or grass on rough land on which implements could not generally be used' led to a reclassification of some 70,000 acres formerly returned as rough grazing [QRL 49]. Similar difficulties arise over the comparison of the acreages under rough grazing in England and Wales before and after 1922 [QRL 3]. Other changes have occurred as a result of the exclusion of statistically insignificant holdings; the acreage returned as rough grazing in Scotland fell by 926,165 acres between 1969 and 1970 largely for this reason [QRL 14]. In Northern Ireland, the change to a computerised census and a different method of raising to account for census schedules which were not returned led to an increase in the estimated area of agricultural land of some 56,000 acres in 1966 [QRL 49].

5.6. Limitations of Census Statistics

5.6.1. Data on agricultural land are required not only nationally but also regionally and locally. Unfortunately, the only up-to-date information which the agricultural departments have about the location of the holdings from whose occupiers information is sought in the agricultural censuses is the address of the occupier, which will normally be that of the farmstead, though local officers will, of course, possess much more detailed information. There are therefore no precise data on the location of land to which the census forms refer. An agricultural holding may cover a large area and more than a third of all agricultural land is in holdings of 300 acres and over; moreover, in the post-war period at least, there have been marked trends towards the enlargement of farms and towards the creation of linked or led farms, i.e., farms run in conjunction with another, often in a subordinate or complementary capacity, as where a hill sheep farm supplies a low ground farm under the same management with stock for fattening and in turn receives fodder and cattle for summering. As farms become larger and as such links develop the usefulness of data located only by a postal address diminishes. The absence of any more precise indicator of location also means that there can be no internal check in the agricultural census that all land is included and it implies that the agricultural data cannot be directly compared with those relating to other land uses, except where these are aggregated in respect of the individual countries or of large parts of them.

5.6.2. The agricultural returns illustrate a further problem affecting the usefulness of land-use statistics, the constraints imposed by considerations of confidentiality, and while this is a characteristic shared with most other public statistics, it is probably more important in land-use statistics because of the significance of location. In order to encourage farmers to make returns, great stress has always been laid on their confidential nature. Under the Agricultural Act 1947 data relating to individual holdings may be disclosed only with the consent of the occupier who provided the information or when the appropriate minister considers that it is in the public interest to do so. Only aggregated data can thus be provided to other government departments, local planning authorities and others who may wish to obtain information on the agricultural use of land. In Great Britain the smallest area for which data are aggregated is the civil parish and in Northern Ireland the rural district (though before 1953 data on enumeration districts were tabulated). In England and Wales such aggregated data can be released only when there are at least three holdings in each parish in order to preserve the confidentiality of individual returns; data for parishes with fewer than three holdings must be amalgamated with those for an adjacent (or any other) parish [B 104]. In Scotland a minimum of five holdings is required [B 99]. There are some 12,000 parishes in England and Wales, but only 891 in Scotland, while there are a mere thirty-three rural districts in Northern Ireland [B 99, 100, 104]. The range of size is also considerable; in Scotland, for example, the largest parish covers more than 250,000 acres and the smallest less than 100 acres. Because of this variation in the size of parishes, and because there are marked regional differences in average size of parish throughout the United Kingdom, the level of generalisation represented by aggregated data for parishes or any other administrative area varies widely; it will be greatest where holdings are small and parishes large and least, subject to the constraints of confidentiality, where farms are large and parishes small [B 19]. It is also probable that large parishes are more heterogeneous than small parishes and contain a wider range of agricultural land types.

5.6.3. There is one further difficulty posed by aggregated data on agricultural land use. Even if they were known, the boundaries of agricultural holdings do not necessarily coincide with those of the administrative areas by which they are aggregated; inspection of the farm boundary maps prepared in the early 1940s for the National Farm Survey [B 80] shows that they frequently do not and that in some instances the discrepancy may be quite considerable. As a result, the agricultural land described by the summary of the agricultural returns for a given administrative unit may not lie wholly within the boundary of that unit, which may in turn enclose land which is in fact recorded in the summaries for other administrative units; in one instance, 34 per cent of the agricultural land in a given parish was returned under other parishes and 34 per cent of the land returned in that parish lay outside its administrative boundaries [B 17]. Such discordance is important chiefly in respect of data for small administrative units, such as parishes, although it may also affect those for individual counties, and the trend towards an increase in average farm size through the amalgamation of farms and the emergence of linked farms, which may be widely separated from their parent holdings, aggravates the seriousness of this problem; it has been estimated that in Scotland as many as 15 per cent of all hill and upland farms are led farms, i.e., parts of multiple holdings [B 54]. Detached portions of farms or separate farms now run as part of a larger unit may thus lie some miles apart. According to the instructions given to occupiers for the completion of the census schedule, holdings which are farmed together as part of the same management unit should be included on a single schedule. In the past the agricultural departments have been very flexible in their attitude towards the number of separate returns made by farmers in an endeavour to ensure that returns were forthcoming [QRL 3], and even today, while the agricultural departments may request occupiers to make only a single return for holdings farmed together, they cannot require them to do so since this decision is one for the occupier alone [B 104]. Such discordance between the location of agricultural land and the limits of administrative areas is in large measure inevitable when the farm is the basic unit for data collection, but this has not been of great concern to those responsible for the collection of statistics because the returns were not intended as land-use data and have been required chiefly at the national level, where such problems do not arise. At parish or township level, however, such discordance may be a matter of considerable importance, especially where farms are large and parishes small, and it implies that the agricultural returns cannot be directly compared with data on any other use, nor can estimates be provided on the proportion of each parish or township devoted to agriculture; similarly, the agricultural data cannot be directly related to data on soil and climate, population, or any other parameter not derived from the agricultural censuses.

5.7. Parish Summaries

These parish summaries for Great Britain are not published, but are available only in manuscript or increasingly as the output from a line printer or in machine-readable form on cards or magnetic tape from the Census Branch of MAFF at Guildford and the Statistics Branch of DAFS in Edinburgh, and appear to be comparatively little used for official purposes; they are largely a legacy from past administrative procedures and represent a stage in the compilation of county and national totals. These latter are published annually in separate volumes of agricultural statistics, *Agricultural Statistics, England and Wales* [QRL 13] and *Agricultural Statistics Scotland* [QRL 14]. Those for Northern Ireland are published in the *Annual Report* of DANI [QRL 59] and in periodic reports, the last of which, covering the period 1966–7 to 1973–4, appeared in 1977 [QRL 49]; results are also published in the *Statistical Review*, produced annually by the Economics and Statistics Division of DANI [QRL 56]. A summary volume, *Agricultural Statistics United Kingdom*, is also published giving data for the whole kingdom and for the constituent countries [QRL 15]. Since 1964, manuscript summaries have also been available in England and Wales for districts of the National Agricultural Advisory Service (now the Agricultural Development and Advisory Service) of which there are now some 380; but these have frequently changed their boundaries, so that the results for different years cannot be compared. Parish summaries for England and Wales for the past 10 years are kept at the Agricultural Censuses and Surveys Branch at Guildford; those for earlier years are now kept at the Public Record Office. Parish summaries for Scotland for all years are kept in the Scottish Record Office in Edinburgh. For Northern Ireland, summaries for urban and rural districts have been publicly available annually since 1962 [B 100]; none is available for the years between 1954 and 1961, while those for 1924–53 have not been published but are available at DANI in Belfast. Summaries for enumeration districts were made annually before 1954 but are regarded as confidential. Several atlases based on these unpublished parish and district data have been produced [B 9, 14, 15, 16, 34, 42, 56]; detailed analyses of horticultural cropping have also been published [QRL 41, 42].

5.8. Other Agricultural Statistics

5.8.1. In addition to the published volumes of statistics, other information is available as press notices and *Statistical Statements*. Press notices are issued in advance of the publication of the annual volumes of statistics, which normally appear a year or so after the census to which they refer but may take longer. For England and Wales, provisional and final results of the June census are issued (as are figures for the quarterly censuses and for the special censuses of horticultural crops discussed below); for Scotland and for Northern Ireland provisional and final figures are issued for both the June and the December censuses. The agricultural departments also issue *Statistical Statements* which provide more detailed advance information on the data subsequently published in the census volumes as well as various kinds of analyses. In England and Wales, county and regional figures for acreages recorded in the June censuses are issued in both provisional and final forms as *Statistical Statements* [QRL 57], though the breakdown of the temporary grass and horticultural acreages is not provided in the provisional statements. In Scotland figures for counties and regions are available in similar *Statistical Statements* [QRL 58] for both the June and December censuses. In Northern Ireland figures appear in *Statistical Statements* [QRL 59] for counties and rural districts for the June census and for counties for the December census.

5.8.2. In addition to the areas under different kinds of land use recorded in the agricultural censuses, various analyses of the census data are also published, both in official publications and in *Statistical Statements*. Annual statements are included in the published census volumes of the number and acreage of holdings in each county in different size groups (as measured both by acreages under crops and grass and by total acreages in England and Wales and in Scotland, and by crops and pasture acreage in Northern Ireland). Frequency tables are also published for the individual countries as a whole showing the breakdown of the acreages by different size groups of holdings (crops and grass acreages) and by crop acreage size groups. No breakdown of the figures for England and Wales or for Northern Ireland is published, but frequency distributions are given for Scottish regions [QRL 14]; regional and occasional county figures for England and Wales are issued as *Statistical Statements* [QRL 57]. The number of units returning a variety of other crops is also published for Scotland as a whole and for the regions [QRL 14]. County figures are also published of the number and acreage of holdings according to the type of tenure in the respective census volumes for England and Wales and for Scotland [QRL 13, 14]; for Northern Ireland such tables are unnecessary as virtually all holdings are owner-occupied. The agricultural departments have been increasingly concerned since the early 1960s to use the agricultural censuses to classify farms according to type, and annual volumes, *Farm Classification* [QRL 39], are now published for England and Wales in which the acreages of the main crops and agricultural land uses on each type of farm are given by three size groups of holdings (as measured by standard man-days), and on spare-time and part-time holdings. Similar figures are published for Scotland as a whole and for the regions [QRL 14]. Average acreages on each type of holding have also been published for England and Wales, Scotland and Northern Ireland in occasional publications [B 64]; for Northern Ireland, where such data are published annually [QRL 56], averages are also published by crops and grass acreage size groups, and for Scotland average acreages have also been computed for regions in 1947 [QRL 63] and for regions and counties in 1962 [B 43]. Maps have also been prepared of the distribution and relative importance of different types of farms [B 12, 97, M6].

5.8.3. Available data on agricultural land are largely confined to the measurement of area. Yields are estimated for the individual crops and for hay from both permanent and temporary grass, but these estimates are not thought to be very reliable and are available only by counties for England and Wales [QRL 13]; in Scotland, the publication even of county estimates was discontinued in 1965 because of doubts about their reliability and because of the introduction of survey methods employing random samples, and only national and regional totals are now given [QRL 14]. Yields in Northern Ireland are published only for the province as a whole [QRL 56]. Yields of horticultural crops are given only for England and Wales, for Scotland and for Northern Ireland [QRL 13, 14, 49]. Estimates of production from rough grazing and from grassland used only for grazing are not regularly made, though differences in carrying capacity (as measured by present stocking) can be computed roughly from the data provided in the census on numbers of livestock. Yields of potatoes have been given by the Potato Marketing Board [QRL 52].

5.8.4. As has already been noted, there are other agricultural censuses than those conducted in June, though only for Scotland [QRL 14] and Northern Ireland [QRL 49] are estimates of land use published. For Scotland county figures of acreages under glass, of orchards and of vegetables for human consumption are given, as well as national and regional totals [QRL 14]; for Northern Ireland only figures for the province are published. In Scotland parish summaries are prepared for the winter census, but unlike those for the June census, these are not available for consultation in the Scottish Record Office. No parish summaries are prepared for the quarterly censuses in England and Wales, which until 1972 were based on samples of every third holding drawn by parishes from the parish list of agricultural holdings [B 104]. Estimates are prepared by counties, but these, too, are not published and are not normally disclosed, since they are liable to sampling errors which may be quite large in the smaller counties. Special censuses of horticultural holdings are also undertaken in England and Wales and county results are published as *Statistical Statements* [QRL 57]. Schedules are sent each October to all occupiers of holdings who return vegetable crops in the June census, to obtain further information about their cropping; before 1972 there were two such censuses, in September and December. Special glasshouse censuses were also undertaken each January and July from all holdings on which glass was recorded in the June census in order to ascertain the patterns of cropping in summer and winter (as well as a biennial inquiry about details of equipment); but, from December 1972, these inquiries have been incorporated in the June and December censuses (with records also obtained from all glasshouse holdings not sampled in December) and the special censuses have been discontinued [B 31]. Periodic censuses have also been undertaken of orchard trees and occasional censuses of irrigated land in England and Wales, and the results have been published in *Statistical Statements* [QRL 57]. Occasionally, special questions have been incorporated in the census, as with that on the acreage under bracken in the June census in Scotland in 1957 [QRL 8].

5.8.5. Miscellaneous statistics on agricultural land use are available from a variety of sources. An *Agricultural Survey of Scotland* in 1946 provided estimates of the amount of improvable land [QRL 16]. Annual figures of acreages affected by improvement schemes are published for Scotland [QRL 14] and for the crofting counties, as are acreages on which crofting grants are paid in those counties. Figures are also published of those crofts used for enlargement and of common grazings apportioned [B 85]. Submissions to Parliamentary inquiries are often a valuable source, particularly those to the Estimates Committee [B 71] and to the Select Committee on Scottish Affairs [QRL 43]. An annual report on smallholdings is produced by MAFF [QRL 26] and much evidence was provided by the Departmental Committee on Smallholdings [QRL 34]. Data are also available for other sources: the Potato Marketing Board, for example, publishes details of the acreages of potatoes of different varieties planted by registered growers [QRL 52].

5.9. Assessment of Official Agricultural Statistics

5.9.1. The chief value of the official agricultural statistics as records of the use of land is the light they throw on changes of use within the agricultural sector [QRL 3, 31]. As a time series extending back over a hundred years, they provide the major source of information for the analysis of change in the larger administrative units, such as the counties, the component countries of the United Kingdom and the Kingdom as a whole; figures for the century from 1866 to 1966 for Scotland and for England and Wales have been conveniently assembled in a single volume, *A Century of Agricultural Statistics, Great Britain 1866–1966* [QRL 31]. Even at this level of aggregation, however, trends must be interpreted with care, especially those covering a long period of time; there are relatively few items which have not been modified in some way since agricultural statistics were first collected [QRL 3]. It is true that some of these changes in definition or administrative procedure have quite small effects. Other changes arise from the increasing complexity of the returns and the effects of these can often be eliminated, with the loss of some detail, by adding the acreages of crops which at some stage have been subdivided; thus, the acreages under turnips and swedes for stock feed and those for human consumption recorded in the 1950 census for England and Wales are comparable with the acreages of turnips and swedes returned in 1870. Such a simple solution is not always possible where a crop was formerly included under the heading of 'other crops'; there is no way in which the acreage under turnips, swedes and fodder beet for stock feed in 1970 can be compared exactly with the acreages recorded before 1953, the year in which the acreage under fodder beet was first enumerated separately (though there is a presumption that this crop was previously not very important). Care is especially necessary when absolute values are being compared, especially those in the smaller administrative areas, since the figures can be affected by increasing accuracy, transfers of land between the summaries for adjacent administrative areas and changes in the basis of collection; for these reasons it is generally advisable to compute mean values for several years (or moving means for time series) or to compare percentage changes.

5.9.2. For reasons already discussed, the published agricultural statistics are of limited value for the study of changes in the extent of agricultural land, particularly where rough grazings account for a large proportion of the total, since these are the least reliable of all the data collected. No conclusion can safely be drawn at any time about changes in the acreage of agricultural land in the smaller administrative areas, and even county and national figures provide a rather uncertain guide to such changes in the period before the mid-1940s. The improvements in the accuracy and completeness of returns in the post-war period suggest that the comparisons of figures for counties and larger areas can give some broad indication of the relative importance of losses of agricultural land in different parts of the country and they have been used for this purpose by Dr. R. H. Best [B 6]; yet even these figures are likely to be affected by changes in administrative procedure which restrict the period over which data are comparable, such as the move to eliminate statistically insignificant holdings from the census in the 1960s, the classification as rough grazing of all deer forests on agricultural holdings in Scotland from 1959 onwards and the collection of the total acreage of agricultural holdings in England and Wales since 1969. Fortunately, the agricultural returns provide an alternative, the change of acreage (formerly occupancy) data, which permit closer analysis of changes in the extent of agricultural land [B 78]; and although such analysis have been published only for individual countries, they are made holding by holding and have been mapped by counties in England and Wales [B 7].

5.9.3. When changes occur in the extent of individual holdings as recorded in successive censuses, occupiers are asked to give the reasons for such changes [QRL 3]. If they cannot be explained by transfers of agricultural land between holdings, local officers of agricultural departments may enquire into the subsequent use of such land. Similarly, when land is gained from other uses, information is sought on the nature of previous uses, though it is probable that data about such gains of agricultural land are less complete than those on losses from holdings already known to the agricultural departments. It is thus possible to compile balance sheets showing the gains from and losses to other uses and hence of the net loss of agricultural land. Four categories of land uses are now given in England and Wales, viz., urban, industrial and recreational development; government departments; Forestry Commission and private woodlands; and other adjustments [QRL 13]; formerly the categories were buildings and development; sports grounds; service departments; forests and woodlands; and a category 'corrections and reclassifications' [QRL 3]. In Scotland data are available on seven categories, viz., roads, housing and industrial development; recreation; mineral workings and water boards; service departments; forestry; and 'other' [QRL 14]. Such data appear to have been collected since 1922 in England and Wales and were the basis of evidence from the Ministry of Agriculture to the Scott Committee, which reported in 1942 [B 90]; subsequent figures have been made public, mainly in answers to Parliamentary questions. Comparable data for Scotland were not available until 1951 and for Northern Ireland until 1961. The data for both Scotland and England and Wales are now published in the respective volumes of agricultural statistics [QRL 13, 14] and are conveniently assembled in the volume prepared to mark the centenary of agricultural statistics [QRL 31]. The agricultural departments have considerable reservations about the accuracy of these data, partly because of a tendency for farmers to copy the last recorded acreage; it has often been the practice to express such transfers as averages for several years and data for England and Wales are given only to the nearest thousand acres [QRL 13]. The categories used are not always wholly satisfactory; for example, losses to allotments have been included with those to forests. Yet, whatever their limitations, these records provide the only reasonable complete information on transfers of land to and from the other uses, a topic of some importance to the farming industry since most of the land required for expanding uses must be taken from that in agricultural use.

CHAPTER 6

FORESTRY

6.1. Types of Forest

The second major use of rural land in the United Kingdom is forestry, although this accounts for little more than a tenth of the acreage devoted to agriculture. As a land-use, it differs from agriculture in a number of respects: the acreage devoted to it has been expanding since the First World War, largely at the expense of rough grazing; most of this expansion has been undertaken by the State, which now has direct responsibility for about two-fifths of the total area under forests (and about half the productive woodland); and forestry is a long-term land use, so that once land has been planted with trees, it tends to remain in that use until the crop has harvested forty or more years later (apart from any replanting that may be necessary to make good losses through fire, wind blow and other hazards). In many ways, too, it is easier to define the area devoted to forestry than to identify agricultural land, since most woodland occupies discrete parcels of land with fairly well-defined boundaries, the areas of which are recorded on large-scale maps of the Ordnance Survey. There are two exceptions to this statement, scrub and cut-over woodland. Scrub consists mainly of woody growth that grades imperceptibly into rough land and is characteristic of upper limits of tree growth and of areas where spontaneous regeneration is taking place, as on abandoned or little-used agricultural land; the point at which tree cover becomes sufficiently discontinuous for the land to be regarded primarily as rough grazing can only be decided arbitrarily. Cut-over land is that on which trees have been felled but no replanting has yet taken place; and since the decision to replant is one that can be taken only by the occupier, the status of such land cannot be determined by observation until preparations for replanting begin. The distinction between scrub and cut-over land on the one hand and rough grazing on the other is made difficult by the fact that much of the land in these two categories is also used as rough grazing [QRL 43].

6.2. Uses of Forests

Trees are grown for a variety of purposes, which include not only timber production, but also cover for game, recreation and the conservation of amenity and wild-life; a proportion of woodland is also land on which grazing or other human-induced pressures are insufficient to prevent the growth of trees. Woods and forests may, and indeed commonly do, serve a number of these uses and it is probable that the proportion of woodland that is in multiple use is much larger than is the case with agricultural land; commercial forestry can readily be combined with many forms of recreation and conservation, though such multiple use may require the occupier to forgo some timber production. Unfortunately, available data are largely confined to measurements of the extent, composition and age of woodlands and throw comparatively little light on the degree to which they are used for purposes other than timber production; for such uses are sporadic and may occur without the knowledge of the owner. In Great Britain the Forestry Commission, which is responsible to the three forest ministers, the Minister of Agriculture, Fisheries and Food in England and the Secretaries of State for Scotland and Wales in those two countries, is the official agency primarily concerned with the implementation of the government's forest policy. In Northern Ireland, which has only 3 per cent of its land surface under woods, forestry is the responsibility of the Forestry Division of the Department of Agriculture, which has similar powers to those of the Forestry Commission to acquire and manage land. It is this department and the Forestry Commission which undertake the collection of data on the use of land for forestry, in respect of both private and State woodland (though the latter term is used by the Forestry Commission to refer only to those forests for which it is responsible, all other forests owned or managed by public bodies, whether national or local, being regarded as part of the 'private' sector).

6.3. Sources of Statistics

6.3.1. Unlike agricultural land, forest land is not the subject of a comprehensive annual census or assessment, although a certain amount of information is collected each year by the forest departments. Since 1970 the acreage of woodlands ancillary to farming has been collected in the agricultural census in England and Wales [QRL 13]; such information has been collected for much longer in Scotland, though the results are not thought to be very accurate [B 99]. Similar information is also collected in Northern Ireland and published by counties [QRL 49]. The main source of information has been censuses at irregular intervals, each census conducted on a somewhat different basis, so that none is strictly comparable with any of the others; the results of the most recent census have been published in *Census of Woodlands 1965–6* [QRL 30]. Other sources, usually derived from these censuses or from other Forestry Commission records, are parliamentary inquiries such as that of the Estimates Committee [B 71] or of the Select Committee on Scottish Affairs [QRL 43].

6.3.2. Understandably, much more is known about State forests than about private forests. Large-scale maps are kept up to date at the Conservancy and District Headquarters of the Forestry Commission showing the extent of the Commission's holdings, and the Commission, like other public agencies, is required to lay an *Annual Report and Accounts* before Parliament [QRL 25]. This report describes the Commission's activities during the forest year (which prior to 1969 ended on 30th September and now ends on 31st March) and gives the acreages of land acquired, planted or replanted, and felled, as well as the reserves of plantable land in hand. Appendices provide information on the land use of each forest, giving the present area, the acreage under plantations, and the plantable reserves. Unfortunately, this latter information is less valuable to those seeking data on the use of land than would at first appear, for the forest is an administrative unit

whose boundaries have changed over the course of time, both through acquisition of
land and through amalgamations for administrative convenience, and although its
general location is given, the land comprising each forest can be accurately identified
only by reference to the Commission's large-scale maps, a very time-consuming task.
Moreover, because forests often straddle county boundaries, published data about the
Commission's forest cannot be directly related to other information for administrative
areas, except for Great Britain as a whole and the three countries. However, the annual
report is only a summary of a large mass of statistics collected annually on such matters
as the age and growth rates of tree crops which, though not formally published, are
available to interested inquirers [B 102]. Land acquired by the Forestry Division of
DANI and that planted is recorded annually for Northern Ireland as a whole, by counties
and by forests [QRL 23, 49, 56]. Some indication of output is provided by sales of produce [QRL 25, 56].

6.3.3. Much less information is available about annual changes in the private sector.
The Forestry Commission's annual report does provide estimates of the scale of private
planting in Great Britain and in the three countries, though these do not separately
distinguish new planting from replanting. The report also gives the acreage transferred
from the private sector to the state sector, most of which will subsequently be replanted.
An annual estimate of the total acreage of woodland in Great Britain is also given in
the *Annual Abstract of Statistics* [QRL 20], from which net gains to forestry can be
calculated, and more detailed information is given in the annual *Scottish Abstract of
Statistics* [QRL 55] and *Digest of Welsh Statistics* [QRL 38]. There is, however, no indication of the scale or nature of any losses from forestry to other uses. The Forestry
Commision does, in fact, possess quite detailed information about those private woodlands (about two-fifths of the total) which participate in either the Approved or the
Dedicated Woodland Schemes, but information about individual estates is understandably regarded as confidential [B 102]. The Commission also has records of virtually all
fellings of private woodlands which are not dedicated, since a felling licence, to which
conditions on replanting may be attached, is required under the Forestry Act 1951 for
all fellings of more than small trees on estates which are not dedicated; this information,
too, is published only as a national total [QRL 25]. The only information regularly
collected about private woodlands in Northern Ireland is that enumerated in the agricultural censuses [QRL 49] but there have been occasional surveys [B 32].

6.4. Forest Censuses

6.4.1. More detailed records of private woodlands and of all land devoted to forestry are
available from the various forest censuses, the first of which was begun shortly after the
establishment of the Forestry Commission in 1919. There are, however, earlier estimates
associated with the agricultural returns and derived from the rate books or valuation
rolls. These sources proved very unsatisfactory and from 1891 information was sought
at intervals from all owners of woodland who were sent schedules for completion;
county data from these inquiries were published in the annual volumes of the agricultural
returns [QRL 3]. A certain amount of statistical data on forestry was also provided in
the reports of the Royal Commission on Coast Erosion and Afforestation [B 92] and of

the Acland Committee [B 68] (which had led to the setting up of the Forestry Commission). The first proper forest census was undertaken between 1921 and 1926, but all acreages were adjusted to the forest year 1924 which was chosen as the census year. Two acres were selected as the minimum size of blocks of woodland for which information would be sought and different procedures were adopted in Scotland and in England and Wales; in Scotland use was made of the Commission's local correspondents and some information was obtained directly by the Commission's staff, while in England and Wales volunteer county organisers were appointed who distributed schedules to individual owners. A summary of the findings was published in *Report of Census of Woodlands and Census of Home Grown Timber, 1924*, but it was recognised that variations in the completeness of the returns and in the interpretations of the questions asked made the undertaking of limited value [B 88]. None of the detailed records from which this report was compiled has survived [B 102].

6.4.2. A second census was begun in 1938. On this occasion, the minimum size of block was 5 acres and data were collected by the Commission's own qualified technical staff. Teams undertook the field inspection of woodlands and their ocular estimates were checked by a contemporaneous sample survey. Unfortunately, the census was incomplete at the outbreak of the Second World War, when only 18 per cent of England and Wales and 50 per cent of Scotland had been covered. It was then decided to institute a method of rapid survey, recording the data for only a sample of woods. This census, too, was thus of limited value, since the records had not been collected on a uniform basis; it did, however, demonstrate how highly skilled staff might collect census data by field observation [QRL 30, B 102]. A report was prepared but not published and the maps and records of the three counties that were completely surveyed in 1938 are kept in the Public Record Office (Lincoln and Montgomery) and the Scottish Record Office (Nairn); records are also available from the 1942 Ministry of Supply survey for Cardigan and Dorset [B 102].

6.4.3. The census undertaken between 1947 and 1949 drew on this experience [B 62]. It, too, employed a minimum block of 5 acres and data were collected in the field by the Commission's staff, who were supplied with 6 inch to 1 mile Ordnance Survey maps. On these they recorded any new forests that had been planted since the date of survey of the map. They then subdivided all blocks of woodland into stands according to their age, composition and productivity, and the boundaries of these were marked on the map and details recorded on field sheets; acreages were calculated by acre grid correct to the nearest acre. A photographic reduction of each sheet was prepared and the data were transferred to punch cards. These sources provide a permanent record of the census, those for England and Wales being housed in the Public Record Office and those for Scotland in the Scottish Record Office [B 102]. Data were aggregated by counties and by countries and detailed reports of the census were published, *Census of Woodlands 1947–1949*, Report Nos. 1, 3, 4 and 5, giving county data in both map and tabular form [B 62, 63]. These data, collected by experienced surveyors in the field, are probably more accurate than most other land-use statistics, although a subsequent sample survey, intended to provide information on small woods of from 1 to 5 acres and on hedgerow timber, did reveal a number of small woods of more than 5 acres which had not been included in the census [B 72].

6.4.4. The census of woodlands under 5 acres was conducted on a sample basis, 441 16-acre strips 1 mile by 2 chains wide being chosen at random and those woods within them measured [B 62]. This report was published as *Hedgerow and Park Timber and Woods under Five Acres* [B 72] and these records are also in the Public Record Office and the Scottish Record Office. Like all other records deposited there, they are subject to the 50-year rule governing disclosure [B 102].

6.4.5. Between 1952 and 1959 several counties were completely resurveyed, but the results of these surveys have never been published in full. The field data, however, have been deposited in the record offices with those of other surveys [B 102].

6.4.6. The most recent census was that conducted between 1965 and 1967 in which data were related to the forest year ending in 1965 [QRL 30]. This census, in which the minimum size of block of woodland was 1 acre, was confined to private woodlands on the mainland of Great Britain and was conducted on a sample basis. After experiments to determine the size of sample which would produce an acceptable standard error, a sample of 15 per cent of the kilometre squares of the National Grid was selected. The squares were chosen at random from within the eighteen marketing regions into which Great Britain had been divided, so that standard errors of the estimates could be computed. Squares in which there were no woodland were first eliminated and the private woodland falling in each of the selected squares were then measured in a similar way to that used in 1947, acreages being again measured by acre grid correct to the nearest acre. Estimates were made of woods under 1 acre, using a 1 in 7930 sample for Central and Southern England only. Because the data are obtained by sampling, reliable estimates can be provided only by conservancies and by countries, though some estimates of total area are given for selected counties. A census report has been published, explaining the methods used and providing data only for the constituent countries and for conservancies [QRL 30]. Because they are collected on a sample basis, these data on private woodlands are also not strictly comparable with those on Forestry Commission woodlands which were available from existing records without the need of further field survey.

6.4.7. It will thus be clear that the data from the different forest censuses are not strictly comparable owing to differences in the basis of collection, minimum size of block, coverage and method of sampling, though the margin of error at national level is unlikely to be large. Preparations for a new census of woodlands have begun, though no details of the methods to be used have yet been published.

6.5. Assessment of Forestry Statistics

None the less, data on land used for forestry are probably more reliable than those available for any other kind of land use. The fact that the targets given to the Commission by the forestry ministers are expressed in terms of area and that its plantings have long been the major cause of changes in land use for forestry and a source of friction with agriculturalists and conservationists implies that accurate records are essential. In the 1960s and early 1970s there was also large-scale afforestation in the private sector, mainly under the aegis of investment groups, and while most of the plantings were undertaken under the Dedicated Woodland Scheme, there are no comprehensive data publicly

available on their location [B 102]. There are also no satisfactory data on transfers of
land from forestry to other uses, though these were estimated at some 7,500 acres annually in 1962, mainly to agriculture, but also to building and other urban uses [QRL 25,
30]. It is true that surveyors in both post-war surveys noted those woodlands shown on
their base maps which could no longer be regarded as forest land, but the value of such
information was limited by the fact that the Commission's staff adopted a different
interpretation of cut-over land from that used by surveyors of the Ordnance Survey, the
former recording as woodland any land still containing stumps, however old these might
be, provided that there was no positive evidence that the land had been transferred to
other uses, whereas the Ordnance Survey surveyors recorded as rough grazing any site
which had become covered with non-tree vegetation (though the area affected is likely
to be small) [B 102, 106]. A further factor was the wide variations in the dates of original
survey of the base maps, some having been surveyed more than 60 years before; it is
thus possible that changes of similar dates to those recorded on such old maps were not
noted on newer maps simply because they took place before these latter were resurveyed.

CHAPTER 7

RECREATION

7.1. Deficiencies in Current Data

Forestry and agriculture account for nearly nine-tenths of the total land area of the United Kingdom, and the urban area for most of the remainder, leaving a relatively small area unaccounted for. Some of this land is occupied by minor uses and some is land which ought properly to be included under one of the other main heads [B 5]. Yet there are many other activities which share the use of rural land with agriculture and forestry, generally in a subordinate role, in various combinations of multiple land use. By far the most important of these, and worthy of separate consideration as a major land use, is outdoor recreation, though there are virtually no data on outdoor recreation which are both comprehensive and reliable, a situation that is as true of long-established field sports as of recent development such as ski-ing and pleasure motoring. There are three principal reasons for this situation: no government agency is responsible for collecting such information; 'outdoor recreation' embraces a very wide range of activities of very diverse character; and many of these activities are junior partners in some form of multiple land use. It is true that the situation is changing with the creation of Countryside Commissions for Scotland (1967) and for England and Wales (1968, replacing the National Parks Commission which had been established in 1949), an Ulster Countryside Committee (1965) and statutory Tourist Boards and Sports Councils; but while these bodies have an interest in many of the activities comprised under the term 'outdoor recreation' and the Countryside Commission does publish a useful *Digest of Countryside Recreation Statistics* [QRL 36], none has the powers nor the statutory duty to collect such information. As a result, much of the information is qualitative and is largely confined to 'guesti-mates' for the component countries of the United Kingdom as a whole or for large parts of them.

7.2. Field Sports

7.2.1. Most of lowland Britain, together with large tracts of the Scottish uplands and parts of those of England and Wales, has long been used for a wide variety of field sports, which include hunting, the shooting of grouse, pheasant and partridge, wildfowling, deer stalking and other shooting. The clientele for such sports is often small, consisting of landowners and their friends and sometimes their tenants. Most field sports depend on other land uses, but their relationships vary, as do their demands on land and the difficulty of measuring these. Shooting in the lowlands, especially of partridge and pheasant, depends largely on the existence of hedgerows, small woodlands and pieces of rough land in a predominantly agricultural landscape and is characteristic of much of eastern England and eastern Scotland. Wildfowling is primarily undertaken on the coastal marshes, which may have some grazing potential but are otherwise significant chiefly for their value to conservation [B 55]. Hunting is characteristic of most parts of the lowlands, taking place mainly on farm land in winter when the risk of damage to crops is small. Grouse shooting is the field sport that interacts most strongly with other land uses, since the grouse depends on heather which must be regularly and carefully burnt to maintain an adequate supply of food; most grouse moors are also grazed by sheep, which benefit from the same management practice, but have less exacting requirements in respect of burning [QRL 43]. Red deer, on the other hand, require little management and live mainly on the poorest upland grazings which are of little value to sheep, though the deer often invade low ground farms in winter when feed is short.

7.2.2. Most shootings are rated and their value, which is based generally on the size of the bag, is recorded in valuation rolls and rate books; but there are no reliable figures on the extent of land so used and it will be clear from the preceding brief description that such estimates are difficult to make. Very rough estimates have been produced of the total area so used in the country, but their bases are uncertain, their reliability unknown and no regional breakdowns are available [B 20]. Grouse moors are roughly coextensive with the area of heather moor and have been estimated to cover some 4.5–5 million acres [B 46]. The boundaries of deer forests have been recorded by G. K. Whitehead, but these are less extensive than the areas where red deer roam, which are thought to cover perhaps twice as large an area [QRL 43, B 55]; the Red Deer Commission does conduct censuses, but these are concerned more with numbers of deer than with the area used by them [QRL 53]. Lists of hunts and descriptions of their territories are available but these provide a picture only of the general locality and do not indicate the land over which hunting actually takes place, which will be determined, at least in part, by the attitudes of individual landowners [B 61].

7.3. Other Rural Recreational Land Uses

7.3.1. Such traditional uses are extensive in their demands on land and important for their interaction with other land uses. However, they represent only a small part of the total volume of recreational use of the countryside. This comprises both the informal visit to the countryside (usually by car) which all surveys show to be the most important category in terms of numbers of participants, and a great variety of activities. Many of the latter are dependent on the availability of particular natural resources, such as uplands suitable for ski-ing or mountaineering, caves for pot-holing, streams and rivers for fishing and canoeing, and lakes for sailing, boating and a variety of other water sports, while other activities, such as golf and team games, are less demanding in their physical requirements but are primarily concentrated in areas close to the main centres of population [B 18, 40]. Although it is possible to indicate in a very broad way where these activities take place, very little information exists about the land used for these various categories of outdoor recreation, in part because of the intrinsic difficulty of providing such data, although attempts have been made to estimate acreages from numbers of facilities [B 47]. A similar approach is possible from estimates, of varying reliability, of numbers of participants.

7.3.2. The availability of information on the use of land for outdoor recreation in the countryside depends more on the legal status of the land than on the nature of the activities, and such estimates necessarily give a very partial view of their relative importance. Very little of the land on which outdoor recreation takes place is used exclusively or even primarily for recreation; in most instances recreation is an occasional or seasonal activity on land which is primarily used for agriculture or forestry. Some recreation takes place on private land with the consent of private owners and/or occupiers, sometimes on payment of a fee or with conditions as to management, repair of damage and the like, and such agreements may be made with clubs and organisations or with individuals; not surprisingly, very little is known about the extent of private land use in this way, since no official consent is required. Secondly, members of the public make use of large tracts of private land for public recreation, though they have no right or permission to do so, because those who own and occupy such land, which is used primarily for agriculture, forestry or private recreation, tolerate such trespass or are unable effectively to prevent it owing to the cost or difficulty of doing so. Such use is probably made of large parts of the one-third of the United Kingdom that is open moorland, but farmland and woodland within motoring range of large centres of population are also likely to be used. Little is known about the recreational use of land of this kind, other than from the protests of occupiers and owners of the land affected, which have tended to grow as the mobility and leisure of the population have increased in the post-war period. Thirdly, public recreation takes place on land over which the public has legal rights of access or is allowed access by virtue of public ownership. The location and area of such land is generally well known to local authorities and to bodies such as the Countryside Commission, though no comprehensive gazetteer is available; there is also little information on the extent to which such land is in fact used for recreation. Fourthly, there are less extensive areas which are used primarily or even exclusively for outdoor recreation. Their location and extent are generally better known because they are in public ownership or contain structures which require planning consent for their erection, or are rateable; alternatively, they are the concern of national bodies of users who publish lists of such facilities for the benefit of their members. Nevertheless, information on the acreages of such land has not been conveniently assembled; the nearest approaches to such an inventory are the estimates made by T. L. Burton and G. P. Wibberley in *Outdoor Recreation in the British Countryside* [B 11] and the summary statistics published by the Countryside Commission [QRL 36, 48].

7.3.3. Land over which the public has rights of access or which it is permitted to use for recreation falls into three categories: land in public or semi-public ownership; certain categories of common land, together with rights of ways; and land over which local authorities have negotiated Access Agreements. The woodlands of the Forestry Commission are generally open to the public along footpaths and forest roads, as is land not suitable for planting and not required for other purposes, subject to restrictions when there is a high risk of fire and to pre-existing commitments, e.g. to shooting tenants; some land which is leasehold may also be subject to restrictions on public use [B 102, QRL 43]. By contrast, little private woodland is open to the public, except insofar as it is traversed by rights of way or enjoys special legal status. In a sense, therefore, the annual reports of the Forestry Commission provide data on one kind of recreational land, and though the extent of land which is in fact used for recreation is not known very accurately, the reports now provide information on numbers of visitors and overnight campers and on facilities on land under the Commission's control. Recreation is of particular importance in the seven Forest Parks, which the Commission created between 1935 and 1955 and in the New Forest which fulfils a very similar role, and an increasing volume of data is available about the recreational use of such areas. Six Forest Parks have also been established in Northern Ireland, where the Forestry Division is also producing opportunities for outdoor recreation in State forests; over fifty such sites had been established by 1973 [B 86]. Apart from land acquired for recreational purposes, most other publicly owned land is no different from private land in respect of access for public recreation, but there are also two important semi-public bodies on whose land recreation plays an important role, the National Trust for England, Wales and Northern Ireland and the National Trust for Scotland, both of which facilitate public recreational use of their land where this is possible, though they are also concerned to conserve the countryside and have obligations to their agricultural and other tenants [QRL 45, 64]. Nevertheless, these properties too can be considered at least in part recreational.

7.4. Commons

While commons, for all practical purposes, now survive only in England and Wales, members of the public do not have rights of access to all common land (contrary to a widespread belief), but only to about a fifth. There are three main categories of common land over which there are public rights of access; those within the Metropolitan Police District, which are subject to the provisions of the Metropolitan Commons Acts, 1866–78; those where such rights have been conferred by deed under Section 193 of the Law of Property Act, 1925 or other legislation; and commons lying wholly or partly in an urban district, which account for about 10 per cent of the total area under commons. It is in this last category that many of the commons in the Lake District fall, for somewhat surprisingly, they lie within the extensive Lakes Urban District [QRL 12]. All commons have now been registered under the Commons Registration Act and their location and extent will be accurately known when appeals have all been heard. Another special class of commons is represented by village greens [B 44]. How far these or other commons are used for recreation is not known accurately; the Royal Commission on Common Land estimated that some 10 per cent of common land was used primarily for recreation and amenity [QRL 12]. L. D. Stamp, J. Wager and D. R. Deman and his collaborators have all provided some information on the recreational use of common land [QRL 12, B 21, 52].

7.5. Access Agreements

Under the Countryside Acts and the National Parks and Access to the Countryside Act, local authorities have powers to negotiate Access Agreements over open land (a concept extended in the Countryside Acts to include woodland) with private or public owners of land, though most authorities have shown no wish to exercise these powers because the public enjoy *de facto* access [QRL 43]. The great majority of Access Agreements in England and Wales, details of which are published in the *Annual Report* of the National Parks (later Countryside) Commission, have been negotiated in respect of land in the Peak District National Park [QRL 21]. Since the 1967 Countryside (Scotland) Act there have been similar powers available to local authorities in Scotland, and several Access Agreements have now been made. The Countryside Acts provide powers for the designation of long-distance footpaths and, though the areas involved are small, such footpaths give access to a much wider range of countryside; in this connection, footpaths in the countryside in general, a legacy from the pre-modern era estimated at some 100,000 miles in England and Wales, similarly provide access to land in the lowlands devoted primarily to agriculture and forestry [B 93]. T. L. Burton and G. P. Wibberley have also included some National Nature Reserves and National Trust properties in their estimates of recreation areas [B 11].

7.6. Recreational Land

7.6.1. Land used exclusively or primarily for recreation tends to be much better known than the categories previously discussed, though there are many gaps and information has not been synthesised in any way; recreational land within the urban fence (and some of that in adjacent countryside) is included in the urban land uses discussed below. Of increasing importance are the Country Parks designated under the authority of the Countryside Acts and under the Amenity Lands Act (Northern Ireland). Those for England and Wales are listed in *Recreation News* [QRL 48], those for Scotland in the annual *Report* of the Countryside Commission for Scotland [B 85] and those for Northern Ireland in the *Report* of the Ulster Countryside Committee [B 86]. Some publicly owned land used for recreation pre-dates the Countryside Acts; for example, the City of London acquired Burnham Beeches and Epping Forest for public recreation in the nineteenth century, Nottingham Corporation purchased Clumber Park and Edinburgh Corporation acquired the land which now forms Hillend Park. Rating valuations and lists compiled by national organisations provide an indication of the location of facilities such as horse, greyhound and motor racing tracks, sports stadia, zoological gardens and other forms of recreation that make relatively large demands on land, though only occasionally, as in the records of zoological gardens, is the actual acreage given, and in none are rural facilities distinguished from urban [B 20]. Lists of golf courses have been published [B 57] and these have been used in conjunction with assumed average acreages to produce estimates of their total area [B 47]. The Scottish Branch of the National Playing Fields Association undertook surveys in 1962 and 1967 of reckonable playing space [QRL 61]. The 1962 survey gives the number of different kinds of pitches, courts, greens, running tracks and playing fields and the total area they occupy in each county, as well as the total area in 1953; the details of the 1962 survey are held at the Scottish headquarters, but no records of the 1953 survey appear to survive. The 1967 survey was similar, though some authorities failed to provide details and estimates were made from the 1962 survey. Partial surveys have been made in England and Wales, but details do not appear to have survived. Numbers of horse-riding schools, which must be licensed, can also be ascertained, though not the acreage of land they occupy, and neither the acreage nor the number of pony-trekking establishments is known accurately. Details of recreational space used by schools and colleges could be supplied by local education authorities and by institutions of higher education, though no official compilations on the information are publicly available for the country as a whole. Some data are also available about the large number of establishments (often country houses) which local authorities and other bodies now own or rent in the countryside for various kinds of field studies and outdoor recreation. The Committee on Environmental Education in England and Wales and the Committee on Education and Countryside in Scotland have sponsored publication of lists of such establishments, which often have quite substantial grounds, though information on acreages is again lacking [B 66, 82]. Data on all these topics are likely to become increasingly available as local authorities become more aware of their responsibilities in respect of outdoor recreation and as the Regional Councils for Sport and Recreation become more firmly established. There are already numerous regional and local surveys of outdoor recreation, some embracing all forms of recreation and others confined to a single activity.

7.6.2. Provision for visitors generally cannot readily be separated from that for outdoor recreation. Caravan sites are now licensed and all local authorities possess lists, while national organisations, such as the Caravan Club and the Camping Club of Great Britain, compile lists of camping and caravan sites for their members [B 94], though, as with most other records, acreages of these sites are not provided. The number of picnic sites designated by local authorities is growing rapidly and these are similarly listed in the *Reports* of the two Countryside Commissions [QRL 21, B 85]. Other categories of land which can be considered broadly recreational are houses and gardens open to the public and ancient and historic monuments; lists of the former are published annually in a variety of sources [B 73] while the Department of the Environment has compiled lists of the latter [B 77]. Although such sites occupy considerable areas, their total acreage is unknown.

7.7. Data Collection

The situation in respect of records of land used for outdoor recreation is clearly unsatisfactory: at the least there are simple records of numbers of sites which occasionally include national estimates of the land they occupy, and at worst there is nothing at all. Moreover, there is a considerable amount of duplication, in that the same land may be used for various forms of recreation, while most recreational land is primarily used for other purposes; nor is it easy from the records available to distinguish between recreational land in urban and in rural areas. T. L. Burton and G. P. Wibberley have attempted to identify the extent of land used for outdoor recreation in the countryside, eliminating duplication where possible; but their estimates contain a wide range of values and some of the assumptions, particularly that areas are available because they are traversed by rights of way and that woodland not suitable for economic management can be regarded as recreational, are questionable [B 11]. The measurement of recreational land will always present difficulty because of the great variability in the incidence of outdoor recreation in both time and space and the subordinate role of many forms of recreation; nevertheless, the principal difficulty appears to be the lack of any clear responsibility for the collection of data on a uniform basis.

CHAPTER 8

OTHER RURAL LAND USES

8.1. Military Uses

There are many less important uses which often combine with farming and forestry, generally as a junior partner in various combinations of multiple or pseudo-multiple use. Two of the most important of these are land required for military purposes and that used for the collection and storage of water, especially to supply urban areas with drinking water. Military establishments themselves have exclusive use of the land they occupy and can be considered part of urban land, but there are much larger areas, generally in the uplands, which are used at intervals for military training and for the testing of equipment; the alternative uses of such land are limited, but most of it is used at other times for grazing. Although the location of such military training land has been shown on Development Plans and is generally known to the public, its location and extent have tended to be regarded as military secrets; national estimates have, however, been given from time to time in response to Parliamentary questions and detailed particulars of a large number of sites have been given in the *Report of the Defence Lands Committee* [QRL 50]. The extent of service land has certainly fluctuated widely in the past 35 years and has been a major item in the changes of occupancy data provided by the agricultural departments [QRL 3].

8.2. Water Collection

Apart from the areas which are actually flooded by reservoirs [QRL 1], most of the land used for the collection of water, whether for drinking purposes or for the generation of hydro-electric power, is also in various forms of multiple use in the uplands, though there are usually constraints on recreational use and on the type of agricultural use on the catchments of supply reservoirs [B 91]. Again, while the individual water authorities know the extent of their land holdings, and the use to which they are put, there is no regular collection or publication of such information; however, the responsible departments in Great Britain, the Department of the Environment (DOE) and the Scottish Development Department (SDD), do have maps showing the extent of gathering grounds and this information is generally included on the Development Plans of local planning authorities, although the latter information is now substantially out of date. The Natural Resources (Technical) Committee also provided an estimate for Great Britain as a whole [B 70].

8.3. Mineral Workings

There are also many 'urban' uses in the countryside, including rural settlements, roads, railways, air fields and power stations, but these will be discussed in the context of urban land, and only two uses, land worked for minerals and derelict land, will be considered here. From a land-use viewpoint (and indeed in respect of tonnage) most active mineral working now takes place in open pits in predominantly rural areas, particularly for the extraction of sand and gravel, clay, chalk and other limestone, and ironstone. Except where workings pre-date the Town and Country Planning Acts, mineral extraction requires the consent of the local planning authorities and the extent of land then being worked for minerals is shown on the Development Plans, as is the land zoned for use in the period of the plan (a situation which will change with the new planning, whereby Development Plans are superseded by Structure Plans and by Local and Action Plans). However, this information is now out of date, and while local planning authorities ought to be able to provide data on the extent of land for which planning consents have been given, such land does not necessarily correspond with land actually being used. Estimates have been made of the annual land requirements for the different minerals, though they are only approximate [B 5]. For each English county, estimates were made in April 1974 for the area under fourteen groups of mineral workings, broken down by spoil heaps, excavations and pits and areas not yet affected [QRL 60]. Less detailed data are available for the Welsh counties and districts [QRL 35]. More detailed information is presumably available from the National Coal Board in respect of open-cast coal workings and, while these are on a much smaller scale than during and immediately after the Second World War, the Board possesses detailed records of the location and extent of land worked and subsequently restored. For underground mining only the tonnage extracted is recorded, though the location of underground workings is clearly important, if only for its possible effects on land uses at the surface. The requirements of the 1951 Ironstone Act have also resulted in the keeping of detailed records on the extraction of iron ore.

8.4. Derelict Land

8.4.1. The composite nature of most sites used for mineral working, embracing working areas, processing or washing plant, mineral storage and land no longer worked, suggests that estimates of the extent of land used for mineral working will always present difficulties. Similar difficulties arise over attempts to estimate the extent of derelict land which, in rural areas at least, is primarily land once used for mineral extraction, though it also includes former industrial sites, land used for waste disposal and that formerly used for transport, such as abandoned railway tracks. There has been growing concern since the late 1950s at the lack of knowledge about the extent and location of such land.

8.4.2. Since 1964 the Ministry of Housing and Local Government (since 1971, the Department of the Environment) has carried out a number of surveys of derelict land in England. Between 1964 and 1971 these surveys were annual and gave the area under spoil heaps, excavations and pits, and other forms of dereliction for administrative counties and county boroughs (except in 1964, when figures for counties only were produced) and for regions; the surveys also showed the amount of derelict land treated in each year [QRL 60]. A special survey in 1972 provided the same categories of information, with the addition of British Rail land that had been restored. A more comprehensive survey was undertaken on 1st April 1974. It identified various categories of derelict land, including derelict military land and abandoned railway land as well as spoil heaps and excavations and pits; figures were also given for the increase in area since the beginning of 1972 and the area restored in that period, land abandoned from mineral working where restoration conditions were unlikely to be fulfilled and land used, or scheduled to be used, for waste tipping [QRL 60]. The information is given by new counties, regions and, for the main categories, districts. An interim survey was made in 1976, covering the period from April 1975 to March 1976 [B 101].

8.4.3. Similar information was collected between 1964 and 1971 in Wales, in the first year by the Ministry of Housing and Local Government and thereafter by the Welsh Office. A more detailed survey was undertaken in 1971 and 1972 by the Welsh Office. The main categories recognised were areas being actively worked for minerals, disused spoil heaps (separately distinguishing those being reworked), disused mineral excavations and disused buildings and installations. Each category was subdivided according to the source of dereliction and information was provided by new counties and districts [QRL 35].

8.4.4. No regular systematic surveys have been undertaken in Scotland. An estimate was made of the total area of derelict land in 1963, and information was collected in 1973 by the Scottish Development Department and the Derelict Land Unit, with the co-operation of local authorities, of all dereliction south of the Caledonian Canal. This initial survey has made use of aerial photographs and ground checks to identify areas of derelict land, but the survey was much wider-ranging than those in England and Wales, including all land that was neglected, derelict or unsightly. The data are being mapped under three major categories, viz., mineral extraction, tipping and handling places; channels and communications (railways, canals, etc.); and other dereliction. More detailed information is being recorded for Glasgow but none of this information has yet been published.

8.4.5. As the different categories indicate, there are major difficulties in defining the extent of derelict land accurately and, with the exception of the 1973 survey of most of Scotland, the true extent of land that is derelict in any visual sense is undoubtedly underestimated; for the figures exclude, *inter alia*, dereliction on sites that are already being worked or for which planning permission for further working has been given or which are subject to conditions in respect of restoration and landscaping (except in some later surveys, which include land where these conditions seem unlikely to be met). One critic, writing in the 1960s, estimated that the area derelict in any visual sense was probably about twice as large as the official figure [B 1]. There has undoubtedly been progress in reducing the area of land made derelict in the past, but new land is also made derelict each year.

CHAPTER 9

CONSERVATION AND AMENITY

9.1. Conservation and Land Use

Another aspect of the use of rural land which has been the subject of increasing public and official concern in recent decades is the conservation of wildlife and the amenity, i.e., the visual quality of the countryside. How far such conservation constitutes a use of land is debatable, though Lord Holford described the enjoyment of beauty as the most important of all uses [B 29]; for the conservation both of amenity and of wildlife is intimately related to the use of land in general and, in most parts of the country, is a by-product of other uses. Sir Dudley Stamp provided both a broad over-view of both kinds of conservation and details of the more important sites, generally including acreages, in each county in England, Scotland and Wales [QRL 10].

9.2. Wildlife and Nature Reserves

9.2.1. Conservation of wildlife can properly be regarded as a use in those areas where it is either the primary or an important consideration in land management. The Nature Conservancy Council (NCC) or, prior to 1973, the Nature Conservancy, has a statutory responsibility in Great Britain for designating National Nature Reserves, which are intended to be representative of the major biological communities and physiographic sites in the country [QRL 43]; in Northern Ireland the conservation of nature is the responsibility of an advisory Nature Reserves Committee, established in 1965 [QRL 47]. Some of the National Nature Reserves have been purchased but the majority are the subject of agreements with landowners, which run for a number of years. Both the location and area of these reserves are known accurately and have been recorded in the *Annual Reports* of the Nature Conservancy (which was established in 1949) and, between 1965 and 1972, of the Natural Environment Research Council [QRL 24]; with the creation of the Nature Conservancy Council in 1973, the reports of that body will in future provide this information [QRL 40]. A detailed review by the NCC, *A Nature Conservation Review: an Account of Biological Sites of Special Importance to Nature Conservation in Great Britain*, was published in 1977 and provides a modern book of all important ecological and physiographic sites, including National Nature Reserves [QRL 46]. All these require that the land also be used for some other purpose, e.g., grazing by sheep; they are thus mostly in some form of multiple use, though the nature of these uses can be established only by examining the individual management plans. Nature Reserves in Northern Ireland are listed, but no acreages are published [QRL 47].

45

9.2.2. In addition to National Nature Reserves there are several other forms of conservation land in Great Britain. Forest Nature Reserves comprise land under trees and already in public ownership, while Local Nature Reserves are designated by local authorities and are generally managed by local naturalists trusts or similar bodies (which may well possess reserves of their own), and acreages and locations of these are available [QRL 43]. Bodies such as the Royal Society for the Protection of Birds and the Scottish Wild Life Trust and county naturalist trusts also own or rent Nature Reserves, and acreages of these by NCC Regions have been published [QRL 36]. The NCC is also responsible for designating Wildfowl Refuges, mainly coastal marshes where large numbers of birds congregate at particular times of the year, and Sites of Special Scientific Interest (SSSIs) [QRL 43]. The latter, which number over 2,000, are widely scattered throughout the country and represent a much lower order of protection, for safeguards are confined to an obligation on local planning authorities to notify the NCC of those proposed land-use changes affecting such sites which require planning approval; the NCC has a complete list of such sites, and local authorities possess similar lists for those SSSIs in the area for which they are responsible. Such lists are not normally published, though many of the sites will be included in the *Nature Conservation Review*; as far as can be ascertained, total acreages have never been computed. In Northern Ireland, Areas of Scientific Interest are noted by the Nature Reserves Committee [QRL 47].

9.3. National Parks and Areas of Outstanding Natural Beauty

In a similar way, areas of high amenity are also statutorily defined, although their extent is much greater and their effect on land-use patterns correspondingly smaller; for while designation confers additional powers in respect of control over land-use changes and for the provision of facilities for access for the enjoyment of the countryside, the existing ownership of the land and existing land uses remain unchanged and land-use controls are restricted to those changes which require planning consent. The most important of such areas in England and Wales have been designated as National Parks; others have been made Areas of Outstanding Natural Beauty, which have been described as second-order National Parks. The location and extent of such areas are recorded in the annual *Report of the National Parks Commission* and of its successor, the Countryside Commission [QRL 21, 51]. No National Parks or Areas of Outstanding Natural Beauty have been designated in Scotland but areas proposed for designation by an official committee are known as National Park Direction Areas, in which there are similar restraints on development; the nature of controls in the interests of amenity in Scotland has been described in the evidence of the Countryside Commission of Scotland to the Select Committee on Scottish Affairs [QRL 43]. Less important areas, known as Areas of Great Landscape or Historic Value, have been incorporated by local planning authorities in their development plans or are the subject of separate proposals; like all of these special areas, their location is known and maps of them have been prepared for the whole of Great Britain [B 18, 50, 83, M 9]. No National Parks have been established in Northern Ireland, though the necessary powers exist; the Ulster Countryside Committee advises on the designation of such parks, as well as of Areas of Outstanding Natural Beauty, of which eight existed in 1973 [B 86].

CHAPTER 10

URBAN LAND

10.1. Deficiencies in Urban Land Data

Although more than four-fifths of the population live in towns, which house most of the economic activities on which the national wealth depends, the use of urban land is paradoxically one of the least well known of all land uses (although it is potentially one that can yield a very rich harvest of data). Indeed, until the maps of the first Land Utilisation Survey were measured, no reasonably accurate estimate even of the total urban area was available, and the acreage of urban land in England and Wales submitted to the Royal Commission on the Distribution of the Industrial Population (the Barlow Commission) by the Ministry of Agriculture and Fisheries (MAF) in 1937 was probably 40 per cent larger than the true acreage because it was a residual figure prepared by deducting known uses from the total land area [QRL 3]. Data on the subdivision of urban land into its component uses has had to await the preparation of Development Plans in the late 1940s and 1950s, and even these are still incomplete; at least one Scottish county still had to submit plans more than 25 years after the Act calling for them and shortly before they were to be abandoned in favour of structure plans and local plans, although the new planning legislation will require local authorities to examine and keep under review 'the principal purposes for which land is used' [QRL 43]. Moreover, while local planning authorities were asked to compile the data on urban land uses in the preparation of their development plans [QRL 3], they have no statutory duty to record annual changes in land use; and although guidance is provided by the central government departments responsible for planning, it is hard to achieve consistent results from large numbers of planning authorities. The difficulty of providing such information is partly due to the complexity and rapidly changing nature of many urban land uses and partly to the fact that responsibility for the collection of data on urban land uses rests on local authorities which vary greatly in their resources, expertise and problems. This situation has changed somewhat with the reorganisation of local government which came into effect in England and Wales in 1974 and in Scotland in 1975. The new local authorities in England and Wales have been asked to provide information of fifteen broad categories of land use change from 1975 to 1976 [B 95], but collection of this information has been deferred because of the need to limit expenditure.

10.2. Definition of Urban Land

capricious or despotic

10.2.1. The definition of urban land is both difficult and arbitrary, for there is a gradation

intensity

of settlements from the large city to the individual isolated dwelling. While effective planning control and the Green Belt policy have tended to sharpen the boundary between town and country in the post-war period by preventing haphazard expansion into the countryside and by encouraging building on any land within the urban fence which is zoned for urban purposes but not previously developed, past urban expansion had already resulted in a continuum of urban development and there is thus an urban penumbra around large cities which is neither town nor country.

10.2.2. Two simple definitions of urban land can be dismissed with little discussion. Urban land is not synonymous with the area of urban administrative districts, which may in fact include large areas of undeveloped land, while extensive tracts of continuously built-up land lie in adjacent rural districts. It was estimated in the early 1950s that 33 per cent of the land in county boroughs in England and Wales was rural, and the figures in urban districts was probably even higher [QRL 3].   These proportions will now have fallen, but an estimate in 1961 indicated that the total administrative area of urban authorities was probably a third higher than the true urban area. Equally, as MAF evidence to the Barlow Commission indicated, an estimate of the urban area cannot be derived as a residual figure, partly because of deficiencies in the existing land-use data and partly because, as the preceding analysis has shown, there are many land uses for which no data exist. It is interesting to note that, under the Countryside (Scotland) Act, countryside (and hence by implication urban land) must be defined and recorded on maps; the proportion has been estimated at 98 per cent [QRL 43 and M9]. Such definition is not required in England and Wales.

10.3. Estimates of Urban Land Use

10.3.1. Because of the difficulties of drawing a line to define urban, the Land Utilisation Survey's estimate of the urban area, obtained by direct measurement of the Survey's maps, related to all built-up land and associated space, and included farmsteads, isolated dwellings and roads and railways in the countryside, mineral workings and derelict land, airfields, industrial plant and large government establishments in rural areas; the results were published in the county reports and in the general account of the survey [QRL 11]. Data on the area of such land on farms, which include the farmstead, or buildings and roads, are in fact now collected by the agricultural censuses, but no other data of this kind are regularly collected [QRL 13, 56, 58]. A similar approach was followed by Dr. R. H. Best, who has provided in *The Changing Use of Land in Britain* the first estimate of the post-war extent of the urban area in Great Britain and the first subdivision of urban land into its component parts [QRL 3]. His estimates, too, cover all built-up land and include open spaces in the towns, as well as the area of roads and railways in the countryside. Indeed, it is an interesting commentary on the significance of apparently minor elements in the land-use pattern that roads and railways outside towns, which appear to be essentially linear features in a national context, were estimated to account for 17 per cent of the total urban area.

10.3.2. Dr. Best's estimates are derived ultimately from the obligation placed upon local planning authorities to undertake surveys and analysis before making their Development

Plans, for which local planning authorities have collected information on broadly comparable bases. Although not all plans had been submitted when Dr. Best made his estimates, sufficient were available for him to establish a relationship between urban area and population for towns of different sizes and hence to estimate the urban area by reference to the known population of the country, although it was not possible to draw a strictly representative sample of towns. No similar data on urban land use are available for Northern Ireland, though an estimate of the area under roads and buildings, obtained from the 1951 census of population, was computed for each county and for the province [B 48].

10.3.3. The bases of Dr. Best's estimates differed for various classes of settlement. For two administrative areas which then existed in England, the counties of London and Middlesex, the urban area had been directly measured in connection with the preparation of development plans, and similar data were available for the four counties of cities in Scotland. Suitable data on urban uses had been assembled for nearly all the 83 county boroughs in England and Wales and the average urban density per 1,000 population (ptp), derived from these was used in conjunction with data from the 1951 census of population to estimate the urban land occupied by such settlements; no similar data were available for large burghs in Scotland and densities computed for England and Wales were used for this purpose. A further category of large settlements was recognised in England and Wales, comprising towns of over 10,000 inhabitants for which town maps were available. Of the 218 settlements for which town maps had been submitted by 1954, 58 had populations of less than 10,000 or had incomplete or unreliable land-use statistics, and were therefore discarded; the remainder were used to estimate an average density of urban land per 1,000 population which was similarly multiplied by the 1951 population. For Scotland, an estimate of land in this category was not computed and all small burghs were regarded as small settlements, even though the population of some exceeded 10,000.

10.3.4. Even with the preparation of development plans, data on small settlements were still very inadequate. Town maps were generally not prepared for such settlements, and nine counties were therefore selected, five in Highland Britain and four in Lowland Britain, to provide sample data. For two areas, East Sussex and the Cupar District of Fife, special data were available; in the former a stratified sample was drawn and in the latter all small settlements were measured. In each of the remaining counties approximately thirty settlements were selected covering a range of population and settlement types. Estimates of urban land ptp were prepared and, owing to the wide range of values, separate estimates of the urban area in England and Wales in this class of settlement were computed for the Highland and Lowland zones; in Scotland, the densities in the Cupar district were used in conjunction with the population for all small burghs or other settlements of lower status. For isolated dwellings, densities estimated for small settlements with between 20 and 100 population were used to compute the urban land occupied by such settlements. It should be noted that the definition of urban land in small settlements is different from that employed in county boroughs and large settlements; for the former excludes mineral workings, military establishments and civil airfields, while the latter includes any acreages of those uses lying within Town map areas. It is also more difficult to determine the urban/rural boundary in small settlements, especially in respect of gardens, paddocks and other open space attached to large houses. Some kind of check should now be possible from the information on urban land now provided by the agricultural censuses.

10.3.5. Estimates of land occupied by roads and railways in the countryside were computed by multiplying representative widths by known mileages, an approach that had previously been used by Sir George Stapledon [B 47] and by the Land Utilisation Survey [QRL 11], and then deducting estimates of the area in roads and railways which had already been included in the urban area [QRL 3]. Data on airfields, also estimated by Stapledon [B 47], have more recently been assembled by Dr. R. N. E. Blake [QRL 5].

10.3.6. These estimates are, of course, liable to errors arising from differences of interpretation and from the different bases of estimation. Moreover, they give totals only for Scotland and England and Wales as a whole and cannot provide insight into regional differences in urban provision which might be expected from what is known of the history of urban expansion in the past two centuries. Some indication of these regional differences is given by the differences in the values for towns of different status, with lower acreages ptp in the county boroughs which are relatively more important in northern England and by the range of values recorded for the small settlements in Highland and Lowland Britain. The data, too, are only broadly referable to 1950 because of the variable dates at which surveys were undertaken. Using a larger sample of 251 towns with populations of more than 10,000 inhabitants and more reliable estimates of the areas of small settlements, Dr. A. G. Champion has been able to provide both regional and county estimates for England and Wales, and has computed a total urban area for England and Wales which is 4 per cent smaller than that estimated by Dr. R. H. Best (though the difference is within the estimated range of error) [QRL 6]. A similar attempt has been made by an Interdepartmental Study Group to provide estimates of the urban areas in each region of England, in Scotland and in Wales [QRL 44].

10.3.7. A different approach to the measurement of the urban area has been adopted by Dr. R. C. Fordham, who has criticised Dr. Best's estimates, particularly on grounds of dependence on suspect data (those derived from the Development Plans) and not being derived from random samples (and hence not amenable to statistical tests) [QRL 68]. Dr. Fordham derived his estimates from systematic point samples of Ordnance Survey maps, using the 1″ to 1 mile maps and 25″ plans for urban administrative areas and the 6″ to 1 mile maps for rural administrative areas. The maps themselves were selected at random, as were sample areas within the selected 25″ plans. Urban land was identified as that occupied by buildings, roads and railways and immediately related open space (gardens, formal recreational land, canals and rivers within urban areas); any large open spaces within the urban fence that could not be identified from the maps as parks or playing fields were excluded. For the 1″ maps the data were obtained from as many post-war revisions as possible and dates of these clustered around the periods 1948–55 and 1958–65; estimates of urban land in urban administrative areas in 1951 and 1961 were derived from these by fitting a straight line between pairs of observations. For the 6″ map, dates of survey clustered around the period 1948–52 and estimates were made of urban land in rural administrative areas in 1951 and 1961 by reference to rates of change of population between those dates. The 25″ plans were used to provide detailed estimates to complement those derived from the 1″ map. Estimates were made for each of the eleven Standard Regions and for the United Kingdom, and coefficients of variation calculated for each estimate; for 1961 the range was 219,000 acres on either side of the estimate of 4,079,000 million acres. His estimate for 1951 was approximately half a million acres lower than Dr. Best's. He also estimated areas for 1971 by linear extrapolation of the trend lines used to produce figures for 1951 and 1961.

10.3.8. Dr. Best recognised that his estimates, based on the first Development Plans, had a number of limitations [QRL 66]. The lack of data on small settlements and limitations on the estimates for isolated buildings and for roads and railways in the countryside meant that the figures used in estimating the urban area for 1950/1 tended to be less accurate the smaller the population and the lower the status of the area in the administrative hierarchy. Where it was difficult to make a reliable estimate every effort was made to err on the side of generosity in choosing parameters, in order that the resulting figure could not be criticised as being an underestimate. His figures for England and Wales were thus maximum figures, so that the availability of more precise data was likely to reduce rather than increase them.

10.3.9. Dr. Best and his associates, particularly Dr. A. R. Jones, have therefore calculated the size of the urban area in 1961, using the same method but employing data derived from later Development Plans and from reviews of those submitted earlier [QRL 66]. In Town Maps submitted after the mid-1950s, local planning authorities had to refer to net areas and to account for the whole of the area surveyed. Furthermore, while the data used to estimate the urban area in 1950/1 were already grouped by what were essentially administrative urban categories that reflected the size of population only in a generalised way, those for 1961 were ungrouped and so could be reliably grouped by size of population. More reliable estimates for small settlements of under 10,000 population had been made by Dr. Best and A. Rogers by direct measurement from maps of the Second Land Utilisation Survey [QRL 4], and the provision of land from the smallest category of such settlements was used to estimate the area of isolated settlements. New estimates of roads and railways in rural areas were also calculated, using representative fence-to-fence widths for different categories, and Dr. Blake had provided an estimate of the area of civil airfields. Because data obtained by direct measurement were lacking in Scotland, estimates derived from those employed to calculate the urban area of England and Wales were used, modified to some extent to take account of the generally higher urban densities in Scotland. The estimates for Scotland are accordingly less reliable than those for England and Wales. This new estimate of the urban area has confirmed the view that the original figure for 1950/1 was probably an over-estimate, since a derived figure for England and Wales from the 1961 base (obtained by using the data on Changes in Land Use discussed in paragraph 5.9.3) is some 290,000 acres lower than the earlier estimate. An estimate of the urban area in 1971 in England and Wales and in Scotland has also been derived from the 1961 estimate by means of the data or Changes in Land Use.

10.3.10. Two other estimates of the urban area in England and Wales have been made, both obtained by using systematic point sampling of intersections of 1 km² cells of the National Grid. Miss M. A. Anderson has based her estimate on the 1:63,360 Agricultural

Land Classification maps of England and Wales (which have a time span from 1952 to 1972 and a modal date of 1962); her figures provide confirmation of Dr. Best's, which lie within the confidence limits of her sample at the 95 per cent level [QRL 65]. Miss A. Coleman and her associates have measured the area under settlements on the maps of the Second Land Utilization Survey, which were surveyed between 1960 and 1970, though mainly in the early 1960s. She gives the date of 1963 for her estimate, which is some 316,000 acres higher than Dr. Best's figure for 1961 [B 115], though she does not indicate the confidence limits of her figure.

10.4. Developed Areas

More recently, the Department of the Environment has commissioned Fairey Surveys Ltd. to produce maps of 'developed areas' in England and Wales, based on panchromatic air photography at a scale of approximately 1:60,000 flown by the RAF in 1969 and Ordnance Survey maps at a scale of 1:50,000 [B 120]. This study is intended to provide a more accurate statement than the small-scale map of Built-up Areas, published in 1958 [M 10], that will permit an assessment of urban land uses, particularly at national and regional levels, and serve as a bench-mark against which future changes can be monitored. Developed areas are defined as all areas of continuous (urban) development of more than 5 acres in extent, though areas of fragmented development are amalgamated where breaks in continuity are less than 50 metres. Roads and railways outside areas of continuous development are excluded and five broad land-use groups are being identified, viz., predominantly residential use; predominantly industrial and/or commercial use; predominantly educational/community/health/indoor recreational use; and transport use. The 1:50,000 maps form the recording base and each parcel is being digitised to permit handling by computer, which is being used to measure areas. Statistics for the South East Region have been produced and those for the remaining regions are expected by the end of 1977 [B 101].

10.5. Estimates of Component Uses of Urban land

10.5.1. The method used by Dr. Best to make estimates of the component uses was essentially the same as that used to estimate the urban area, though no suitable data were available for Scotland or Northern Ireland and estimates have therefore been made only for England and Wales [QRL 3]. Data from the county borough development plans and for the town map areas in England and Wales had been assembled under four main heads: residential, the most important category; open space, the second largest; industrial; and educational. Apart from residential land, these categories are not wholly satisfactory, for education land includes school playing fields which are in one sense recreational; open space includes both allotments and cemeteries, as well as public and private recreation land and land valued for its landscape; and the category for industrial land is largely confined to manufacturing industry. Residential land is defined as the net residential area, which includes not only house plots but also local roads and small included areas of open space. These four main categories vary greatly in their contribution and there was also a residual category which was generally larger than any of the main categories except residential land. No data on urban uses were available in respect of small settlements, but a separate survey had been conducted by the Planning Department of East Sussex County Council of such settlements in that county. This survey showed that densities were lower than in larger settlements and that densities declined with declining rank of settlement; but it was recognised that the figures for this county were atypical and could not be expected to provide estimates for the small settlements of England and Wales as a whole. Dr. Champion has also shown that *per capita* provision for each of the main categories in England and Wales shows considerable regional variation, with twice as much land per thousand population for housing and for education and open space in the most favoured regions by comparison with the least favoured. There is, moreover, a considerable range within regions [QRL 7].

10.5.2. In later development plans and town maps in England and Wales more detail was provided on the residual category, which includes transport, commerce, administration, derelict land and unused land, but this information has never been analysed, and A. R. Jones, who has examined 205 town maps, ranging in date of survey from 1955 to 1965, has also had to restrict his analyses to the four main categories [B 103]. However, for some areas, more elaborate data are available. Full details of land used as allotments in England and Wales have been collected by a Departmental Committee in *Departmental Committee of Inquiry into Allotments: Report* [QRL 32]. Separate estimates have also been made of industrial land [B 2] and better data are available for New Towns [QRL 2].

10.5.3. As with measurement of the urban area, these estimates of the composition of the urban area derived from town maps and development plans are also liable to error which is due both to the nature of the original data and to the way in which the estimates have been computed. The data contained in the original land-use statistics are for zones rather than for individual properties, so that each contains 'impurities', i.e., other uses; furthermore, where buildings with more than one storey contain a number of uses, only the most important has been considered, and this decision itself may have been made arbitrarily; for example, residential land generally excludes those living in multistorey accommodation in central areas. There are also undoubtedly differences of interpretation by planning authorities, especially in respect of the categories of educational land and open space. Nonetheless, whatever their weaknesses, these data have been compiled specifically as land-use records and they represent the best that are currently available. The Ministry of Housing and Local Government also computed estimates from the first round of Development Plans, similarly relating broadly to about 1950, but no published data for any of the component countries of the United Kingdom are available for any later date, and as far as is known, no further analyses have been undertaken by the planning ministries [B 87]. It is true that more recent submissions of town maps, whether as revisions or for the first time, contain a complete statement of land uses for the whole area covered by each map, but no analyses of these maps have been published and, since the acreages are net while earlier figures are gross, they are not strictly comparable. Of course, these and additional data are available for the areas for which individual planning authorities are responsible.

10.5.4. Dr. Fordham has also made estimates of fifteen individual uses within the urban area for each of the eleven Standard Regions, though only the figures for buildings, transport land and open land have been published. Owing to differences of definition, his estimates cannot be compared with those made by Dr. Best and his associates.

10.6. Changes in Urban Land Use ✓

10.6.1. Changes in the extent of urban land have been estimated partly by comparison of estimates of the area at different points in time and partly by means of the data on Changes in Land Use (paragraph 5.9.3), which are obtained from the agricultural census. The estimates from the two Land Utilisation Surveys of England and Wales are not strictly comparable and Miss Coleman has attempted to adjust her figures (derived from a systematic point sample) and those from the First Land Utilisation Survey (obtained by direct measurement by means of squared paper) to make them compatible; the methods of adjustment are not described and, apart from the addition of a figure for civil airfields, are based on complex estimates from a number of sources [B 98, QRL 67]. Direct comparisons of estimated urban areas in the eleven Standard Regions in 1951, 1961 and 1971 have also been made by Dr. Fordham [QRL 68].

10.6.2. Dr. Best has related the data on Changes in Lane Use to his estimates of the urban area in England and Wales in 1950/1 [QRL 3] and 1961 [B 112, QRL 66] to provide comparable estimates of its extent at various dates since 1901; he has also compared the rates of conversion from agricultural to urban land in the period since 1922 [B 113]. Similar estimates for changes in Scotland have been made since 1960. Dr. Best and Dr. Champion have also used these data to calculate changes in the constituent regions and counties [B 7]. Both the Interdepartmental Study Group and Dr. Champion have used these data on change of use to update estimates of the urban area for 1950-1. The Study Group has estimated totals for the English regions, for Scotland and for Wales, while Dr. Champion has provided estimates for both regions and counties in England and Wales in 1960 and 1970 [QRL 6, 44]. The request to local authorities to provide data on land use changes under fifteen heads (agriculture and fisheries; community and health services; defence; education; recreation and leisure; manufacturing; mineral extraction; offices; residences; retail distribution and servicing; storage; transport; utility services; wholesale distributions; and unused land, water and buildings) will help, assuming that comparable data can be collected [B 95]. It is intended that the minimum recorded should include the address, coordinate reference, site area, previous and new uses and date of change, and it is expected that local authorities will be able to draw on a number of sources such as rating and planning records. On past experience, however, it is likely that several years will elapse before consistent and reliable estimates are available.

10.7. Assessment of Data on Urban Land Use

10.7.1. In the absence of official data on urban land, several researchers have made ingenious attempts to provide reliable estimates. They have been handicapped in their efforts both by the nature of the data available to them and by the inherent difficulties in defining urban land. In the circumstances, the closeness of the various estimates is a matter of congratulation, for many of the discrepancies can be explained, at least in part, by differences in data, in definition and in method. Professor Stamp had drawn attention to differences in the definition of urban land adopted by the First Land Utilisation Survey and that used by Dr. Best, but thought the latter's estimates "very near the truth" [QRL 11]. Professor P. G. Hall, on the basis of comparisons between Dr. Best's figures and those derived by direct measurement of maps of the Second Land Utilisation Survey, thought the former were probably over-estimates [B 25] (a likelihood that Dr. Best himself accepted), while Dr. Fordham thought they were as much as 646,000 acres too high [QRL 68]. Part of this discrepancy was eliminated by the revision of Dr. Best's figure for 1951 on the basis of calculations on better data, and Dr. Best was confident that the difference was largely explicable by differences in definition (arising largely from the different data sources) and by the nature of the data [QRL 66]. Discrepancies between Dr. Best's estimates and those of Dr. Champion and Miss Coleman can also be largely explained by differences in definition. It is unfortunate that the nature of the data derived from the Development Plans does not permit estimates of statistical reliability to be made, for the data chosen were those that were available and usable; but in view of the difficulties of definition and identification, statistical rectitude is no guarantee that the resulting data are any more reliable.

10.7.2. The data on Changes in Land Use are recognised as having serious weaknesses [QRL 13], though those changes that provide the basis for the Scottish data are confirmed with both parties to the change [B 114], and Dr. Best's estimates of the urban area in England and Wales for 1931 and 1939, derived from these data, are consistent with figures from the First Land Utilisation Survey [QRL 66]. Dr. Fordham's estimates of the differences between the urban area in England and Wales in 1951 and 1961 imply a rate of change (36,900 acres p.a.) that is very similar to that computed by Dr. Best for the 1950s from the Change of Land Use data (37,100 acres p.a.). It is true that widely different views have been expressed about the scale of transfers from agricultural uses to urban uses (e.g., [B 109, B 110, B 111, B 113, B 115, QRL 67]), but it must be appreciated that urbanisation is a continuing process that varies with economic circumstances and with attitudes towards land-use planning. The process of transfer must always lead to the occurence of land that is apparently unused or derelict, and it is not clear from the available evidence at what point such land ceases to be regarded, both by the occupier and by census officials, as no longer in agricultural use. Land-use changes on the urban fringe are probably the most difficult to monitor accurately. It does not seem possible from present land-use data to identify satisfactorily a category of unused or idle land, though there is little doubt that some land awaiting transfer to urban uses is allowed to run down and may appear derelict or even abandoned. The amount of such land is also likely to increase in periods of financial stringency when activity in the civil engineering industry is restricted. Nor is it possible to identify changes within the urban area through redevelopment (which may similarly result in apparent waste land) except by air photographs and field mapping. The collection of adequate data on urban land and land-use changes is always likely to present difficulties.

CHAPTER 11

LAND UTILISATION SURVEYS

11.1. First Land Utilisation Survey

11.1.1. As has already been noted, the only record of land use for the whole country referable to a particular point in time is the first Land Utilisation Survey, the summary results of which were published in *The Land of Britain—its Use and Misuse* [QRL 11]. Even this survey, which was organised by the late Sir Dudley Stamp, was spread over 10 years from 1931 to 1941, though the great bulk of the field work was done between 1931 and 1934 [QRL 11]; 1-inch-to-1-mile maps have been prepared for the whole of Great Britain, which is also covered by *County Reports* in which the results of the survey are analysed and estimates of the land use are tabulated [B 33]. A similar survey of Northern Ireland was undertaken between 1938 and 1946 under the direction of Mr. D. A. Hill, though most of the field work was completed in the 1930s; while all the 1-inch maps were issued, only one memoir was published as *The Land of Ulster I. The Belfast Region* and no estimates appear to have been made of the areas under the different uses [B 28]. The record of land use provided by these surveys is a simple one, but it has the great merit of being both roughly contemporaneous and comprehensive; all land is accounted for and there are no blanks on the maps. Information was collected by observation and recorded on 6-inch-to-1-mile maps, each field or other parcel being labelled according to its predominant land use. Six major categories were identified, viz., forest and woodland; grassland; arable land; heathland, moorland and rough hill pastures; gardens (including allotments, orchards and nurseries); and land agriculturally unproductive. Surveyors were also encouraged to supply additional information, woodland, for example, being subdivided into high forest, coppice, scrub and cut-over land; unfortunately, the information obtained was not sufficiently consistent for the subcategories to be included in either the county or the national analyses. Surveyors were volunteers, many of them secondary school pupils and students at university and training colleges, and were often not skilled either in the interpretation of land uses or in map reading; sheets were examined for consistency of information at the margins with adjacent sheets, obvious errors were checked and sheets were occasionally resurveyed. Particular difficulty must have been experienced in areas where one use graded into another, e.g., where fields were being invaded by scrub or bracken, or where there had been substantial changes to the base maps, as when new housing estates had obliterated former field patterns. In Northern Ireland grassland and moorland were subdivided where substantial proportions (but less than half) were occupied by rough growth and good grass respectively [B 48].

11.1.2. When maps had been checked, information in the six major categories was transferred to 1-inch-to-1-mile maps in preparation for publication. In Great Britain processes of reduction and transfer were done by eye on to maps of the outline edition of the 4th edition of the Ordnance Survey 1-inch map, the boundaries between different classes of land use being sketched in. The acreages of the different categories of uses were then measured from the 1-inch map by means of transparent squared paper. There are thus three possible sources of error in the tables printed in the summary volumes and in the individual county reports: those of interpretation and location by the field surveyors; errors in transferring the information from the 6-inch to the 1-inch scale; and errors of measurement. How large these were is not known, but records were at least intended to provide information on land use and were the product of direct observation in the field, so that there is no reason to suppose that errors in measurement show any particular bias. For the 1-inch maps that were not published, manuscript, hand-coloured copies are held in the map collection of the Royal Scottish Geographical Society [QRL 11]. Some 4-mile-to-1-inch maps were also produced for a few areas and a map for the whole of Great Britain at a scale of 1:625,000 was published as part of the National Atlas series; but this latter map is generalised and land-use data were again transferred by eye to the smaller scale map from the 1-inch maps, a tenfold reduction [M 7]. The original field sheets at a scale of 6 inches to 1 mile have not all survived; those that do are held in the Department of Geography, London School of Economics. In Northern Ireland 1-inch maps were published by the Ordnance Survey of Northern Ireland [M 2]. The field sheets of this are held in the Department of Geography, Queen's University.

11.1.3. Paradoxically, although the main emphasis in this survey was the measurement of rural land uses, its most valuable contribution has been the provision of the first reliable estimate of the urban area, and similar estimates can be made for any part of the country by measuring the appropriate maps. The other categories provide a check on the land uses recorded from official censuses, but surveyors faced the same difficulties as those responsible for these censuses in defining what was agricultural land. The Land Utilisation Survey recorded over a million acres more grassland than was enumerated in the agricultural returns, but the survey included grassland which was not used for agricultural purposes, especially on the fringes of towns, e.g., in Surrey [B 45]. The measurement of woodland was also likely to have been affected by difficulties of defining the boundaries between rough grazing and scrub. The category of heathland, moorland and rough hill pasture similarly included all rough land covered with non-tree vegetation irrespective of whether it was used for grazing or not. There is thus no reason to prefer the records of rural land use provided by the Land Utilisation Survey to those from official censuses. The agricultural returns have an advantage that they provide a wealth of information both on crops and more especially livestock which can be related to the data on land use, while the forestry censuses were all undertaken by skilled personnel. The records of the Land Utilisation Survey, on the other hand, though considerably out of date, form a convenient baseline from which post-war changes can be measured and have been used for this purpose by P. Hall and his associates [B 25]. They also have the considerable merit of being more accurately located than those of any data from the agricultural censuses.

11.2. Second Land Utilisation Survey

A second land use survey of Great Britain, begun in 1960 and largely completed for England and Wales in the 1960s, will provide a much greater range of data, since there are sixty-four categories of information, although this survey, too, has a rural bias [B 13]. The published maps are also at a scale of 1:25,000, at which field boundaries are shown, so that greater precision of measurement will be possible. The accuracy of the maps has yet to be established and the information relates to a wide span in time; for while most sheets covering England and Wales were completed in the early 1960s, the survey of England (except Foulness, since surveyed) was mapped in 1969 and that of Wales in 1970; only a small part of Scotland has been surveyed. Maps covering 15 per cent of England and Wales have been published but no small-scale maps for the whole country are yet available. Estimates of acreages under different land uses have been made from systematic point samples and those for England and Wales have been published [QRL 67]. An attempt has also been made to make data from the two surveys comparable by incorporating data from other sources, a process involving fourteen different adjustments [B 98]. This survey is potentially more valuable than its predecessor and should be able to provide data on land uses which are inadequately covered by official statistics, notably industrial and mineral land; there is also a category of tended but unproductive land which is broadly equivalent to open space. A book describing the survey and giving estimates of land in different categories in each country is being prepared [B 98]. Several areas have since been resurveyed to provide estimates of the rate of change.

CHAPTER 12

LAND CAPABILITY

12.1. Agricultural Land Capability

Limited data are also available on the capability of land for different uses. The first comprehensive attempt to assess land capability was made by the late Sir Dudley Stamp, in response to a request from the Royal Commission on the Distribution of the Industrial Population, and the resulting map was published as part of the Ordnance Survey's National Atlas series at a scale of 1:625,000 [QRL 11, M 8]. It is highly generalised and was prepared from physical and land-use maps; while nominally a general land classification map, it is essentially a map on which land is classified according to its suitability for agriculture. Estimates of the proportion of the country covered by the different classes of land were computed and published both by the Ordnance Survey, in a booklet which accompanies the map, and in Sir Dudley Stamp's summary of the work on the Land Utilisation Survey [QRL 11]. In the lowlands of Scotland, a more detailed survey was undertaken by staff of DAFS in the 1940s in which the agricultural quality of each parcel was recorded on a seven-point scale on maps at a scale of 6 inches to 1 mile; most of lowland Scotland has been covered and manuscript maps are held by DAFS [B 99]. In England and Wales maps of agricultural significance were prepared between 1966 and 1974 by staff of the Agricultural Land Service (now the Land Service) and were published at a scale of 1 inch to 1 mile (1:63,660); these maps show agricultural land on a five-point scale according to its relative importance for agriculture and are intended primarily to guide the transfer of land from agriculture to other uses [M 8]. Estimates of the proportion of land in each grade in Wales and seven MAFF regions in England have been published [B 60]; proportions on each map sheet will be given in the reports which are being prepared for each sheet. Maps of land capability, at a scale of 1 inch to 1 mile, are also being prepared by the Soil Surveys of England and Wales and of Scotland, a few sheets have been published; though other uses are considered, these too are primarily maps of land quality [M 8, B 8]. A land-capability map has been prepared for Northern Ireland by Dr. L. Symons and Dr. J. G. Cruickshank at a scale of 1:375,000 [B 48], using a similar approach to that adopted in Scotland.

12.2. Land Capability for Other Uses

Much less attention has been paid to the preparation of maps of land capability for other uses. The Forestry Commission, in conjunction with DAFS and MAFF, has surveyed the suitability of large tracts of Highland Britain for forestry, but the maps are not published and are not available for consultation [B 102]. Experimental work is in progress on the classification of land according to its scenic value and its suitability for wildlife conservation, but no systematic surveys are in progress; a variety of such maps has, however, been prepared by individual local planning authorities.

CHAPTER 13

MAPS AND AIR PHOTOGRAPHS

13.1. Ordnance Survey Maps

There are two potential sources of land-use data which have never been adequately exploited, the maps of the Ordnance Surveys and air photographs. The large- and medium-scale maps of the Ordnance Survey provide information for Great Britain on nearly all the categories recorded by the first Land Utilisation Survey, with the exception of the division of agricultural land into arable and permanent grassland, though the dates of survey vary widely; orchards and glasshouses are separately distinguished and more information is provided on urban areas, especially in relation to public buildings [M 1]. A small-scale land-use map has, in fact, been produced in the *Atlas of Great Britain and Northern Ireland*, based on the 1-inch-to-1-mile series [B 9], and the preparation of a developed areas map has already been noted [B 101]. Little information is readily available on the criteria used by surveyors in recording the different uses. The period necessary to survey the whole country is also longer than that taken by the Land Utilisation Survey. Resurvey is not undertaken on a uniform basis, areas of rapid change, particularly in the urban sector, being resurveyed more frequently than those where little change occurs [B 106]. Prior to 1880, the parish Area Books, produced in conjunction with the 25-inch plans, did give the acreage and use of each parcel, and from 1925 the Ordnance Survey recorded the areas under ten headings; the practice was discontinued after the Second World War, during which most of the existing records were destroyed, the surviving records covering only one-tenth of the country. However, the Ordnance Survey does now undertake continuous revision of its maps and this information is available in manuscript form and could provide a basis of regular assessments of changes in land use, particularly between agriculture, forestry and urban land. The maps of the Ordnance Survey of Northern Ireland provide similar information to their counterparts in Great Britain.

13.2. Other Maps

Apart from the maps of the two Land Utilisation Surveys, several other land-use maps have been published, notably in the Planning Maps series of the Department of the Environment and the Scottish Development Department. They are listed after the Bibliography. Maps of parts of the country have been prepared by various agencies and researchers.

13.3. Air Photographs

The potential of air photography as a source of land-use data is considerably greater. Aerial photographs provide a permanent record of a large number of land uses and also have the merit of permitting doubtful interpretations to be referred back, though it is true that interpretation is a highly skilled task for which ground control is essential when interpretation keys are being formulated. Professor D. Thomas has produced estimates of land uses in the London Green Belt from sample air photographs to provide what is probably the most comprehensive set of land-use data yet available for that area [B 49]. Air photographs have also been used for mapping derelict land, for forest inventory and for estimating recreational use, and the United States Department of Agriculture is currently experimenting with the use of air photographs in the collection of agricultural census data. Apart from problems of interpretation, the chief limitation on their present use for the supply of data on land use is their uneven coverage in space and time. The last complete cover of the whole of the United Kingdom by the Royal Air Force (RAF) was flown in the late 1940s and prints are, by modern standards, of poor quality. Air cover of large areas has been flown in the past 20 years to assist the Ordnance Survey with their map revision, and these photographs are generally of high quality. Most of the country was again covered by an RAF survey in 1969 [B 101]. A great deal of other cover is flown for local authorities, government agencies, private companies and the like, and it seems probable that a substantial part of the country is covered in any quinquennial period, especially in the more populous parts; unfortunately, there is at present no comprehensive machinery for co-ordinating these records, although the Department of the Environment, the Scottish Development Department and the Welsh Office are now filling this role in the public sector by maintaining Central Registers of Air Photographs. Furthermore, prior to the making of the developed areas map, no attempt had been made to extract land-use data from this photographic cover in any systematic way. Broad estimates of land uses may also be forthcoming from satellite imagery. The Department of the Environment is developing techniques to automate the classification of urban features from computer tapes of Landsat imagery, with encouraging results [B 101, B 119]. The feasibility of using this approach will be improved when resolution increases from its present limit of 79 metres to 20 metres in 1980–1 [B 101].

CHAPTER 14

IMPROVEMENTS IN LAND-USE RECORDS

14.1. Possible Improvements in Data Collection

14.1.1. The present position in respect of land-use data in the United Kingdom is clearly unsatisfactory. Coverage is inadequate and patchy, there are large gaps, data are rarely collected primarily as land-use records and few of the sources that are available have been properly evaluated. The inadequacy of the present position is widely recognised, especially in the planning profession, and has now been recognised by Ministers [B 95, QRL 43]. There is less agreement about what needs to be done, for to some extent the desire of the planner to have more and better information is in conflict with the administrator's concern to limit the cost of obtaining it and the politician's awareness of public sensitivity over data collection and of the need to keep demands for information to a minimum. Yet is is equally undesirable that decisions should be made on the basis of inadequate data.

14.1.2. On one point there would probably be little disagreement, the need for some public agency, possibly the Central Statistical Office (CSO), to have the responsibility for considering land use as a whole and for co-ordinating the attempts of various public agencies to collect data that bear on the use of land. One of the first tasks of such an agency would be to examine critically the data currently collected and the way in which they are obtained, bearing in mind both the purposes they are intended to serve and those which they might serve if the agencies responsible for their collection took account of the needs of other public bodies. The principal question in respect of the data now obtained in various ways would be how far they could be made compatible with other data so that gaps (arising from lack of any responsible agency or from remits that are too narrowly drawn) and ambiguities could be kept to a minimum. For those uses for which there are currently no data, the chief questions would be the kind of information which should be collected, the agency which should be responsible and the users from whom it should be collected.

14.1.3. A critical decision that would have to be decided if this collection of data was to be rationalised in this way would be the level of policy- and decision-making at which different kinds of information on land use are required; for this would determine the acceptable degree of accuracy with which data could be collected and their location specified. It is clear that a large part of the data currently collected in, for example, the agricultural returns, is little used at the local level, except by academics, though in part this may be due to the difficulty of handling data at this level of detail (a difficulty that computer-based information systems and the use of automated cartography may help to remove).

Such decisions on the level at which data are required have obvious implications for the growing concern with confidentiality and the trend towards the increasing use of sampling in data collection. Considerations of confidentiality impose restraints on the availability of data, requiring that they be disclosed only at a level of aggregation at which information about individuals cannot be identified (though, in principle, all such information could be obtained simply by observation); yet such aggregation, usually by administrative areas, has made for loss of flexibility of use in the resulting data, especially where the original data are destroyed, for they cannot then be recombined to make them compatible with other data sets. Sampling, too, requires that data be computed only for fairly large areas so that the resulting estimates have an acceptable level of accuracy; such sampling will also ensure that confidentiality is preserved. If data are required only at a high level of generalisation, e.g., for the country as a whole or for individual regions, there will be advantages in respect of confidentiality and cost/benefit ratios in collecting only sample data; for this will reduce costs and, though less certainly, improve the accuracy by permitting scarce resources of skilled manpower to be used to better advantage. On the other hand, if data are required for local use, e.g., in planning, neither sampling nor rigid rules to maintain confidentiality will be appropriate; it will be desirable to collect data from the whole population and to retain the original data so that a wide range of different aggregations of data (each preserving confidentiality) would be possible. Understandably, sampling appeals to both politicians and statisticians, since it reduces both demand on users and the costs and the volumes of data to be handled. Yet sampling will be a false economy if detailed data are subsequently needed at lower levels; information from the 1965–7 forestry census cannot be employed by local planning authorities because the results are not sufficiently precise to be used as valid estimates of private woodlands at that scale.

14.1.4. Investigations into the use of computerised data banks for planning purposes have in fact led to recommendations that, as far as possible, data be kept unaggregated so that they can be used flexibly, though this procedure involves costs in the storage and processing of data [B 74]. If this is done, it will be possible to reduce costs, while rules can be devised to ensure that confidentiality is always safeguarded; for appropriate samples can be drawn from the stored data whenever sampling produces an acceptable level of accuracy.

14.1.5. In the light of this analysis of data requirements at different levels, further consideration could also be given to the possibility of making greater use of air photographs for the collection of land-use data, particularly through comprehensive cover of the whole country at regular intervals, though there are admittedly difficulties posed by the variability of weather conditions in the United Kingdom. In addition to the advantages which have already been noted, remote sensing has the additional merit that it makes no demands on individual users of land. There is clearly scope for co-ordinating air photography so that coverage is both complete and compatible, though there will continue to be a need for special surveys. Possibly the Ordnance Survey could play this co-ordinating role, for data abstraction and analysis might well go hand in hand with map-making and map-revision; at present the Ordnance Survey's interest in land use is only incidental to its role as map-maker but its work in digital mapping, in air photography and in continuous revision have given it a much greater capability of playing a key role in monitoring land use. Since data on land use are generally of limited value unless they can be related to other data, there will be obvious advantages in co-ordinating such comprehensive air photography with collection of other data, notably the census of population. Such coverage will not, of course, obviate the need for field survey and postal inquiries, but it will make a greater range of up-to-date information available, provide a desirable check on data collected in other ways, and allow special inquiries which could be answered from air photographs, to be mounted more speedily.

14.1.6. The use of air photographs would be facilitated, as would many other ways of collecting data on land use if there were publicly available and up-to-date records of the ownership and occupation of land, especially in rural areas where the units of decision-making cover large areas. Such a task would pose considerable practical problems, although it should be noted that the boundaries of rural estates in Scotland have been mapped single-handed by Dr. R. Millman [B 35, 36, 37]. Such a record of land ownership would also lessen the risk that land might be omitted from censuses of land use. The Government has recently become aware of its lack of knowledge of ownership of farm-land and has appointed the Northfield Committee to investigate the matter.

14.1.7. The emphasis throughout this analysis of British land-use statistics has been on the areal extent of such uses, but it has also been clear that there are great variations in the intensity with which land is used. While area is an important attribute in a country where there is only 1 acre of land per head of population, it is by no means the only one. Unfortunately, data on intensity of use are even less adequate and sampling is probably the only feasible way of improving the quality of such data in the short run.

14.2. Trends in Land Use

Co-ordination of the collection of data on land use could also lead to more adequate analyses of trends in land use. A possible approach would be an elaboration of the type of information recorded on the change of occupancy data, in which an annual land budget would be presented, showing the gains and losses between the various uses, not only for the United Kingdom as a whole, as has been attempted by Miss A. M. Edwards and Professor P. G. Wibberley [B 23], but also for regions and for local planning authority areas. It is difficult to see how the effectiveness of present land-use policies can be evaluated unless the resulting changes are monitored; it is, for example, surprising that there is no firm knowledge whether 20 years of government encouragement of bracken eradication in Scotland has changed either the total acreage of bracken or its distribution [QRL 43]. Nor is it easy to see how governments can formulate adequate policies to deal with problems presented by, say, derelict land without fairly reliable data, not only on the spatial distribution of such land, but also on the rate at which its extent and distribution are changing. The need for information on change is now recognised by government, but we still lack adequate information of the existing situation to provide a context for assessing the significance of rate of change; furthermore, as in planning generally, the proposed method of collecting data from local authorities emphasises urban rather than rural changes. Nevertheless, such developments are to be welcomed and the situation will be further improved if expectations of the potential of satellite imagery for monitoring land-use changes are fulfilled. While better land-use statistics will not usher in the millennium, they are necessary for the proper conduct of both central and local government.

QUICK REFERENCE LIST

Description

The Quick Reference List is ordered in approximately the same way as the text and relates mainly to the area of land under different land uses. In general the tables for the United Kingdom contain the same information as those in the corresponding publications for England, Wales, Scotland and Northern Ireland, but there are sometimes small differences and some information may be available for one or more of the constituent countries but not for the United Kingdom as a whole. Many of the sources described in the monograph are not produced regularly or are estimates derived from incomplete data or inferred from other sources not relating directly to land use and are excluded from this list.

Of major importance in land-use statistics is the break-down of statistics by administrative areas. The county is normally the smallest area for which statistics are published, though in forestry details of individual state forests are given; details of smaller areas are, subject to rules governing disclosure of confidential information, generally available from the responsible agency. In particular, full parish details of the agricultural censuses in England, Wales and Scotland are available, the former from the Agricultural Census Branch of the Ministry of Agriculture, Fisheries and Food at Guildford (past 10 years) or the Public Record Office, the latter from the Scottish Record Office. All agricultural statistics are derived from the June censuses unless otherwise stated.

Statistics of both area and production from the main kinds of land use listed in this section are published in the *Annual Abstract of Statistics*, the Scottish, Welsh and Northern Ireland versions of this, and some appear in *Britain: an Official Handbook* or in the *Ulster Yearbook*. These sources will not be repeated in the sections which follow.

The sources refer to 1972. The machinery of collection, the name of the responsible agency and the name of the publication have sometimes changed. Thus prior to 1900, *Agricultural Statistics, England and Wales* and *Agricultural Statistics, Scotland*, were formerly in a single volume. *Agricultural Returns for Great Britain;* similarly, agricultural statistics for Northern Ireland were formerly printed in *Agricultural Statistics Ireland*. The changes are often complex and are not recorded in this section.

Data on trends are provided in most of these sources, but definitions and administrative areas have often changed, so that only for large areas and broad categories is it possible to examine long-term trends.

Column 5 provides a number in square brackets, and this is the number in the Quick Reference List Key which follows the Quick Reference List, listing in numerical order the publications which have been reserved in this paper. The final column in the Quick Reference List identifies by number the section of the text of this paper dealing with the appropriate entry.

QUICK REFERENCE LIST—TABLE OF CONTENTS

QUICK REFERENCE LIST

Type of statistics	Breakdown/details of analysis	Areas	Frequency	Publication	Text reference
Agricultural land quality					
Area	Land by classes	E,W,S, counties	*ca.* 1931–9	[QRL 11]	12.2
	Land by classes	Scot., districts	*ca.* 1941	[QRL 16]	12.2
AGRICULTURAL LAND					
Area	Crops, grass, rough grazing, woods, other land	UK	Annual	[QRL 15]	5.1–5.2, 5.9
Area	Crops, grass, rough grazing, woods, other land for agriculture	E, Eng. counties W, Welsh counties	Annual	[QRL 13]	5.1–5.2
Area	Crops, grass, rough grazing, woods, roads, yards, buildings	Scot., regions, counties	Annual	[QRL 58]	5.1–5.2
Area	Crops, grass, rough grazing, woods, roads, buildings and wasteland	North. Ire. counties	Annual	[QRL 49]	5.1–5.2
Area	Crops, grass, rough grazing (from 1891)	GB, E & W, Scot.	1866–1966	[QRL 31] ·	5.9
Crops and fallow					
Area	Total crops and fallow and each crop	UK, E & W, Scot. GB, North. Ire.	Annual	[QRL 15]	5.3
Area	Total crops and fallow and each crop	E, Eng. counties W, Welsh counties	Annual	[QRL 13]	5.3
Area	Total crops and fallow and each crop	Scot., regions, counties	Annual	[QRL 14]	5.3
Area	Total crops and fallow and each crop	North. Ire.	Annual	[QRL 23]	5.3
Area	Total crops and fallow and each crop	North. Ire. counties	Annual	[QRL 49]	5.3
Area	Total crops and fallow and each crop	North. Ire. counties, rural districts	Annual	[QRL 59]	5.3
Yields	Each cereal and root crop, sugar beet, hops	UK, E & W, Scot., GB, North. Ire.	Annual	[QRL 15]	5.8
Yields	Each cereal and root crop	E, Eng. counties W, Welsh counties	Annual	[QRL 13]	5.8
Yields	Each cereal and root crop	Scot.	Annual	[QRL 17]	5.8
Area	Total crops and principal crops	GB, E & W, Scot.	1866–1966	[QRL 31]	5.9
Area	Potatoes, area planted 1st, 2nd earlies, main crop	E,W,S, counties	Annual	[QRL 52]	5.8
Yields	Each cereal and root crop	Scot., regions	Annual	[QRL 14]	5.8
Yields	Each cereal and root crop	North. Ire.	Annual	[QRL 56]	5.8
Yields	Each cereal and root crop	North. Ire.	Annual	[QRL 23]	5.8
Yields	Principal crops	GB, E & W, Scot.	1888–1966	[QRL 31]	5.9
	Potatoes, varieties	E,S,W,	Annual	[QRL 52]	5.8

Type of statistics	Breakdown/details of analysis	Areas	Frequency	Publication	Text reference
Grass					
Area	Temporary grass, permanent grass, for mowing, not for mowing	UK, E & W, Scot., GB, North. Ire.	Annual	[QRL 15]	5.4
Area	Temporary grass, permanent grass, for mowing, not for mowing	E, Eng. counties W, Welsh counties	Annual	[QRL 13]	5.4
Area	Temporary grass, permanent grass, for mowing, not for mowing	Scot. regions	Annual	[QRL 14]	5.4
Area	Temporary grass, permanent grass, for mowing, not for mowing	North. Ire.	Annual	[QRL 23]	5.4
Area	Temporary grass, permanent grass, for mowing, not for mowing	North. Ire. counties	Annual	[QRL 49]	5.4
Area	Temporary grass, permanent grass, for mowing, not for mowing	North. Ire. counties, rural districts	Annual	[QRL 59]	5.4
Area	Permanent grass, temporary grass, for hay (1885–1866)	GB, E & W, Scot.	1866–1966	[QRL 31]	5.9
Yields	Hay (total)	UK, E & W, Scot., GB, North. Ire.	Annual	[QRL 15]	5.8
Yields	Hay (perm. grass)	E, Eng. counties W, Welsh counties	Annual	[QRL 13]	5.8
Yield	Hay (temp. grass)	North. Ire.	Annual	[QRL 56]	5.8
Yield	Hay (temp. grass)	GB, E & W, Scot.	1885–1966	[QRL 31]	5.9
Horticultural crops					
Area	Vegetables, individual crops, crops under glass, hardy nursery stock, flowers, orchards, small fruit	E, Eng. counties W Welsh counties	Annual	[QRL 13]	5.3. 5.8
Area	Vegetables, individual crops, hardy nursery stock, flowers, orchards (December), soft fruit	Scot., regions, counties	Annual	[QRL 14]	5.3, 5.8
Area	Vegetables, individual crops, orchards, small fruit, winter veg. (December)	North. Ire.	Annual	[QRL 49]	5.3, 5.8
Area	Vegetables, individual crops (generally 1941–66)	E & W, often E,W,S, principal counties	1964	[QRL 41]	5.8
Area	Fruit, flowers, individual crops (generally 1947–64)	E & W, sometimes, E,W,S, and principal counties	1964	[QRL 42]	5.8

Type of statistics	Breakdown/details of analysis	Areas	Frequency	Publication	Text reference
Horticultural crops—*contd.*					
Yields	Vegetables, individual crops, orchards, individual crops, small fruit, individual crops	UK, E & W, Scot., GB (where appropriate)	Annual	[QRL 15]	5.3, 5.8
Yields	Vegetables, individual crops, orchards, individual crops, small fruit, individual crops	E & W	Annual	[QRL 13]	5.8
Yields	Vegetables, individual crops, orchards, small fruit, individual crops	Scot.	Annual	[QRL 14]	5.8
Yields	Vegetables, principal crops, apples, other tree crops, individual small fruit crops	North. Ire.	Annual	[QRL 49]	5.8
Rough grazing					
Area	Total, inc. common grazing	UK, E & W, Scot., GB, North. Ire.	Annual	[QRL 15]	5.4, 5.5
Area	Total, sole rights, common	E, Eng. counties W, Welsh counties	Annual	[QRL 13]	5.4, 5.5
Area	Total, inc. common grazing	Scot., regions, counties	Annual	[QRL 14]	5.4, 5.5
Area	Common grazings	Scot., regions, counties	Annual	[QRL 58]	5.4, 5.5
Area	Total	North. Ire. counties	Annual	[QRL 49]	5.5
Area	Common land	E, W, counties	1956–8	[QRL 54]	5.5
Frequency distributions					
Area	Principal crops	E & W	Annual	[QRL 13]	5.8
Area	Principal crops	E, W, regions	Annual	[QRL 57]	5.8
Area	Principal crops	Scot., regions	Annual	[QRL 14]	5.8
Area	Principal crops	North. Ire.	Annual	[QRL 56]	5.8
Area	Principal crops	North. Ire., counties	Annual	[QRL 59]	5.8
Area	Principal vegetables	E & W	1962	[QRL 41]	5.8
Area	Principal fruits	E & W	1966	[QRL 42]	5.8
Type of farming					
Area	Area of each crop, by type of farm, by size groups, mean acreage by type	E & W	Annual	[QRL 39]	5.8
Area	Area of each crop, by type of farm, by size groups	Scot. regions	Annual	[QRL 14]	5.8
Area	Mean acreage of principal crops by type of farm and size group	North. Ire.	Annual	[QRL 56] and [QRL 49]	5.8
Area and number	Number of farms of each type and mean acreage of principal land uses	Scotland	1947	[QRL 63]	5.8
Holdings					
Area	Agricultural holdings, by total area and by crops and grass area, by size groups	E, Eng. counties W, Welsh counties	Annual	[QRL 13]	5.8

Type of statistics	Breakdown/details of analysis	Areas	Frequency	Publication	Text reference
Area	Agricultural holdings, by total area and by crops and grass area, by size groups	Scot., regions, counties	Annual	[QRL 14]	5.8
Area	Agricultural holdings, by total area and by crops and grass area, by size groups	North. Ire.	Annual	[QRL 59]	5.8
Area	Agricultural holdings, by crops and grass area, by size groups	North. Ire., counties	Annual	[QRL 49]	5.8
Area and number	Number and area of statutory smallholdings provided by local authorities	E, W, counties	1964	[QRL 33]	5.8
Area and number	Other statutory smallholdings			[QRL 34]	5.8
Area and number	Area under smallholdings, land acquired and disposed of, and number of holdings, by size groups	E, W, counties	Annual	[QRL 26]	5.8
Area and number	Area and number of holdings, by crops and grass size groups	E, W, Scot.	At intervals 1875–1966	[QRL 31]	5.9
Tenure					
Area	Land owned by occupier, land rented	E, regions, counties	Annual	[QRL 13]	5.8
Area	Land or holdings owned or mainly owned by occupier	Scot., regions, counties	Annual	[QRL 14]	5.8
Area	Land let in conacre, and crops grown on conacre land	North. Ire.	Annual	[QRL 56]	5.2
Area and number	Area and number of holdings under different kinds of tenure	E & W, Scot.	At intervals 1887–1966	[QRL 31]	5.9
Area	Common grazings, common land	E & W, counties	1956–8	[QRL 12]	5.5
Area and number	Land use, principal crops, land improved on crofts and number of crofts and working units	Crofting counties, counties	1970	[QRL 43]	5.8
Area and number	Area of land improved and number of working units	Crofting counties, counties	Annual	[QRL 22]	5.8
Area	Land managed by Dept. of Agriculture and Fisheries for Scotland	Scot.	Annual	[QRL 17]	5.8

Type of statistics	Breakdown/details of analysis	Areas	Frequency	Publication	Text reference
Tenure—*contd.*					
Area and number	Land capable of improvement by inclusion in rotation, application of fertiliser and drainage and number of farms capable of growing particular crops	Scot., districts	*ca.* 1941	[QRL 16]	5.8
Area	Area subject to ploughing grants	UK, E,S,W,NI	1963–6	[QRL 62]	5.8
Area	Area of land improved with grant-aid	Crofting counties	Annual	[QRL 22]	5.8
Area	Ploughing grant	Scotland	Annual until 1973	[QRL 17]	5.8
Losses of agricultural land					
Area	To urban, industrial and recreational; govt. depts; FC and private woodlands; other adjustments	E & W	Annual	[QRL 13]	5.9
Area	To roads, housing, industrial developments; recreation, mineral workings; hydro-electric and water boards; forestry; service depts.; and other losses	Scotland	Annual	[QRL 14]	5.9
Area	Estimated change in urban area 1950–70 by changes in land-use statistics	GB, E,W,S, Standard regions	1950–70	[QRL 44]	10.0
Area	Estimated changes in urban area 1950–60 and 1960–70 by changes in land-use statistics	E & W counties	1950–60–70	[QRL 6]	10.0
Area	Estimated changes in urban area by changes in land-use statistics	E & W	At intervals 1901–71	[QRL 66]	10.6.2
Area	Total	UK, std. regions	1951–61–71	[QRL 68]	10.6.1
Area	Total, settlement, airfields, tended open space, agricultural land, woodland, other cover land, water	E & W	*ca.* 1933, *ca.* 1963	[QRL 67]	10.6.1
FOREST LAND					
Area	Total state	GB, UK, North. Ire.	Annual	[QRL 20]	6.3
Area	Forestry Commission land, area under plantations and land planted by FC	GB, E, W, Scot. conservancies, forests	Annual	[QRL 25]	6.3

Type of statistics	Breakdown/details of analysis	Areas	Frequency	Publication	Text reference
Area	FC land acquired by FC land planted, area of land burned, area of land felled, area of private planting under grant and, area of private woodland licensed for felling	GB, E, W, Scot.	Annual	[QRL 25]	6.3
Area	Estimated planting without grants	GB	Annual	[QRL 25]	6.3
Area	Land in State owner-ship and under plantations	North. Ire. counties and forests	Annual	[QRL 23]	6.3
Area	Woodland ancillary to farming	E, Eng. counties W, Welsh counties	Annual	[QRL 13]	6.3
Area	Woodland ancillary to farming	Scot. counties	Annual	[QRL 14]	6.3
Area	Woodland returned in agricultural census	North. Ire. counties	Annual	[QRL 49]	6.3
Yield	Sales of timber by FC	GB	Annual	[QRL 25]	6.3
Yield	Sales of forest produce by Forestry Division, NI	North. Ire.	Annual	[QRL 56]	6.3
Area	Land under woods, status, composition	GB, E, W, Scot., conservancies	Occasional	[QRL 30]	6.4

RECREATION LAND

Type of statistics	Breakdown/details of analysis	Areas	Frequency	Publication	Text reference
Area	Land in National Parks, Areas of Outstanding Natural Beauty, country parks and and picnic sites	E & W individual National Parks and areas of outstanding natural beauty	Annual	[QRL 21] (before 1968 [QRL 51])	7.4, 9.3
Area and number	Area of National Parks and Areas of Outstanding Natural Beauty, National Park Direction Areas, number of country parks and picnic sites	E, W, Econ. Planning Regions, Scotland	1973	[QRL 36]	7.6
Area and number	Area of Forest Parks and number of camp sites, picnic sites and car parks on Forestry Commission land	GB, E,W,S,FC conservancies	1974	[QRL 36]	7.3
Area	Area of National Parks, access land, land purchased for access purposes, Ministry of Defence land, land with rights of use only	E & W, individual parks	1973	[QRL 36]	7.3
Area and number	Area of reckonable playing space and number of pitches, courts and greens	Scot., counties and counties of cities	1962–67	[QRL 61]	7.6

Type of statistics	Breakdown/details of analysis	Areas	Frequency	Publication	Text reference
RECREATION LAND—*contd.*					
Area and number	Area and number of newly designated Areas of Outstanding Natural Beauty, country parks and picnic sites	Areas in E & W	Monthly	[QRL 48]	7.6, 9.3
Deer forests					
Area and number	Areas surveyed and deer counted	Scot. counties	1957	[QRL 14]	7.2
CONSERVATION LAND					
Area	Land in National Nature Reserves	E, W, Scot.	Annual	[QRL 24] until 1973	9.2
Area	Land in National Nature Reserves and local nature reserves	E, W, S, and each reserve	1973–75	[QRL 40]	9.2
Area	Land in County Trust, Scottish Wildlife Trust or Royal Society for the Protection of Birds reserves	GB, W, S, and NCC regions in Eng.	n.d.	[QRL 36]	9.2
Area and number	Wildfowl refuges, national and regional	Each reserve	*ca.* 1960 *ca.* 1970	[QRL 1] [QRL 9]	9.2
Area	National Trust properties	Each property in E, W, NI	Annually	[QRL 45]	7.3
Area	National Trust properties	Each property in S	Annually	[QRL 64]	7.3
Area and number	National Trusts' properties owned and protected by covenant, and number of gardens, houses and open to public	GB, E, W, S, and Economic Regions in E	1973	[QRL 36]	7.3
Area and number	Commons and village greens	E, counties	1962	[QRL 12]	7.4
DEFENCE LAND					
Area	Area of land and foreshore, freehold and leasehold and over which rights of use, by army, navy, air force, territorial army	UK, E, W, S, NI, individual sites	1971–3	[QRL 50]	8.1
Area	Ministry of Defence land, freehold, leasehold and rights of use, and foreshore	GB, W, S, and Economic Regions	n.d.	[QRL 36]	8.1
LAND IN MINERAL WORKINGS					
Area	Spoil heaps, excavations and pits, areas not yet affected, sub-divided by whether restoration conditions or not, for 14 groups of mineral workings	E counties, National Parks and Areas of Outstanding Natural Beauty	1974	[QRL 60]	8.3
Area	Active mineral workings, by type	W, counties, districts	1971–2	[QRL 35]	8.3

Type of statistics	Breakdown/details of analysis	Areas	Frequency	Publication	Text reference
DERELICT LAND					
Area	Derelict land, increase, restored, reclaimable, abandoned mineral workings, refuse, tipping, spoil heaps, excavations, military, railway land	E, districts, counties, regions	1974	[QRL 60]	8.4
Area	Derelict land, causes of increase, agency restoring	E, counties, regions	1974	[QRL 60]	8.4
Area	Disused spoil heaps, reworked heaps, excavations, buildings, by type	W, counties, districts	1971–2	[QRL 35]	8.4
Area	Derelict land and land reclaimed in 1972	GB, E, W, S, and Econ. Regions	1971	[QRL 36]	8.4
WATER-GATHERING GROUNDS					
Area	Area, ownership and sporting rights of gathering grounds	Each reservoir E & W	1969	[QRL 18]	8.2
Area	Area, ownership and sporting rights of gathering grounds	Each reservoir in S	1971	[QRL 19]	8.2
URBAN LAND					
Area	Houses and gardens, agriculturally unproductive land	GB, E, W, S, counties	1931–9	[QRL 11]	10.3
Area	Estimated area in large and small settlements, isolated dwellings, railways and roads in countryside	GB, E & W, S	*ca.* 1950	[QRL 3]	10.3
Area	Housing, industry, open space, other uses for large settlements	E & W	*ca.* 1950	[QRL 3]	10.5
Area	Total and four main uses in New Towns	E & W, S	1960–1	[QRL 2]	10.5
Area	Total and four main uses by size groups and standard regions	E & W, std. regions	*ca.* 1950	[QRL 7]	10.3
Area	Total and four main uses in large and small settlements	E & W	1961	[QRL 66]	10.3.9
Area	Total in large and small settlements	GB, S	1961	[QRL 66]	10.3.9
Area	Total	E & W	*ca.* 1962	[QRL 65]	10.3.10
Area	Total	UK, std. regions	1951–61–71	[QRL 68]	10.3.7
Area	Total, civil airfields, tended open space	E & W	*ca.* 1933, *ca.* 1963	[QRL 67]	10.3.10
Area	Total, buildings, transport land, open land	UK, std. regions	1961	[QRL 68]	10.5.4

Type of statistics	Breakdown/details of analysis	Areas	Frequency	Publication	Text reference
Urban land—*contd.*					
Area	Total and four main uses for small settlements (− 10,000 inhabitants) by size groups	E & W, std. regions	*ca.* 1961	[QRL 4]	10.5
Area	Total, large and small settlements	E & W, Regions, counties	*ca.* 1950, 1960, 1970	[QRL 6]	10.6
Area	Total	GB, E, W, S, regions	*ca.* 1950, 1970	[QRL 44]	10.6
Area and number	Allotments, varied statistics on growth, change of use, based partly on official statistics and partly on questionnaire surveys of urban and rural authorities	E & W, urban and rural, counties	1965	[QRL 32]	10.5
Area	Roads and railways (estimates)	E & W	*ca.* 1950	[QRL 3]	10.3
Area	Civil airports	E & W	*ca.* 1950	[QRL 5]	10.3

Note: In addition to the statistics listed here, there are others which may be available from the agricultural departments, generally providing greater spatial disaggregation than is acceptable for published statistics.

QUICK REFERENCE LIST KEY TO PUBLICATIONS

Reference number	Author or organization responsible	Title	Publisher	Frequency of date	Remarks
[QRL 1]	Atkinson-Willes, G. L. (ed.)	Wildfowl in Great Britain	HMSO	1963	Monographs of the Nature Conservancy No. 3
[QRL 2]	Best, R. H.	Land for New Towns	Town & Country Planning Association	1964	
[QRL 3]	Best, R. H. and Coppock, J. T.	The Changing Use of Land in Britain	Faber	1962	
[QRL 4]	Best, R. H. and Rogers, A. W.	The Urban Countryside	Faber	1973	
[QRL 5]	Blake, R. N. E.	'The impact of airfields on the British landscape.' Geographical Journal 135, 508–27	Royal Geographical Society	1969	See also [B 3]
[QRL 6]	Champion, A. G.	An Estimate of the Changing Extent and Distribution of Urban Land in England and Wales, 1950–70	Centre of Environmental Studies	1975	Research Paper No. 10. See also [B 3, B 4, B 6 and B 7]
[QRL 7]	Champion, A. G.	Variations in Urban Densities Between Towns of England and Wales	School of Geography, Oxford University	1972	Research Paper No. 1. See also [B 25]
[QRL 8]	Hendry, G. F.	'The size of Scotland's bracken problem.' Scottish Agricultural Economics, 8	HMSO	1958	
[QRL 9]	Sedgwick, N. M., Whitaker, P. and Harrison, J.	The New Wildfowler in the 1970s	Barrie & Jenkins	1970	
[QRL 10]	Stamp, Sir Dudley	Nature Conservation in Britain	Collins	1969	
[QRL 11]	Stamp, L. D.	The Land of Britain: Its Use and Misuse	Longmans	1962	3rd Edition
[QRL 12]	Stamp, L. D. and Hoskins, W. G.	The Common Lands of England & Wales	Collins	1963	See also [B 21]
[QRL 13]	Ministry of Agriculture, Fisheries & Food	Agricultural Statistics, England and Wales	HMSO, London	Annual	
[QRL 14]	Department of Agriculture & Fisheries for Scotland	Agricultural Statistics Scotland	HMSO, Edinburgh	Annual	
[QRL 15]	Ministry of Agriculture, Fisheries & Food; Dept. of Agriculture & Fisheries for Scotland	Agricultural Statistics, United Kingdom Agricultural Censuses and Production	HMSO, London	Annual	(Before 1974, Min. of Agriculture, Northern Ireland.)

[QRL 16]	Department of Agriculture for Scotland	*Agricultural Survey of Scotland*	HMSO	1946	Out of print
[QRL 17]	Department of Agriculture & Fisheries for Scotland	*Agriculture in Scotland*	HMSO, Edinburgh	Annual	
[QRL 18]	British Waterworks Association	*Amenity Use of Reservoirs Survey, Analysis of Returns*	British Waterworks Association	1969	See also [B 70]
[QRL 19]	British Waterworks Association	*Amenity Use of Reservoirs in Scotland, Analysis of Returns*	British Waterworks Association	1972	See also [B 70]
[QRL 20]	Central Statistical Office	*Annual Abstract of Statistics*	HMSO, London	Annual	
[QRL 21]	Countryside Commission	*Annual Report*	HMSO, London	Annual	
[QRL 22]	Crofters Commission	*Annual Report*	HMSO	Annual	
[QRL 23]	Department of Agriculture, Northern Ireland	*Annual Report*	HMSO, Belfast	Annual	
[QRL 24]	Natural Environment Research Council	*Annual Report*	HMSO, London	Annual	(From 1974 Nature Conservancy Council)
[QRL 25]	Forestry Commission	*Annual Report and Accounts*	HMSO, London	Annual	See also [B 32]
[QRL 26]	Ministry of Agriculture, Fisheries & Food and Department of Agriculture & Fisheries for Scotland	*Annual Report on Smallholdings*	MAFF	Annual	
[QRL 27]	General Register Office	*Census, England and Wales, County Reports*	HMSO, London	Decennial	
[QRL 28]	General Register Office, Scotland	*Census, Scotland, County Reports*	HMSO, Edinburgh	Decennial	
[QRL 29]	General Register Office, Northern Ireland	*Census, Northern Ireland, County Reports*	HMSO, Belfast	Decennial	
[QRL 30]	Forestry Commission	*Census of Woodlands (1965–6)*	HMSO, London	Periodic	See also [B 62, 63, 72, 84]
[QRL 31]	Ministry of Agriculture, Fisheries & Food and Department of Agriculture & Fisheries for Scotland	*A Century of Agricultural Statistics, Great Britain 1866–1966*	HMSO	1968	Cmnd. 2936
[QRL 32]	Ministry of Housing & Local Government and Welsh Office	*Departmental Committee of Inquiry into Allotments: Report*	HMSO	1969	Cmnd. 4166
[QRL 33]	Ministry of Agriculture, Fisheries & Food	*Departmental Committee of Inquiry into Statutory Smallholdings, First Report*	HMSO	1966	Cmnd. 2936
[QRL 34]	Ministry of Agriculture, Fisheries & Food	*Departmental Committee of Inquiry into Statutory Smallholdings, Final Report*	HMSO	1967	Cmnd. 3303
[QRL 35]	Welsh Office	*The Derelict Land Survey of Wales*	Welsh Office	1975	

Reference number	Author or organization responsible	Title	Publisher	Frequency of data	Remarks
[QRL 36]	Countryside Commission	*Digest of Countryside Recreation Statistics*	Countryside Commission	Occasional	(1974) Countryside Commission Publication 86. See also [B 11]
[QRL 37]	Department of Finance, Northern Ireland	*Digest of Statistics, Northern Ireland*	HMSO	Annual	(Before 1974, Ministry)
[QRL 38]	Welsh Office	*Digest of Welsh Statistics*	HMSO	Annual	
[QRL 39]	Ministry of Agriculture, Fisheries & Food	*Farm Classification*	HMSO, London	Annual	
[QRL 40]	Nature Conservancy Council	*First Report 1 November 1973-31 March 1975*	HMSO	1975	Subsequent reports annually for 1st April to 31st March
[QRL 41]	Ministry of Agriculture, Fisheries & Food	*Horticulture in Britain, Part 1, Vegetables*	HMSO	1967	
[QRL 42]	Ministry of Agriculture, Fisheries & Food	*Horticulture in Britain, Part 2, Fruit & Flowers*	HMSO	1970	
[QRL 43]	Select Committee on Scottish Affairs	*Land Resource Use in Scotland, Report, Evidence and Appendices*	HMSO	1972	House of Commons Paper 511. Five volumes
[QRL 44]	Department of the Environment	*Long Term Population Distribution in Great Britain*	HMSO	1971	Report by an Interdepartmental study group See also [B 73]
[QRL 45]	National Trust for Historic Interest or Natural Beauty	*National Trust Properties*	National Trust	Annual	
[QRL 46]	Nature Conservancy Council	*A Nature Conservation Review: an Account of Biological Sites of Special Importance to Nature Conservation in Great Britain*	Cambridge University Press	1977	
[QRL 47]	Nature Reserves Committee	*Nature Reserves Committee Annual Report*	HMSO, Belfast	Annual	
[QRL 48]	Countryside Commission	*Recreation News*	Countryside Commission	Monthly	
[QRL 49]	Department of Agriculture, Northern Ireland	*(Ninth) Report on Agricultural Statistics*	HMSO, Belfast	Periodic	(Before 1974, Ministry.) See also [B 64]

[QRL 50]	Ministry of Defence	*Report of the Defence Lands Commission 1971–73*	HMSO	1973	See also [B 75]
[QRL 51]	National Parks Commission	*Report of the National Parks Commission*	HMSO	Annual to 1967	
[QRL 52]	Potato Marketing Board	*Report on the Operation of the Potato Marketing Scheme*	Potato Marketing Board	Annual to 1962	Replaced by Annual Report & Statement of Accounts containing much less detail.
[QRL 53]	Red Deer Commission	*Report of the Red Deer Commission*	HMSO	Annual	See also [B 55]
[QRL 54]	Royal Commission on Common Land	*Report of the Royal Commission on Common Land 1955–58*	HMSO	1958	
[QRL 55]	Scottish Office	*Scottish Abstract of Statistics*	HMSO	Annual	
[QRL 56]	Department of Agriculture, Northern Ireland	*Statistical Review of Farming in Northern Ireland*	HMSO, Belfast	Annual	
[QRL 57]	Ministry of Agriculture, Fisheries & Food	*Statistical Statements*	MAFF, Guildford	Annual	
[QRL 58]	Department of Agriculture & Fisheries for Scotland	*Statistical Statements*	DAFS, Edinburgh	Annual	
[QRL 59]	Department of Agriculture, Northern Ireland	*Statistical Statements*	DANI, Belfast	Annual	
[QRL 60]	Department of the Environment (Planning, Regional & Countryside Directorate)	*Survey of Derelict and Despoiled Land in England*	Department of the Environment	1975	Summary section, Section II (Derelict land and Waste(Refuse Tipping) Section III Mineral Working)
[QRL 61]	National Playing Fields Association, Scottish Branch	*Surveys of Reckonable Playing Space*	Details held at Scottish Headquarters	1962 1967	
[QRL 62]	Select Committee on Estimates	*Tenth Report of the Estimates Committee on Improvement of Agricultural Land*	HMSO	1967	House of Commons Paper 549
[QRL 63]	Department of Agriculture for Scotland	*Types of Farming in Scotland*	HMSO	1952	Out of print See also [B 43]

Reference number	Author or organization responsible	Title	Publisher	Frequency of data	Remarks
[QRL 64]	National Trust for Scotland	*Year Book National Trust for Scotland*	National Trust for Scotland	Annual 1977	
[QRL 65]	Anderson, M. A.	'A comparison of figures for the land-use structure of England and Wales in the 1960s', *Area* **9**, 43–5			
[QRL 66]	Best, R. H.	'The extent and growth of urban land', *The Planner*, **1**, 8–11		1976	
[QRL 67]	Coleman, A.	'Is planning really necessary?', *Geographical Journal*, **142**, 411–30		1976	
[QRL 68]	Fordham, R. C.	*Measurement of Urban Land-Use*	Dept. of Land Economy Cambridge University Press	Occasional (1974)	

BIBLIOGRAPHY

Much of the information in this review is derived from personal discussion with officials or from correspondence with the appropriate agencies, and not from published sources. Among the latter, the most useful complement to this review is the contributions to Studies in Official Statistics, No. 14, *Agricultural and Food Statistics*, HMSO, 1969.

[B 1]   Barr, J. *Derelict Britain*. Penguin, London, 1969.
[B 2]   Beaver, S. H. 'Changes in industrial land use 1930–67.' *Land Use and Resources: Studies in Applied Geography*, Special Publication No. 1, Institute of British Geographers, pp. 101–9. London, 1968.
[B 3]   Best, R. H. 'Competition for land between rural and urban uses.' *Land Use and Resources: Studies in Applied Geography*, Special Publication No. 1, Institute of British Geographers, pp. 89–100, London, 1968.
[B 4]   Best, R. H. 'Extent of urban growth and agricultural displacement in post-war Britain.' *Urban Studies*, **5**, 1–23. Oliver & Boyd, London, 1968.
[B 5]   Best, R. H. *The Major Land Uses of Great Britain*, Studies in Rural Land Use No. 4, Wye College, University of London, 1959.
[B 6]   Best, R. H. 'Recent changes and future prospects of land use in England and Wales.' *Geographical Journal*, **131**, 1–12 1965.
[B 7]   Best, R. H. and Champion, A. G. 'Regional conversions of agricultural land to urban use in England and Wales, 1945–67.' *Transactions of the Institute of British Geographers*, **49**, 15–32 1970.
[B 8]   Bibby, J. S. and Mackney, D. *Land Use Capability Classification*, Technical Monograph No. 1, The Soil Survey, Rothamsted and Craigiebuckler, 1969.
[B 9]   Bickmore, D. P. and Shaw, M. A. *Atlas of Great Britain and Northern Ireland*, Clarendon Press, Oxford, 1963.
[B 10] Bruce, M. W. 'An analysis of urban land use in England and Wales since 1950 from Development Plans.' Unpublished M.Phil. thesis, University of London, 1967.
[B 11] Burton, T. L. and Wibberley, G. P. *Outdoor Recreation in the British Countryside*, Studies in Rural Land Use No. 5. Wye College, London University, 1965.
[B 12] Church, B. M., Boyd, D. A., Evans, J. A. and Sadler, J. E. 'A type of farming map based on agricultural census data.' *Outlook on Agriculture*, **5**, 191–6 1968.
[B 13] Coleman, A. 'The Second Land Use Survey: progress and prospect.' *Geographical Journal*, **127**, 168–86 1961.
[B 14] Coppock, J. T. *An Agricultural Atlas of England and Wales*, 1st edition. Faber & Faber, London, 1964.
[B 15] Coppock, J. T. *An Agricultural Atlas of England and Wales*, 2nd edition. Faber & Faber, London, 1976.
[B 16] Coppock, J. T. *An Agricultural Atlas of Scotland*, John Donald, Edinburgh, 1976.
[B 17] Coppock, J. T. 'Farm and parish boundaries.' *Geographical Studies*, **2**, 12–26 1955.
[B 18] Coppock, J. T. 'The geographer and the Countryside (Scotland) Act.' *Scottish Geographical Magazine*, **84**, 201–11 1968.
[B 19] Coppock, J. T. 'The parish as a geographical/statistical unit.' *Tijdschrift voor Economische en Sociale Geografie*, pp. 22–25. 1960.
[B 20] Coppock, J. T. 'The recreational use of land and water in rural Britain.' *Tijdschrift voor Economische en Sociale Geografie*, **57**, 81–96 1966.
[B 21] Denman, D. R., Roberts, R. A. and Smith, J. J. F. *Commons and Village Greens*, Leonard Hill, London, 1967.
[B 22] Edwards, A. M. and Rogers, A. W. (eds.). *Agricultural Resources*, Faber & Faber, London, 1974.
[B 23] Edwards, A. M. and Wibberley, G. P. *An Agricultural Land Budget for Britain 1965–2000*, Studies in Rural Land Use No. 10, Wye College, London University, 1971.

[B 24]   Gasson, R. *The Influence of Urbanisation on Farm Ownership and Practice*, Studies in Rural Land Use No. 7. Wye College, London University, 1966.

[B 25]   Hall, P. *et al. The Containment of Urban England*, 2 vols. Allen & Unwin, London, 1973.

[B 26]   Harrison, A. *The Farms of Buckinghamshire*, Department of Agricultural Economics, University of Reading, 1966.

[B 27]   Hart, J. E. *The British Moorlands*, University of Georgia Monographs No. 2. Athens, Georgia, 1955.

[B 28]   Hill, D. A. *The Land of Ulster. I. The Belfast Region*, Belfast, HMSO, 1948.

[B 29]   Holford, Lord. Unpublished address to a National Trust meeting London, 25th February, 1963.

[B 30]   Horscroft, P. G. 'Changes envisaged for the agricultural census in England and Wales.' *Statistical News*, **6**. London, HMSO, 1969.

[B 31]   Horscroft, P. G. and Orton, C. R. 'Reshaping of the agricultural census for England and Wales.' *Statistical News*, **19**. London, HMSO, 1972.

[B 32]   Jack, W. H. 'Private forestry in Northern Ireland.' *Agriculture in Northern Ireland*, pp. 170–2. September, 1960.

[B 33]   Lebon, J. H. G. and others (1936–46). *County Reports, Land Utilisation Survey*, Nos. 1–92, Geographical Publications, London, 1937.

[B 34]   Messer, M. *An Agricultural Atlas of England and Wales*, 2nd edition. Ordnance Survey, Southampton, 1932.

[B 35]   Millman, R. 'The landed properties of northern Scotland.' *Scottish Geographical Magazine*, **86**, 186–203 1970.

[B 36]   Millman, R. 'The landed estates of southern Scotland.' *Scottish Geographical Magazine*, **88**, 126–33 1972.

[B 37]   Millman, R. 'The marches of the Highland estates.' *Scottish Geographical Magazine*, **85**, 172–81 1969.

[B 38]   Moisley, H. A. 'The Highlands and Islands—a crofting region?' *Transactions of the Institute of British Geographers*, **31**, 83–95 1962.

[B 39]   Orton, C. R. 'The development of stratified sampling method for the agricultural census of England and Wales.' *Journal of the Royal Statistical Society* (Series A), **135** 1972.

[B 40]   Patmore, J. A. *Land and Leisure*, David & Charles, Newton Abbot, 1970.

[B 41]   Peters, G. H. 'Land use studies in Britain.' *Journal of Agricultural Economics*, **21**, 171–214 1970.

[B 42]   Pryse-Howell, J. *An Agricultural Atlas of England and Wales*, 1st edition. Ordnance Survey, Southampton, 1925.

[B 43]   Scola, P. M. 'An economic classification of Scottish farms based on the June census 1962.' *Scottish Agricultural Economics*, **15**, 298–329. Edinburgh, HMSO, 1965.

[B 44]   Stamp, L. D. 'The common lands and village greens of England and Wales.' *Geographical Journal*, **130**, 145–69 1964.

[B 45]   Stamp, L. D. *Surrey*, Part 81, Land of Britain. Geographical Publications, London, 1942.

[B 46]   Stapledon, R. G. *The Hill Lands of Britain*, Faber & Faber, London, 1937.

[B 47]   Stapledon, R. G. *The Land Now and Tomorrow*, Faber & Faber, London, 1935.

[B 48]   Symons, L. (ed.) *Land Use in Northern Ireland*, University of London Press, London, 1963.

[B 49]   Thomas, D. *London's Green Belt*, Faber & Faber, London, 1970.

[B 50]   Thomas, D. 'Statutory protection of the countryside.' *Zeitschrift für Wirtschaftsgeographie*, **6**, 34–38 1962.

[B 51]   Thomas, E. and Elms, C. E. *An Economic Survey of Buckinghamshire, Part I*, Department of Agricultural Economics, University of Reading, 1938.

[B 52]   Wager, J. 'How common is the land?' *New Society*, July 1964.

[B 53]   Wallwork, K. L. *Derelict Land*, David & Charles, Newton Abbot, 1974.

[B 54]   Whitby, H. 'Some developments in Scottish farming since the War.' *Journal of Agricultural Economics*, **21**, 1–16 1970.

[B 55]   Whitehead, G. K. *The Deer Stalking Grounds of Great Britain and Northern Ireland*, Hills & Carter, London, 1960.

[B 56]   Wood, H. J. *An Agricultural Atlas of Scotland*, Gill & Sons, London, 1931.

[B 57]   *An Addicts's Guide to British Golf*, St. Paul's Publications, Langley, 1959.

[B 58]   Interdepartmental Committee on Social and Economic Research. *Agricultural and Food Statistics*, Guides to Official Sources No. 4. London, HMSO, 1958.

[B 59]   Ministry of Agriculture, Fisheries and Food. *Agricultural and Food Statistics*, Studies in Official Statistics, No. 14. London, HMSO, 1969.

[B 60]   Ministry of Agriculture, Fisheries and Food. *Agricultural Land Classification of England and Wales*, Agricultural Land Service, London, 1974.

[B 61]   *Baily's Hunting Directory*, J. A. Allen, London, Annual.

[B 62] Forestry Commission. *Census of Woodlands 1947–1949*, Census Report No. 1, London, HMSO, 1952.

[B 63] Forestry Commission. *Census of Woodlands 1947–1949*, Census Reports Nos. 3, 4 and 5, County Details. London, HMSO, 1952.

[B 64] Ministry of Agriculture, Fisheries and Food, Department of Agriculture and Fisheries for Scotland, and Ministry of Agriculture, Northern Ireland. *The Changing Structure of Agriculture 1968–75*, London, HMSO, 1977.

[B 65] Ministry of Housing and Local Government. *Derelict Land and Its Reclamation*, Technical Memorandum, No. 7. The Ministry, London, 1956.

[B 66] Council for Environmental Education. *Directory of Centres for Outdoor Studies in England and Wales*, The Council, London, 1973.

[B 67] Department of Agriculture, University of Cambridge. *An Economic Survey of Hertfordshire*, Report No. 18. Department of Agriculture, University of Cambridge, 1931.

[B 68] Reconstruction Committee, Forestry Sub-Committee (Acland Committee). *Final Report*, Cd. 8881. London, HMSO, 1918.

[B 69] Ministry of Housing and Local Government. *First Review of Approved Development Plans*, Circular No. 9/55. London, HMSO, 1955.

[B 70] Natural Resources (Technical) Committee. *Forestry, Agriculture and Marginal Land*. London, HMSO, 1957.

[B 71] Select Committee on Estimates. *Forestry Commission*, 7th Report, House of Commons Paper 272. London, HMSO, 1964.

[B 72] Forestry Commission. *Hedgerow and Park Timber and Woods under Five Acres, 1951*, Census Report No. 2. London, HMSO, 1953.

[B 73] Country Life. *Historic Houses, Castles and Gardens in Great Britain and Northern Ireland*, ABC Historic Publications. London, Annual.

[B 74] Joint Local Authority, Scottish Development Department and Department of the Environment Study Team. *General Information System for Planning*, London, HMSO, 1972.

[B 75] 'Land for the army.' *Town and Country Planning*, **25**, 341–4 1957.

[B 76] Department of Agriculture and Fisheries for Scotland. *Land use in the Highlands and Islands*, Edinburgh, HMSO, 1964.

[B 77] Department of the Environment. *List of Ancient Monuments in the Care of the Department open to the Public*, London, HMSO, 1974.

[B 78] 'Losses and gains of agricultural land in England and Wales.' *Agriculture*, **56**, 233–6 1949.

[B 79] Royal Automobile Club. *Motor Sports Year Book*, RAC, London, Annual.

[B 80] Ministry of Agriculture and Fisheries. *The National Farm Survey—a Summary Report*, London, HMSO, 1946.

[B 81] Joint Local Authority, LAMSAC, Scottish Development Department and Department of the Environment Study Team. *National Land Use Classification System*, 3 vols. Department of the Environment, London, 1972.

[B 82] Committee on Education and the Countryside. *Outdoor Studies Centres in Scotland*, Scottish Education Department, Edinburgh, 1971.

[B 83] Ministry of Housing and Local Government. *Planning Atlas of England and Wales*, The Ministry (since 1971, Department of the Environment), London, 1953.

[B 84] Forestry Commission. *Post-War Forest Policy*, Cmd. 6477. London, HMSO, 1943.

[B 85] Countryside Commission for Scotland. *Report*, The Commission, Perth, Annual.

[B 86] Ulster Countryside Committee. *Report*, Belfast, HMSO, Annual.

[B 87] Ministry of Housing and Local Government. *Report, 1958*, Cmnd. 737, Appendix XXII. London, HMSO, 1959.

[B 88] Forestry Commission. *Report of Census of Woodlands and Census of Production of Home Grown Timber, 1924*, London, HMSO, 1928.

[B 89] Ministry of Agriculture, Fisheries and Food. *Report of the Committee Appointed to Review the Provincial and Local Organisation and Procedure of the Ministry of Agriculture, Fisheries and Food*, Cmd. 9732. London, HMSO, 1956.

[B 90] Ministry of Works and Planning. *Report of the Committee on Land Utilization in Rural Areas* (Scott Report), Cmd. 6378. London, HMSO, 1942.

[B 91] Ministry of Health. *Report of the Gathering Grounds Sub-Committee of the Central Advisory Water Committee*, London, HMSO, 1948.

[B 92] Royal Commission on Coast Erosion and Afforestation. *Reports, Minutes of Evidence and Appendices*, Cd. 3683, 3684, 4460, 4461, 4708, 4709, London, HMSO, 1908.

[B 93] Select Committee on Sports and Leisure. *2nd Report and Minutes of Evidence*, House of Lords Paper 193. London, HMSO, 1973.

[B 94] Caravan Club of Great Britain and Ireland. *Sites Directory and Handbook*, Caravan Club, London, Annual.

[B 95] Department of the Environment and Welsh Office. *Statistics of Land Use Change*, DOE Circular 71/74, Welsh Office Circular 114/74. London, HMSO, 1974.

[B 96] 'Statistics relating to the use of land in the United Kingdom.' *Journal of the Royal Statistical Society, Series A (General)*, **116**, 424–30. 1953.

[B 97] Ministry of Agriculture, Fisheries and Food. *Type of Farming Maps of England and Wales*, London, HMSO, 1969.

[B 98] Coleman, A. Personal communication, 1977.

[B 99] Department of Agriculture and Fisheries for Scotland. Personal communication, 1973.

[B 100] Department (formerly Ministry) of Agriculture, Northern Ireland. Personal communication, 1973.

[B 101] Department of the Environment. Personal communication, 1977.

[B 102] Forestry Commission. Personal communication, 1973.

[B 103] Jones, A. R. Personal communication, 1973.

[B 104] Ministry of Agriculture, Fisheries and Food. Personal communication, 1973.

[B 105] Nature Conservancy Council. Personal communication, 1974.

[B 106] Ordnance Survey. Personal communication, 1974.

[B 107] Ordnance Survey, Northern Ireland. Personal communication, 1974.

[B 108] Scottish Development Department. Personal communication, 1976.

[B 109] Best, R. H. 'Laying the land-use myths'. *New Society*, **15**, 556–8 1970.

[B 110] Best, R. H. 'Land conversion to urban use'. *SSRC Newsletter*, **19**, 11–3 1973.

[B 111] Best, R. H. 'Building on farmland', *New Society*, **19**, 287–8 1974.

[B 112] Best, R. H. 'The changing land-use structure of Britain'. *Town and Country Planning*, **44**, 171–6 1976.

[B 113] Best, R. H. 'Agricultural land loss, myth or reality'. *The Planner*, **2**, 15–16 1977.

[B 114] Centre for Agricultural Strategy. *Land for Agriculture*, CAS Report 1, University of Reading, 1976.

[B 115] Coleman, A. 'Land-use planning. Success or failure?' *Architects Journal*, **165**, 96–134 1977.

[B 116] Dickenson, G. C. and Shaw, M. G. 'What is land-use?' *Area*, **9**, 38–42 1977.

[B 117] Gilg, A. W. 'Development control and agricultural land quality'. *Town and Country Planning*, **43**, 387–9 1975.

[B 118] Locke, G. M. L. *The Place of Forestry in Scotland*. Research and Development paper 113, Forestry Commission, Edinburgh, 1976.

[B 119] Smith, T. F. 'Breaking through the clouds over England', *Geographical Magazine*, **47**, 737–43 1975.

[B 120] Smith, T. F, van Genderen, J. L. and Holland, E. W. 'A land-use survey of developed areas in England and Wales'. *Cartographic Journal*, **14**, 23–9 1977.

LIST OF MAPS

Ordnance Survey

[M 1] **Topographic**
  Complete coverage of Great Britain:
    1:10,000   or 1:10,560
    1:50,000   or 1:63,360
    1:250,000 or 1:253,440
    1:625,000
  The 1:25,000 series covers a large part of Great Britain except the Highlands and Islands of Scotland, and coverage will be gradually extended.
[M 2] **Land Use**
    1:63,360   Ordnance Survey of Northern Ireland.
    1:625,000 (2 sheets).
[M 3] **Land Classification**
    1:625,000 (2 shects).
[M 4] **Grassland**
    1:625,000 for England and Wales only.
[M 5] **Vegetation**
    1:625,000 for Scotland only.
[M 6] **Type of Farming**
    1:625,000 (2 sheets).
  The thematic maps in the 1:625,000 series are accompanied by explanatory booklets.

Other

[M 7] **Land Use**
    1:63,360   Land Utilisation Survey.
  For parts of Scotland for which there are not published maps, hand-coloured manuscript maps are kept in the map collection of the Royal Scottish Geographical Society, Edinburgh.
    1:253,440   Land Utilisation Survey (destroyed), limited areas only.
[M 8] **Land Classification**
    1:63,360   Ministry of Agriculture, Fisheries and Food, England and Wales only.
    1:250,000   Ministry of Agriculture Fisheries and Food, England and Wales only.
    1:1,900,000   Ministry of Housing and Local Government (Planning maps series).
    1:10,560   Department of Agriculture and Fisheries for Scotland, for most of lowland Scotland.
    1:25,000   Soil Survey. A small number of sheets for England and Wales.
    1:63,360   Soil Survey. A small number of sheets for Scotland.
    1:375,000   Land Utilisation Survey of Northern Ireland [B 48].
[M 9] **Type of Farming**
    1:1,900,000   Ministry of Housing and Local Government (Planning maps series).
[M 10] **Conservation**
    1:1,220,000   Map of cherished land, *Geographical Magazine*.
    1:1,900,000   Department of the Environment (Planning maps series).
    1:460,000 Scottish Development Department (Planning maps series).
[M 11] **Built-up Areas/Countryside**
    1:1,460,000   The Countryside, Scottish Development Department (Planning maps series).
    1:1,900,000   Built-up areas, Ministry of Housing and Local Government (Planning maps series).

Air Photographs

Records of the coverage of air photographs are kept in Central Registers in the Department of the Environment, the Scottish Office and the Welsh Office.

APPENDIX

Please read
notes
enclosed and
return form
promptly

Ministry of Agriculture, Fisheries and Food

Agricultural and Horticultural Census: Return for 2nd June, 1975

NOTICE REQUIRING INFORMATION

To be completed and sent back by 9th June, 1975

Agricultural Censuses and Surveys Branch,
Government Buildings (Block A),
Epsom Road, Guildford, Surrey, GU1 2LD
23rd May, 1975

Agriculture Act 1947, section 78 (as amended)

On behalf of the Minister of Agriculture, Fisheries and Food I hereby give you notice that he requires you to complete in writing, in respect of the land occupied by you, the enclosed form of agricultural and horticultural return. The information asked for, as specified in Schedule 1 of this notice, is to be given in accordance with the "Notes for Guidance" set out in Schedule 2. The information is to relate to the position on 2nd June 1975, except where the information is required in respect of the periods described on the form. The completed form must be sent to the Collecting Officer at the above address **within 7 days from 2nd June 1975.** THIS RETURN IS COMPULSORY and under section 81 of the above Act penalties may be imposed for failure to make a return or for knowingly or recklessly furnishing false information.

Except as specified in section 80 of the above Act and section 12 of the European Communities Act 1972, no information which you give on the return may be published or otherwise disclosed without your prior written consent.

A. D. NEALE, Secretary

In any correspondence please quote the reference number of your holding.

PLEASE RETURN IN ENVELOPE PROVIDED

CHANGE OF ADDRESS

If the name (or description in the case of a registered joint stock company) or postal address shown alongside is materially inaccurate, please enter correct particulars in BLOCK LETTERS below:-

....
....
....
....

Holding
Reference Number

OTHER HOLDINGS IN THE SAME OCCUPANCY

Please list here any other holding reference numbers under which you make agricultural census returns. *(See note 1)*

| 169 | F9 |

....
....
....

O	O	crops and grass	total area
B.R. 12	I.C. 13		

J.75

CHANGE IN ACREAGE

1. According to the census records, the most recently recorded acreage of your holding is as shown above. If this is no longer correct, please give below your present acreage (to the nearest ¼ acre). Include land on this holding let by you for seasonal grazing but not land on another holding used by you for this purpose.

crops and grass   total area

....

2. Please give details of acreage transfers to account for any change recorded in para. 1.
(a) Acreage acquired:

Acres........................... Date.....................

Name and address of previous occupier:

....
....

(b) Acreage disposed of:

Acres........................... Date.................

Name and address of new occupier:

....
....
....

(c) Any other reason for a change in the area of your holding:

....
....
....

DECLARATION

I declare the particulars given in this return to be correct to the best of my knowledge and belief.

Signature of
Occupier ....

Date................................1975

The present occupier should complete and sign this return even if he has only recently taken over the holding and the name given on the form is not his. If an accredited agent signs the form the name of the actual occupier should also be shown.

Form C412G/CSS   1   CONTINUED ON NEXT PAGE

SCHEDULE 1 AGRICULTURAL AND HORTICULTURAL CENSUS JUNE 1975

CROPS AND GRASS (including Bare Fallow) — *See note 3*
and other areas of land within the holding

Please enter all acreages to the nearest ¼ acre		Statute Acres
Wheat	1	
Barley	2	
Oats	3	
Mixed corn for threshing *See notes 3(e), 3(f) and 3(h)*	4	
Rye for threshing *See notes 3(g) and 3(h)*	5	
Maize for threshing	6	
Maize fed green or for silage (for sweet-corn see item 200)	7	
Potatoes — Already harvested or intended for harvesting by 31st July	8	
Potatoes — Intended for harvesting after 31st July	9	
Sugar Beet, *not* for stockfeeding	10	
Hops, statute acres, *not* hop acres	11	
Horticultural crops (to agree with item 249 on page 4)	12	
Beans for stockfeeding	13	
Turnips, Swedes and Fodder Beet for stockfeeding	14	
Mangolds	15	
Rape (or Cole) for stockfeeding *See note 3(c)*	16	
Rape grown for oilseed *See note 3(c)*	17	
Kale for stockfeeding	18	
Cabbage, Savoy and Kohl Rabi for stockfeeding	19	
Mustard for seed, fodder or ploughing in	20	
Other Crops — for stockfeeding (include Vetches and Tares but not Lucerne, Grasses or Maize) *See note 3(h)*	21	
Other Crops — not for feeding to farm livestock *See notes 3(i), 3(c), 3(d), 3(e) and 3(f)*	22	
Bare Fallow *See note 3(a)*	23	
Lucerne *See Items 34-38 and note 3(j)*	24	
All Grasses (temporary and permanent), Clover and Sainfoin *See note 3(k)* — sown in 1971 or later	25	
All Grasses (temporary and permanent), Clover and Sainfoin *See note 3(k)* — sown in 1970 or earlier	26	
TOTAL CROPS AND GRASS (including Bare Fallow) (Items 1-26)	27	
Rough Grazings on which you have the SOLE grazing rights *See note 3(l)*	28	
Total Woodland on the holding *See note 3(m)*	29	
All other land not included under items 27-29 e.g. farm roads, buildings, ponds, derelict land etc. *See note 3(n)*	30	
TOTAL AREA OF YOUR HOLDING (Items 27-30)	31	

See 'Change of Acreage' on page 1

LAND RENTED AND/OR OWNED *See note 4*

		Statute Acres
Area of this holding rented by you	32	
Area of this holding owned by you	33	

Form C412G/CSS   2

ALL GRASSES (TEMPORARY AND PERMANENT), CLOVER AND SAINFOIN

AREA OF GRASS SOWN IN 1971 OR LATER
of the acreage returned at item 25 estimate how many acres were—

		Statute Acres
Sown in 1975 without a nurse or cover crop	34	
Sown in 1974 as a one year ley	35	
Sown in 1974 to be left down longer than one year	36	
Sown in 1971-1973	37	
TOTAL (to agree with total at item 25)	38	

AREA OF GRASS SOWN IN 1970 OR EARLIER
of the acreage returned at Item 26 estimate how many acres were—

Sown in 1967-1970	39	
Sown in 1966 or earlier	40	
TOTAL (to agree with total at item 26)	41	

GRASS INTENDED FOR MOWING THIS SEASON
which you expect to use for hay, silage or drying or to cut for seed (already included at items 24, 25 and 26)

All Grasses (temporary and permanent but excluding rough grazings), Clover, Sainfoin and Lucerne for mowing this season — Sown in 1971 or later	42	
— Sown in 1970 or earlier	43	

ARTIFICIALLY DRIED GRASS (other than barn-dried hay)

		Please answer 'Yes' or 'No'
Have you a Grass Drying Plant on the holding to which this return relates?	44	
		Key: 1 for Yes, 2 for No

HAY

		Tons
Quantities of HAY on the holding on 2nd June (excluding this season's crop)	45	

SEED CROPS

		Please answer 'Yes' or 'No'
Is it likely that you will harvest any of the following crops for seed this year?		
(a) Grasses or clovers	46	
(b) Root fodder or vegetable crops (excluding potatoes and cereals)	47	
		Key 1 for Yes, 2 for No

FARMERS AND WORKERS—*See note 5*
(include yourself as occupier—*see note 5(k) (ii)*)

				Number
Farmers, partners and directors	Whole-time	*See note 5(c)*	50	
	Part-time		51	
	Salaried Manager(s) *See note 5(e)*		52	
Persons engaged on your holding on 2nd June	Family Workers	Regular Whole-time	Male	53	
			Female	54	
		Regular Part-time	Male	55	
			Female	56	
	Hired Workers	Regular Whole-time	Male	57	
			Female	58	
		Regular Part-time	Male	59	
			Female	60	
	Seasonal or Casual Workers (hired or family)		Male	61	
			Female	62	
TOTAL FARMERS AND WORKERS				69	

SCHEDULE 1 (continued)   LIVESTOCK   JUNE 1975

See note 6

CATTLE

			Number
Cows and Heifers in milk	Mainly for producing milk or rearing calves for the dairy herd	70	
	Mainly for rearing calves for beef	71	
Cows in Calf but not in milk	Intended mainly for producing milk or rearing calves for the dairy herd	72	
	Intended mainly for rearing calves for beef	73	
Heifers in Calf (first calf)	Intended mainly for producing milk or rearing calves for the dairy herd	74	
	Intended mainly for rearing calves for beef	76	
Bulls for Service	2 years old and over	78	
	1 year old and under 2	79	
All other Cattle and Calves	2 years old and over — Male (excluding bulls for service)	80	
	2 years old and over — Female — intended for slaughter	81	
	2 years old and over — Female — For dairy or beef herd replacements	82	
	1 year old and under 2 — Male (excluding bulls for service)	83	
	1 year old and under 2 — Female — intended for slaughter	84	
	1 year old and under 2 — Female — for dairy herd replacements	85	
	1 year old and under 2 — Female — for beef herd replacements	86	
	6 months old and under 1 year — Male (including bull calves for service)	87	
	6 months old and under 1 year — Female	88	
	Under 6 months old — Intended for slaughter as calves	89	
	Under 6 months old — Others — Male (including bull calves for service)	90	
	Under 6 months old — Others — Female	91	
TOTAL CATTLE and CALVES		92	

If NONE of the cattle and calves entered at item 92 belongs to the holding to which this return relates please enter a tick against item 93	93	

Key 1 if ticked, Skip if blank

Heifers in calf (first calf)

			Number
Of the heifers in calf returned at items 74 and 76 above, how many were aged:—	2 years and over	75	
	under 2 years	77	

Intensive Rearing

Cattle being reared intensively on your holding for slaughter at 8 to 14 months (already included under "All other Cattle and Calves" at items 83-91)	Male	94
	Female	95

Irish Stores

Store Cattle on your holding which have been imported from the Irish Republic (already included under "All other Cattle and Calves" at items 80-86)	96

Calvings

Number of Calvings on your holding during March, April and May 1975 *See note 6(e)*

Heifers that calved for the first time during March, April and May 1975	97
All other Cows that calved during March, April and May 1975	98

PIGS

				Number
Breeding Pigs	Sows in pig	100	&0	
	Gilts in pig	101	&1	
	Other Sows (either being suckled or dry sows being kept for further breeding)	102	&2	
	Boars being used for service	103	&3	
	Gilts 110 lb and over (liveweight) not yet in pig but expected to be used for breeding	104	&4	
Barren sows for fattening		105	&5	
All other Pigs (not entered above) — Pigs weighing (liveweight)	240 lb and over	106	&6	
	175 lb and under 240 lb	107	&7	
	110 lb and under 175 lb	108	&8	
	45 lb and under 110 lb	109	&9	
	Under 45 lb	110	A0	
TOTAL PIGS		111	A1	

SHEEP

Lambs under 1 year old		112	A2	
Sheep 1 year old and over	Ewes kept for breeding (do not include two-tooth ewes—see item 114, or draft and cast ewes—see item 116)	113	A3	
	Two-tooth Ewes (Shearling Ewes or Gimmers) to be put to the ram in 1975	114	A4	
	Rams for service	115	A5	
	Draft and cast Ewes (do not include at item 113)	116	A6	
	Wethers and other sheep 1 year old and over	117	A7	
TOTAL SHEEP & LAMBS		119	A9	

POULTRY Do not include the same birds under more than one heading and do not include game birds

Hens and Pullets kept mainly for producing eggs for eating	Growing pullets (from day old to point of lay)	120	B0	
	Birds that have been in the laying flock for less than 12 months	121	B1	
	Birds that have been in the laying flock for 12 months or more	122	B2	
Fowls for breeding	Hens and Pullets of all ages kept mainly for producing eggs for hatching	123	B3	
	Cocks and Cockerels of all ages kept for breeding	124	B4	
Broilers (chicken for killing up to 10 weeks of age)		125	B5	
Other table fowls (not guinea fowls)		126	B6	
Ducks of all ages		127	B7	
Geese of all ages		128	B8	
Turkey Hens used for breeding		129	B9	
All Other Turkeys (including stags)		130	C0	
TOTAL POULTRY		139	C9	

HORSES

Horses used for agricultural or horticultural purposes		146	D6
All other Horses and Ponies		147	D7

GOATS

Milch goats (in kid or in milk)		148	D8
All other goats		149	D9

SCHEDULE 1 (continued)   HORTICULTURE   JUNE 1975

IF YOU GROW HORTICULTURAL CROPS
PLEASE COMPLETE—the return on this page for those grown in
the open; and item 205 on this page and the return on page 5 for
those grown under glass etc.

Please enter all acreages to the nearest ¼ acre

VEGETABLES
Grown in the open, for human consumption
See note 7(a)

				Statute Acres
Brussels Sprouts	for market	170	G0	
	for processing	171	G1	
Remaining spring cabbage (planted in 1974)		172	G2	
Cabbage	summer and autumn (e.g. Primo & Winnigstadt)	173	G3	
	winter (e.g. Xmas Drumhead, January King and Dutch Whites)	174	G4	
Savoys		175	G5	
Summer and autumn cauliflower (for marketing up to 31 December)		176	G6	
Winter cauliflower (heading broccoli), sprouting broccoli and kale *See note 7(a) (ii)*		177	G7	
Carrots	for market — early (intended for marketing by mid-September)	178	G8	
	for market — maincrop	179	G9	
	for processing	180	H0	
Parsnips		181	H1	
Turnips and Swedes (not for stockfeeding)		182	H2	
Beetroot (red beet—*not* sugar beet or fodder beet)	for market	183	H3	
	for processing	184	H4	
Onions	for salad	185	H5	
	for harvesting dry	186	H6	
Broad Beans	for market	187	H7	
	for processing	188	H8	
Runner beans (pinched)		189	H9	
Runner beans (climbing)	for market	190	i0	
	for processing	191	i1	
French Beans	for market	192	i2	
	for processing	193	i3	
Peas for harvesting dry		194	i4	
Green Peas	for market	195	i5	
	for processing	196	i6	
Celery		197	i7	
Lettuce (not under glass)		198	i8	
Watercress		199	i9	
Other vegetables and mixed areas (including maize for sweet-corn) *See note 7(a) (iii)*		200	"0	
TOTAL VEGETABLES grown in the open		201	"1	

GLASSHOUSE AREA
(not including lights and cloches)

Total area (acres) under glass or plastic structures *See note A on page 5*	205	"5	

MUSHROOMS

			Please answer Yes or No
Do you grow mushrooms?	203	"8	
			Key 1 for Yes, 2 for No

ORCHARDS

				Statute Acres
Orchards, grown commercially (include area of young non-bearing orchards but not fruit stock—see item 230)	Dessert apples	209	"9	
	Cooking apples	210	J0	
	Cider apples *See note 7(c)*	211	J1	
	Pears	212	J2	
	Perry pears *See note 7(c)*	213	J3	
	Plums	214	J4	
	Cherries	215	J5	
	Other top fruit (including nuts)	216	J6	
Orchards, not grown commercially		217	J7	

SMALL FRUIT *See note 7(d)*
Include at items 218-225 (but not at 226) any area of small fruit grown under orchard trees

Strawberries	Open grown only	218	J8	
	under cloches, tunnels, etc.	219	J9	
Raspberries		220	K0	
Blackcurrants	for market	221	K1	
	for processing	222	K2	
Gooseberries		223	K3	
Other Small Fruit (including grapes)		225	K5	
TOTAL ORCHARDS AND SMALL FRUIT (items 209-225 less any area of small fruit grown under orchard trees)		226	K6	

HARDY NURSERY STOCK

Fruit trees, bushes and canes, strawberries for runner production and other fruit stock for transplanting		230	L0	
Field grown	Roses (including stock for budding)	231	L1	
	Shrubs, conifers, hedging plants and Christmas trees (not roses)	232	L2	
	Ornamental trees	233	L3	
	Herbaceous plants (not for cut flowers)	234	L4	
Other hardy nursery stock and mixed areas		235	L5	
TOTAL HARDY NURSERY STOCK		236	L6	

			Number to nearest 100
Container grown plants (include acreage in item 235)	237	L7	

BULBS (corms, tubers and rhizomes) and FLOWERS in the open

				Statute Acres
Bulbs grown in the open for cut flowers or bulbs	Gladioli	240	M0	
	Irises	241	M1	
	Others, including remaining daffodils (narcissi) and tulips	242	M2	
Other flowers (in the open) for cutting		243	M3	
TOTAL BULBS and FLOWERS		244	M4	

TOTAL HORTICULTURAL CROPS (to agree with item 12 on page 2)	249	M9	

4

SCHEDULE 1 (continued)   GLASSHOUSES   JUNE 1975

TO BE COMPLETED BY GROWERS WITH 1,000 SQ. FT. OR MORE OF GLASS OR PLASTIC STRUCTURES

Notes for Guidance (Glasshouse)

A. "Glasshouse" includes any fixed or mobile structure of a height sufficient to allow persons to enter in an upright position and which is glazed or clad with film or rigid plastics or other glass substitutes. In the case of mobile structures return only the area covered by the structures themselves and not the total area of the sites that could be covered by moving the structures.

B. Enter at items 250-251 any fixed or mobile structures covered by glass or by glazed lights. Exclude Dutch lights used as frames on the flat, cloches and Dutch light structures unglazed at the date of return.

C. Enter at items 252-253 any fixed or mobile structures covered by film or rigid plastics or other glass substitutes providing the plastic cladding is in a satisfactory state for crop production. Exclude cloches, low tunnels and other forms of plastic coverage which do not allow people to enter in an upright position, or which are not capable of completely covering the crop as necessary.

D. (i) "Tomatoes, heated crop" means plants being grown with the aid of artificial heat during the whole or part life of the planted out crop.

(ii) "Tomatoes, unheated crop" means plants being grown without the aid of artificial heat after planting.

E. Plants in pots — give the total area of glasshouse floor space, not the total area of benches or beds.

F. Bedding plants — the number of boxes recorded should be in terms of a standard size 14 inches x 9 inches.

TOTAL AREA OF GLASSHOUSES
(whether in use or not—See note A)

				Square feet
Area covered by glass See note B	With heating equipment	250	N0	
	Without heating equipment	251	N1	
Area covered by plastics or other glass substitutes See note C	With heating equipment	252	N2	
	Without heating equipment	253	N3	
TOTAL AREA (to agree with total at 272)		254	N4	

Mobile Glasshouses (those structures on wheels, rails or other sliding devices which can be moved to cover a succession of areas)—already included in item 254	273	P3	

AREA OF CROPS IN GLASSHOUSES
(do not include crops under lights or cloches—See notes B and C)

					Square feet
VEGETABLES	Tomatoes	heated crop See note D(i)	255	N5	
		unheated crop See note D(ii)	256	N6	
	Cucumbers		257	N7	
	Other vegetables and herbs		258	N8	
FLOWERS	Carnations		259	N9	
	Roses		260	O0	
	Chrysanthemums	year round production (cut bloom only)	261	O1	
		for sale as pot plants	262	O2	
		for use or sale as cuttings	263	O3	
		early flowering (i.e. harvested May/June)	264	O4	
		all other chrysanthemums	265	O5	
	Plants in pots See note E	flowering plants other than chrysanthemums	266	O6	
		for foliage	267	O7	
	All other flowers, foliage crops, nursery crops, seedlings and bedding plants		268	O8	
FRUIT	Peaches, nectarines, strawberries, grapes and any other fruit		269	O9	
Remaining Glasshouse area at 2nd June	Estimated area which you expect to crop in 1975		270	P0	
	Estimated area which you do not expect to crop in 1975		271	P1	
TOTAL AREA (to agree with total at 254 above)			272	P2	

BEDDING PLANTS IN GLASSHOUSES

			Number of boxes
Bedding plants grown in boxes during the current season See note F	274	P4	

5

SUBJECT INDEX TO LAND-USE STATISTICS

15: TOWN AND COUNTRY PLANNING

L. F. Gebbett

Department of Planning and Transportation
Greater London Council

REFERENCE DATE OF SOURCES REVIEWED

This review is believed to represent the position, broadly speaking, as it obtained at 31st December 1975. Later revisions have been inserted up to the proof-reading stage (Nov 1977) taking account, as far as possible, of any major changes in the situation.

INDEX TO INITIALS USED IN THE TEXT

BAA	British Airports Authority
BOT	Board of Trade
BRB	British Rail Board
BSO	Business Statistics Office
BURISA	British Urban and Regional Information Systems Association
CSO	Central Statistical Office
DAFS	Department of Agriculture and Fisheries of Scotland
DANI	Department of Agriculture for Northern Ireland
DE	Department of Employment
DHSS	Department of Health and Social Security
DI	Department of Industry
DOE	Department of the Environment
DTI	Department of Trade and Industry
ED	Enumeration District
EFA	Effective Floor Area (net floor space)
ER	Employment Return
FES	Family Expenditure Survey
GISP	General Information System for Planning
GLC	Greater London Council
GLDP	Greater London Development Plan
HMSO	Her Majesty's Stationery Office
IDC	Industrial Development Certificate
IMTA	Institute of Municipal Treasurers Association
IR	Inland Revenue
LOB	Location of Offices Bureau

LTE	London Transport Executive
MAFF	Ministry of Agriculture, Food and Fisheries
MANI	Ministry of Agriculture for Northern Ireland
MPBW	Ministry of Public Building and Works
MD	Ministry of Development (Northern Ireland)
MHLG	Ministry of Housing and Local Government
MLH	Minimum List Heading
MOL	Ministry of Labour
MOT	Ministry of Transport
NAAS	National Agricultural Advisory Service
NES	New Earnings Survey
NI	National Insurance
NLGSLC	National and Local Government Statistical Liaison Committee
NLU	National Land Use
ODP	Office Development Permit
OPCS	Office of Population Censuses and Surveys
OS	Ordnance Survey
PAG	Planning Advisory Group
PAYE	Pay As You Earn
RCA	Reduced Cover Area (gross floor space)
RG	Registrar General
RRL	Road Research Laboratory
RSE	Regional Statistics of Earnings
RTPI	Royal Town Planning Institute
RUC	Royal Ulster Constabulary
RV	Rateable Value
SCLSERP	Standing Conference on London and South East Regional Planning
SDD	Scottish Development Department
SIC	Standard Industrial Classification
SPI	Survey of Personal Income
WE	Workers' Earnings

CONTENTS OF REVIEW 15

108

ADDENDA ON RECENT DEVELOPMENTS

Section 4.1.3. Stock of Dwellings

1971 Census data held for 1-km squares was first made available late in 1976. The Census Research Group at Durham University, funded by the Social Science Research Council has been working on them. The records for the whole of Great Britain are available on the university computer. Further details can be obtained from *1971 Census Grid Square Statistics Explanatory Notes* (OPCS, 1977) and *CRU Working Papers 9, 10 and 11*, obtainable from, the Department of Geography, Durham.

Section 5.2.13. Office Decentralisation

It should be noted that the role of the LOB has now been extended to advising on the location of offices within the London area as well as on the location of offices outside London.

Section 10. Transport

In 1977 the DOE was split into the DOE and Department of Transport.

Section 11.1.3. Land Use Changes

The DOE has asked for 1976/7 returns to be completed on new forms which can be used as input documents for computer processing but there has been no change in the actual data requirements.

Section 11.2.1. Planning Permissions

Continuing economic stringencies have made it difficult for all authorities to meet fully all the requirements of DOE circulars of recent years and the DOE has abandoned for the time being its proposals for more comprehensive and integrated development control returns in England and Wales. At the same time the returns of counts of planning permissions and refusals (see Section 3.2.1) have been considerably simplified. From 1977 onwards it will no longer be necessary under Circular 32/75 to provide details of certain individual sites where planning permissions are outstanding.

Some 95% of the English Authorities were able to make full or partial returns in response to Circular 32/75 and provisional estimates of the amount of land with planning permission for private sector housing on 1 July 1975 are now available for the English regions. These estimates have been published in *Statistics of Land with Outstanding Planning Permissions*, (HMSO London) and include areas of land, numbers of dwellings, and annual averages of dwellings started.

CHAPTER 1

INTRODUCTION

1.1. Evolution of Town and Country Planning

1.1.1. Town and country planning has been on the statute book since 1909 but the real foundation of modern law and practice was the 1947 Town and Country Planning Act. This introduced the two features of the preparation of detailed development plans and the control of development by local planning authorities. These formed the starting point of the needs of planners and research workers covering a very wide range of topics. The general approach has been substantially retained in the more recent Town and Country Planning Acts of 1962 and 1971 though now the detailed development plans formerly required have given way to the less detailed structure plan associated with continuous monitoring. Now local authorities are charged with a very wide range of social, economic and environmental issues.

1.1.2. A general introduction to planning is given in *Town and Country Planning in Britain* by J. B. Cullingworth [B 9] and this includes an historical account of its development. *The Evolution of British Town Planning* by G. E. Cherry [B 6] covers the development of planning legislation, the evolution of planning practice and the history of the Royal Town Planning Institute (RTPI). Control of development in Northern Ireland has not followed post-war legislation in Great Britain and plans have been prepared on a non-statutory basis. Mackenzie summarises the new planning law (1972) in Northern Ireland in [B 29].

1.2. Planning Authorities

1.2.1. For the greater part of the last 20 years the Ministry responsible for the administration of planning in England and Wales was the Ministry of Housing and Local Government (MHLG). The responsibilities of the MHLG were transferred in 1970 to the Department of the Environment (DOE) on the amalgamation of the MHLG with the Ministry of Transport (MOT) and the Ministry of Public Building and Works (MPBW). The authority with central responsibility for planning in Scotland is the Scottish Development Department (SDD) and in Northern Ireland the Ministry of Development (MD). From 1st October 1973 the responsible authority for planning in Northern Ireland is the Department of Housing, Local Government and Planning. There will also be a Department of the Environment (Belfast) distinct from the DOE London.

111

1.2.2. Planning authorities comprising County Councils and County Borough Councils have been responsible for local planning. The Local Government Act of 1972 introduced radical alterations from April 1974 in England and Wales. Instead of the 145 county borough planning authorities there are some 340 new authorities outside London and the metropolitan areas. Such changes obviously have wide implications for planners who wish to develop statistical time-series for the new areas. A new two-tier structure in Scotland came into existence in 1975. A guide to local government reorganisation is being produced by the Social Survey Division (R. M. Blunden and Sheila Gray) of the Office of Population Censuses and Surveys (OPCS) with the title New Districts for Old. This will eventually appear in three volumes, the first two being devoted to England and Wales and the third to Scotland. Volume I was published in 1974. The volumes will include population and acreage figures of the new districts by new counties and the contents of each new district in terms of former local authorities and their counties. For further details see 27.22 of [B 54].

1.3. Structure Plans and Monitoring

1.3.1. The key publication foreshadowing the change from detailed development plans to a new hierarchy of structure plans, district plans and action area plans is *The Future of Development Plans* [B 42] prepared by the Planning Advisory Group (PAG) in which the MHLG, MOT and SDD were represented. The Town and Country Planning Act of 1968 and the equivalent Scottish Act of 1969 incorporated the PAG proposals on structure plans and *Development Plans. A Manual on Form and Content* [B 38] for England and Wales and a Scottish Interim Manual [B 39] give detailed guidance, emphasising the need to cover the totality of environment, continuous review of plans and public participation. Development plans are no longer attempts to prepare detailed land use patterns for 15–20 years ahead. They are now procedures for deciding on a set of policies and strategies, subject to approval by the responsible Minister, to guide development at local authority level. Within this framework the local planning authorities take short-term decisions as solutions to immediate problems.

1.3.2. The introduction of structure planning requires planning authorities to review the implementation of plans. [B 38] states that: 'By keeping data under review, authorities will be able to detect significant trends which may invalidate assumptions basic to the plans, so leading them to alter the structure and local plans affected. Monitoring data in this way, ensuring that policies and proposals in the plans are based on up to date information which will be a continuous process.' An example of an approach to monitoring appears in *The Planner* [B 19] in June 1974. R. Harris and D. Scott describe a system for the sub-region of Notts/Derby with further references to monitoring.

1.4. Survey for Plans

1.4.1. As part of the process of preparing a development plan for approval by the responsible Minister, local authorities are required to carry out a survey of their area and make an analysis. Many statistical sources are used to supplement data obtained by survey and the great majority of these will have been developed without the specific needs of town planners in mind. These non-planning sources have given and continue to give much useful information about people, their homes, workplaces and associated land uses. Surveys, some of them on a considerable scale in the conurbations, have been carried out directly by or on behalf of local authorities to give statistics of land use, traffic, housing, employment and so on. These surveys tend to be on an *ad hoc* basis and even where they have become part of a regular series the statistics generated have been invariably only on a local authority basis or at best for a conurbation. A number of authorities have incorporated surveys, national and local sources of statistics into local information systems and descriptions of some of these ('Profiles') appear in various issues of *BURISA* [B 36], the newsletter of the British Urban and Regional Information Systems Association.

There has generally only been limited co-ordination of data obtained by local authorities either with respect to the topics covered or to the definitions and measurements involved. To the outside observer it may seem surprising that surveys and analysis of data by local authorities are not as yet centrally co-ordinated or extended by the DOE to provide statistical series at various levels for wider planning and use. As an example, the control of development, that is the granting or refusal of applications for development within the framework of planning, gives an excellent opportunity to measure general commitments and to forecast development as well as monitoring development plans. This has not been done except by individual local authorities and so there are as yet no comprehensive returns of planning permissions at the national level. The only returns local authorities have been required to make, at least until 1975, have related to counts of planning applications for different types of planning permissions and refusals. The real wealth of information that could be drawn from planning permissions and refusals concerning housing, offices, industry, shops, etc., remains a largely untapped source and a number of assertions appear in the daily press and elsewhere about delays in granting planning permissions which only too often cannot be either confirmed or refuted, let alone be judged against statistics showing the wider context of the implementation of planning permissions.

1.4.2. There are preliminary stages in the planning process which do yield statistical series. Industrial Development Certificates (IDCs) and Office Development Permits (ODPs), for example, have to be issued by central government in certain areas for varying levels of proposed development before certain planning applications can be entertained by local authorities. While they produce useful indicators of planning pressures in certain areas they have been restricted as a statistical source not merely because they only apply to parts of the UK but because offices and industry are only two of the many land uses competing for available land. The statistics generated hitherto at a national level by the planning process do not amount to much more than this and are thus rather meagre. The DOE has been very concerned in recent years with trying to improve this situation and various parts of this review will indicate the various requests for planning statistics being made of local authorities by the DOE. These requests are concerned with land-use changes and information contained in planning permissions.

1.4.3. A new statistical series has appeared under the general title *Statistics for Town* *and Country Planning* but has tended to be sporadic. The first of the series [QRL 59] contains simple counts of planning decisions and has already been referred to. The second [QRL 60] is drawn from Inland Revenue (IR) records and the third population projections based on the national censuses. The series is an interesting development but as we shall see is as yet of limited scope. The IR returns are a classical example of the problems that arise for planners when they try to use statistics whose source and definitions have quite different purposes from those of planning practice.

1.4.4. Planning authorities are consulted to an increasing degree by central government before such undertakings as national censuses of population and distribution take place and there is considerable evidence of awareness on the part of central government of the value of local knowledge and skills in improving the usefulness of the data collected by central agencies. This is very desirable for one of the chief complaints of local planning authorities is that statistics are often unreliable below the county conurbation district and borough levels and that central government sources ought to be able to provide more often reliable information for smaller areas such as redevelopment zones, shopping centres and Census Enumeration Districts (other than from the Census itself) subject to any limitations required for confidentiality of sources. The National and Local Government Statistical Liaison Committee (NLGSLC) is an important body set up in 1970 for the consideration of such difficulties. For the terms of reference and a description of the particular subjects being investigated by NLGSLC see the article by Cooke and Peretz [B 7]. Mention should also be made of the various standing conferences on planning which have been set up by local authorities to co-ordinate regional planning and which have attempted to set up simple monitoring systems. The first of these, now known as the Standing Conference on London and South Eastern Regional Planning (SCLSERP), publishes papers [B 53] on various topics which give useful insight into the assembly and use of statistics for planning at a regional level.

1.4.5. One major problem for planners in using national sources is the relative infrequency of data collection for national censuses and the delays which occur in publishing the results. National population censuses processing delays, as in 1961–71, still result in situations where planning authorities preparing strategic plans may be compelled to use statistics already 7 or 8 years out of date. A full census requires at present several years for complete processing including any special tabulations which may be needed by local planning authorities. All strategic plans making use of sources which are several years out of date can turn out to be highly unsatisfactory.

1.4.6. Planning authorities do not have direct control over such matters as employment levels and population densities. They must exercise indirect control through the amount of physical development they permit on specific sites based on their knowledge of probable densities of employment and population. The two principal measures of change they must consider are the uses to which the land is to be put and the intensity with which it is used. The first measure involves general considerations as to whether the use of the site should remain as it is and concerns the site itself and its environs. The second measure will involve specification of numbers and size of dwellings, amount of floor space, numbers of parking spaces and so on. The various sources of statistics on housing given in [B 11] and [B 14] give a fair amount of information about the intensity of use for this important land use but this is not for the most part directly related to statistics of the original planning permissions. We will also see that the statistics of floor space as a measure of intensity of use for offices, shops, commerce and industry is not nearly so well provided for as housing.

1.4.7. In 1968 a study team drawn from central and local government was set up to produce a national land-use classification, the absence of a standard classification having led to innumerable problems of inconsistency and incompatibility in land-use statistics collected locally and regionally for development plans and other purposes. The study was then widened to consider the larger problems of organising information for planning. The resulting report by the Joint Local Authority, SDD and DOE study team was published as *General Information System for Planning* (GISP), HMSO, 1972 [B 44]. While there may not be general agreement about all the conclusions reached with regard to the nature and practicability of the type of system proposed, the report incorporates definitive statements on the statutory background, local authority statistics and problems, monitoring and other matters referred to briefly in this introduction and is necessary reading for anyone working in this field.

1.5. Scope of Statistical Sources

1.5.1. The statistics used in planning are very wide-ranging as may be seen, for example, in the *Greater London Development Plan—Report of Studies* (GLDP) [B 45] which offers specific illustrations of the use of both national and local statistics in the preparation of a strategic plan. A more general guide to the many aspects of planning information is *Sourcebook of Planning Information* by B. White [B 34].

1.5.2. It is far beyond the general scope of a single review in this series to give a detailed or, in some instances, even a limited consideration of all the possible statistical sources which planners and research workers in planning may wish to use. Companion reviews in the series will give more detailed treatment of a number of subjects introduced here, e.g. employment and transport. Reference to some of these reviews is made in the main text and in addition attention is drawn to [B 26] by Lewes and Parker and [B 27] by Lickorish. Details of other relevant fields such as population, public expenditure and social services have had to be omitted. Fuller details have been given where it was thought the content was unlikely to be treated in detail in other reviews, e.g. Section 4 on Industrial and Commercial Properties. Given the necessary selectivity of this review it still brings together a substantial number of sources of value in town and country planning.

CHAPTER 2

PROBLEMS OF DEFINITION AND MEASUREMENT

2.1.1. The main problems may be summarised as follows:
  (a) Changes in definitions of administrative areas and other areas such as regions, wards and EDs.
  (b) Changes in central government classifications such as the Standard Industrial Classification (SIC) and occupational classification and absence of national classifications.
  (c) Differences between definitions in planning and other government sources.
  (d) Incomplete coverage of the UK by central government sources.

2.1.2. *Changes in area definitions*

There have been innumerable changes in administrative boundaries in the last 25 years and these create problems in developing time-series. With the creation of a two-tier structure in local government in England and Wales in 1974, consequent upon the 1972 Local Government Act, and an even more radical reorganisation in Scotland in 1975, these problems will grow rather than diminish for some years to come. Some sources, such as the population censuses, are being reprocessed, so that existing data will be available for the new administrative areas on an exact or estimated basis. This means that it will be possible to make some comparisons for the new administrative areas over a period of years. For example, when the GLC came into existence in 1965, thirty-two London boroughs were created which were amalgamations of former boroughs, parts of boroughs, urban districts and rural districts. The Registrar General (RG) was able to process the 1961 Census results for the new administrative areas and comparisons were thus possible with the 1966 Census results. A similar situation but on a much bigger scale arises with the creation of the new two-tier authorities. Provision has been made for processing the 1971 results for the new areas but it remains to be seen how many other sources can be reprocessed in the same way in order that existing data can be fully used as part of a time series.

Regional areas and various smaller areas are of considerable interest to planners and although there has been considerable rationalisation in the presentation of regional statistics figures are still provided by some public bodies for geographical areas used for special administrative purpose which do not correspond to the standard regions and local authority administrative areas. The development of statistical regions in the UK is discussed by Kent-Smith and Pritchard [B 24].

The availability of information from population censuses by wards and EDs has its

116

drawbacks as well as its attractions. The definitions of wards are not under the control of OPCS and have been liable to considerable change. Much of the Census and other material accumulated for wards has only been of value for limited periods because of subsequent changes in ward boundaries. For smaller areas reprocessing is a more difficult and expensive process. OPCS does have control over the definition of EDs but these too change from one census to the next. Section 4.1.3 refers to this problem and attempts being made to solve it by coding to grid squares.

2.1.3. *Classifications*

The key to national returns are universally accepted classifications. Two classifications widely used by planners not only in adapting central government sources but also for local surveys are the Standard Industrial Classification (SIC) [B 52] and the Classification of Occupations [B 37]. Both are, however, modified periodically and these changes can cause problems of interpretation (see Section 6.1.8). The essence of the SIC is that it is based on industry rather than occupation. Ideally planners need both but a great deal of employment data has only used the SIC. The first version of the SIC appeared in 1948 and revised versions have appeared in 1958 and 1968. The Classification of Occupations has also been modified as recently as 1972.

   The problems of using these classifications have, however, not been as troublesome as those in the field of land use where in the absence of a national land-use classification individual classifications have flourished with the inevitable absence of a national source of land use statistics. The new classification discussed by Coppock [B 8] has had a mixed reception from local planning authorities and despite its enormous detail, which includes such esoteric categories as dolls' hospitals, cross-country running courses and *son et lumière* places, presents a number of practical problems particularly in urban areas.

2.1.4. *Differences between planning and other definitions*

It cannot be too strongly emphasised that definitions of major land uses such as offices, industry, shops and warehousing (sometimes referred to as commerce) are highly variable and that different definitions can produce very different figures for what superficially appear to be the same thing. This emerges particularly strongly in Chapter 5 on Industrial and Commercial Properties when comparisons are made between definitions applying to Office Development Permits (ODPs), Industrial Development Certificates (IDCs), planning permissions and Inland Revenue (IR) floorspace statistics. A knowledge of the definitional differences is especially important for anyone trying to compare sources such as [QRL 60] with those assembled by local authorities from planning permissions and land-use surveys. Local authority planners will obviously tend to base their definitions on planning law and practice. These are sometimes very different from the requirements of a particular government department deriving statistics of administrative processes such as the fixing of rateable values [QRL 60]. A possible criticism of GISP [B 44] is that it assumes that with the widespread establishment of general information systems serving planners and others it will be a relatively straightforward matter to absorb and interpret existing sources.

2.1.5. *Incomplete coverage*

A number of sources discussed in this review which are the responsibility of central government do not give complete coverage of the UK. Quite apart from the general problem of differences between England and Wales and the rest of the UK or Great Britain and Northern Ireland, there are those returns which apply only to certain areas for limited periods as, for example, ODPs [QRL 24] (see Section 5.2.7), IDCs [QRL 62] (see Section 5.1.7) and Housing Land Availability [QRL 39] (see Section 4.3.1).

CHAPTER 3

LAND USE AND PLANNING DECISIONS

3.1. Land Use

3.1.1. Although, as we have seen in the Introduction, town and country planning is now extremely wide-ranging, the control of land use remains its essential basic function so that the statistics of land use are fundamental. There are, however, no comprehensive and regular series of statistics on land use currently available. The companion review on Land Use Statistics in the UK by Coppock [B 8] gives detailed information on the present sources and should be referred to particularly for land-use statistics on farming, forestry and other rural activities. Urban land use statistics in terms of floorspace areas of office, industrial, shopping and warehouse uses are described in the next section of this review. The final section of the review refers to the new DOE requirements for annual returns by local authorities of land use changes.

3.1.2. *Administrative areas*

Local authorities carry out land-use surveys with widely varying definitions and coverage. Common to all these surveys is a need to check on the measurement and totals of individual parcels, properties and hereditaments against any known measurements of total areas. On whatever basis land-use surveys may be carried out in future the same considerations will apply.

3.1.3. Useful checks of total areas are provided by the Ordnance Survey (OS). A convenient reference for these are the Census County reports [QRL 18] and [QRL 19] which give the total acreages for counties, boroughs and districts at the time of the census. Since 1971 these have been available in hectares instead of acres. It should, however, be borne in mind that these figures are for land and inland water only since tidal water and foreshore are excluded from the totals. The figures of these exclusions are available from the OS.

3.1.4. The Ordnance Survey has also measured the area of all parcels given on the 1:1250 scale maps in urban areas and 1:2500 maps in rural areas. Changes in administrative boundaries mean that the statistics given in [QRL 18] and [QRL 19] become out of date, and more especially so in recent years. The OS notifies local authorities of any new measurements resulting from these changes. These are not published by the OS but can be provided at a nominal charge.

3.1.5. *Allotments*

While this may be regarded as a topic of relatively minor importance, it is included here from a viewpoint which may not be expressed elsewhere in this series. Allotments were primarily regarded in wartime as making a useful contribution to the supply of food and the total land given to this use grew considerably. In more recent years allotments have been regarded more as a recreational activity. At the same time considerable areas of allotments have been vanishing, especially in urban areas, to be replaced by housing. This, in turn, has led to growing waiting lists for any allotments becoming available.

3.1.6. Local urban authorities are required to send annual returns in England and Wales as at 30th September of allotments in three categories, viz. statutory, temporary and private. Statutory allotments are those on land bought or appropriated by a local authority for use as allotments. Temporary allotments are those on land held by the council on lease or council-owned land not bought or appropriated for allotments. Private allotments are those on land let by other organisations than the council but do not include railway allotments. The statistics obtained for each of these categories include the total site areas, the number of plots subdivided into occupied and unoccupied plots. Another feature of the returns is the numbers of applicants for allotments on local authority lists. Rural authorities are only required to provide returns every 4 years. A degree of estimation is involved in the statistics for some returns. When this is known to be the case the summaries compiled by the DOE give brief comments on the items estimated.

3.1.7. The data are not normally published by the DOE. Tables of returns are, however, released sometimes for publication elsewhere as, for example, in the GLC *Annual Abstract of Greater London Statistics* [QRL 5]. There are no published statistics on allotments in Scotland and Northern Ireland.

3.2. Planning Decisions

3.2.1. *Statistics for Town and Country Planning*, Series I, Planning Decisions [QRL 59], is the only current national source of statistics for England and Wales on the outcome of planning applications. This particular series began in 1968 and continued a similar series which first appeared in 1962 as *Statistics of Decisions on Planning Applications*. Until 1974 the statistics were returned by local planning authorities on a calendar year basis but from 1st April 1974 onwards they were returned on a financial year basis so that the newly constituted authorities as at that date were not required to produce returns for the preceding 3 months. The returns are confined to simple counts of numbers of planning permissions and refusals. The figures exclude applications referred to the DOE for decision and decisions following appeal cases. (See Addenda).

3.2.2. Each planning permission or refusal is allocated to a particular use group within one of the two main categories of building and engineering operations or changes of use. This is a little arbitrary as only the dominant use can be counted for many urban sites and buildings involving more than one use. More serious, of course, is that large developments are quite indistinguishable from small developments so that the tables only provide general indicators of planning authorities, work loads. However, in the absence of more detailed information these statistics have at least reflected the considerable fluctuations in recent years of planning commitments (permissions granted) and pressures (applications received). For a discussion on the use of these statistics see [B 2] by Blake who points out that there is no breakdown of the category 'all other classes' which accounts for over a quarter of all decisions.

3.2.3. In Scotland local authorities return counts of planning decisions to the SDD in a form similar to that required in England and Wales. Summaries for Scotland are published in the *Annual Report of the Scottish Development Department*, Cmnd. 5274 [QRL 9]. The *Ulster Year Book* [QRL 64] gives Northern Ireland totals of applications, approvals, conditional approvals, and refusals. However, from 1st October 1973 onwards the new Department of Housing, Local Government and Planning is obtaining quarterly returns from the Divisional Planning Offices which show the number of applications and decisions for each of the twenty-six District Council Areas in Northern Ireland. The returns show the applications and decisions classified in various ways, e.g. residential-urban/rural, commercial, industrial, civic/cultural, recreational open space. The applications are further broken down between demolitions and extensions. No statistics have yet been published but information can be obtained from the Department at Castle Grounds, Belfast.

3.2.4. *Appeals statistics*

For the year 1962 onwards statistics compiled from its own records by the DOE of planning appeals for England and Wales were published in the *Handbook of Statistics* [QRL 36]. This was last published for the records of 1970 although similar unpublished figures are held by the DOE for later years. It is the intention of the DOE to publish these in a new series similar to [QRL 36] with a title on the lines of Local Government Planning and Miscellaneous Statistics. [QRL 36] includes numbers of allowed and dismissed appeals analysed by class of development as well as a number of tables covering enforcement notices, control of advertisements and established use certificates. Summaries of appeals in Scotland compiled by the SDD are given in Cmnd. 5274 [QRL 9]. The *Ulster Year Book* [QRL 64] gives Northern Ireland totals of appeals received and allowed. Following reorganisation appeals in Northern Ireland are the responsibility of the Planning Appeals Commission which was set up on 1st October 1973. A monthly bulletin will be published by the Commission giving the total of appeals, lodged and decided. Copies of the bulletin will be obtainable from The Secretary, Planning Appeals Commission, Carlton House, 1 Shaftesbury Square, Belfast BT2 7LB.

3.2.5. *Preservation of historic buildings*

[QRL 59] gives the statistics for England and Wales of the outcome of applications related to buildings, listed for historical and architectural importance. These figures are broken down into (a) demolitions and (b) alterations and extensions. The new returns of the District Councils in Northern Ireland (see Section 3.2.3) include listed buildings applications and decisions. There is, however, no breakdown between demolitions and alterations and extensions. The remarks on the publication of the statistics in Section 3.2.3 apply to listed buildings.

3.2.6. A useful secondary source of some of the planning statistics (acreages, development applications, appeals, etc.) in England and Wales is *County Planning Statistics* [QRL 24] compiled by the County Planning Officers' Society and the Society of County Treasurers. Additionally statistics are given of the professional, technical and administrative expenses as well as other planning expenses of counties in England and Wales.

CHAPTER 4

HOUSING

This topic has been dealt with in detail in the companion reviews [B 11] by Farthing and [B 14] by Fleming. In consequence brief references only are given here for the sake of completeness to the most important sources discussed fully by Farthing and Fleming. This section also refers to some aspects of housing of additional interest to planners, such as land availability for housing, with some suggestions of improvements that could be made using local authorities own records of planning permissions for housing developments.

4.1. Stock of Dwellings

4.1.1. The main sources quoted and discussed by Farthing and Fleming are the *Census of Population in Great Britain* [QRL 18] and *Housing and Construction Statistics* [QRL 38]. For Northern Ireland the main source quoted is the *Census of Population, Northern Ireland* [QRL 19]. For planning the published reports are of great value but further analyses are required from the censuses for smaller areal units such as enumeration districts (EDs). This need has generated vast quantities of unpublished tables provided directly by OPCS, and formerly by the Registrar General (RG), as well as by further processing of basic Census records by local authorities. The use of magnetic tapes provided by OPCS are, however, subject to various confidentiality restrictions.

4.1.2. OPCS has given planning authorities increasing opportunities over the years in the delineation of EDs. This has made it possible to aggregate EDs into meaningful planning areas, subject to OPCS criteria on size, location, ward boundaries, etc., being satisfied.

4.1.3. Considerable problems arise with comparisons over a number of years because of changes in borough and ward boundaries. The problem becomes much worse at ED level because the size of the ED has depended to some extent on the coverage of a particular census. Thus the more questions are asked the more work is created for the enumerator and this leads to a reduction in the number of households to be included in an ED. In order to get round the unsuitability of the ED, or the ward for that matter, as a basis of comparison between successive censuses, the OPCS introduced in the 1971 Census the coding of data to 100-m, 500-m, and 1-km squares on the national grid. The problem of confidentiality can obviously arise in analyses of such areas as with EDs and to overcome the problem OPCS adopted the bizarre device of adding to each non-zero cell in some tables 1, −1 or zero according to a quasi-random pattern.

This has obvious disadvantages in validation procedures for planning authorities producing tables for small areas. (See Addenda).

4.1.4. One of the most notable deficiencies in housing statistics for planners is the absence of a central government sources of statistics about housing densities. Planners are interested in housing density which may be expressed in terms of number of dwellings, habitable rooms or indirectly persons per acre or hectare. Planning permissions for larger developments are frequently expressed in such terms and yet there are no generally available statistics of the density of the housing stock against which the density of changes to the stock can be judged. Farthing [B 11] gives details of local authority housing developments densities. The best that can generally be done is to use the housing figures given in the population censuses [QRL 18] and [QRL 19] and relate these to site areas of housing obtained from local land-use surveys. However, care needs to be taken because of the problem of definition of a dwelling which Farthing [B 11] discusses. For a recent examination of this see Wheller [B 33]. This is a perennial problem and changes have taken place between successive censuses in the rules for counting the numbers of habitable rooms particularly with regard to kitchens. Therefore any attempt to relate census figures to local data must take note of the basis of room counting if proper comparisons are to be made.

4.2. Changes to the Stock of Dwellings

4.2.1. While changes to the stock of dwellings appear regularly in *Housing and Construction Statistics* [QRL 38] and *Housing Return for Northern Ireland* [QRL 40] there are no national statistics of potential changes in the stock implied by the granting of planning permissions for housing developments. This is a subject of considerable interest if only to judge from statements made through the press by developers about land not being released quickly enough for house building and counter-statements to the effect that planning permissions for housing are not being fully or quickly used by developers. The developers point out that statistics on land available for housing are not very meaningful since they take insufficient account of ownership, density restrictions, availability of main services and existing land uses. These differing viewpoints can indeed rarely be resolved one way or the other by any appeal to reliable statistics. The Standing Conference on London and South East Regional Planning (SCLSERP) has carried out an investigation of such planning permissions granted by some of its member authorities [B 53]. There is a clear need for such statistics to by systematically collected at the national level.

4.2.2. Planning permissions for housing could be used not only to give national statistics of potential change but also from the implementation of the permissions as a measurement of the rate of change. Hartley has prepared an unpublished paper for the DOE [B 21] which analyses housing density for various size ranges of planning permissions granted in 1970–2 for London boroughs and the entire Greater London area. The data source is described by Gebbett in [B 16]. An individual permission will normally only give details of the numbers and size of the dwellings proposed to be built so that further information on dwellings lost on redevelopment, housing and otherwise would need to be additionally recorded. Subsequently implementations could be used to produce not only returns of completions for *Housing and Construction Statistics* [QRL 38] but also to produce statistics of outstanding and lapsed permissions which are topics hitherto shrouded in mystery. Such returns by planning authorities ought also to incorporate statistics of conversions which in terms of numbers of permissions comprise a substantial proportion of all permissions in the conurbation areas. *Housing and Construction Statistics* [QRL 38] gives local authority returns of conversions of existing dwellings from improvement grant figures but some conversions resulting from planning permissions will be carried out without an improvement grant.

4.3. Housing Land Availability

4.3.1. Planning authorities in the West Midlands and South-east England (excluding Greater London) were requested in Circular 102/72 to provide details of the undeveloped sites in their areas on the whole, or part of which, residential development (including both public and private sector housing) could start within a 5-year period from October 1972. The circular distinguished between sites which already had planning permission at October 1972 and on which building could start, sites for which planning permission could become effective and building could start in the next 2 years. A further classification was made of new sites over 3 acres, new sites under 3 acres, redevelopment sites and sites under construction. These returns have been analysed but not published by the DOE and some further analyses have been made by the Standing Conference [B 53]. Planning authorities were asked to maintain records of the land-availability situation in their areas.

4.3.2. While Circular 102/72 only sought information from authorities in the West Midlands and the South East, the statistics obtained are of general interest and the DOE wishes to collect similar information for England and Wales from 1975 onwards.

4.3.3. Problems arose in compiling the results of 102/72. The chief difficulties were that the returns had to be made by some authorities from existing records in which the form of the data did not correspond precisely with the definitions in the Circular with respect to dates or categories.

4.3.4. The Economist Intelligence Unit in association with Halpern and Partners was commissioned in June 1973 by the DOE and the Housing Research Foundation to make a study of the supply of land for new houses. The results of this study appear in *Housing Land Availability in the South East* [QRL 39]. Appendix 6.1 of this report explains the method of data collection which was based on the information of Circular 102/72 but which involved further data collection and analysis. The consultants decided to confine their study to four counties—Buckinghamshire, Kent, Surrey and West Sussex— selected as being both representative of the different planning situations in the region and with records suitable for the type of analysis proposed.

4.3.5. The scope of [QRL 39] varies with the amount of data available in individual counties but the tables give useful statistics on the progress of site work on sites with outstanding housing permissions and progress on allocated sites. This is the first time that an authoritative analysis of this nature has been undertaken and its significance will clearly extend beyond the particular areas involved.

CHAPTER 5

INDUSTRIAL AND COMMERCIAL PROPERTIES

The chief source for the floorspace statistics of industrial and commercial properties in England and Wales is *Statistics for Town and Country Planning*, Series II [QRL 60] obtained from Inland Revenue (IR) Valuation Lists by the DOE. There are no sources of floorspace statistics of industrial and commercial floorspace for Scotland and Northern Ireland comparable with [QRL 60]. The basic data unit in [QRL 60] is the hereditament and *Local Government Administration* by Hart [B 20] states that 'The unit for the purpose of assessment is the hereditament which may be defined as each parcel of land, buildings, mines, sporting rights, etc., separately occupied.' Separate occupation implies that individual buildings, especially in town centres where a number of firms may occupy a single building, can contain a number of hereditaments. [B 20] gives further background information on rating and hereditaments including the treatment of unoccupied hereditaments. Floorspace in IR tables is defined in terms of what is called Effective Floor Area (EFA) of the rateable hereditaments and is elsewhere often referred to as net floorspace. It is the internal area of the buildings and excludes walls, staircases, lifts, corridors, w.c.'s, etc. Canteens are included if they are part of the hereditaments. There are two other sources of floorspace data, ODPs and IDCs, and these are granted on a floorspace basis called Reduced Cover Area (RCA) by IR. This definition produces areas based on external measurements of buildings multiplied by the number of storeys and basements with areas such as courtyards excluded. It is more generally known as gross floorspace and local authorities carrying out land-use surveys will normally measure floorspace on this RCA/gross basis.

Series II [QRL 60] is potentially a useful source especially for those authorities who have not carried out their own floorspace surveys. It has the merit of being the only source that could be used for local authority and regional totals over the whole of England and Wales. If some of the considerable definitional problems could be overcome so that floorspace could be expressed in a form closer to the definitions of planning permissions, ODPs and IDCs, the value of [QRL 60] would be greatly increased. In such a situation there would be a considerable demand for statistics below the local authority level. The DOE says that the question of confidentiality which might have prevented the distribution of results for smaller areas will be overcome. Such distribution would give researchers useful insight into the significance and consistency of the IR definitions.

5.1. Stock of Industrial Floorspace

5.1.1. Series II [QRL 60] gives floorspace figures on an EFA basis for local authorities

126

down to local authority level for the first time in No. 2 of the series. No. 1 in the series was limited to changes in stock only. No. 2 gave the total stock as at 1st April 1967 and the changes for the financial year 1967–8. No. 3 was again limited to changes in stock, this time from April 1967 to March 1969 whilst No. 4 gave stock as at 1st April 1974.

5.1.2. The description of the floorspace data in [QRL 60] as stock is a little misleading since some new floorspace which is unoccupied may not be counted in the stock since it does not appear in the current valuation list. On the other hand, if a local authority chooses to exercise its powers to levy rates on vacant property unoccupied premises may then be included in the stock. The quoted stock therefore is an underestimate of the true stock. No separate figures are quoted of vacant industrial floorspace and this is one of the most serious shortcomings of the source.

5.1.3. The Series II [QRL 60] tables show the numbers of hereditaments and any hereditament included in the complete tables is allocated in its entirety to one and one only of the four uses of industry, shops, offices and warehousing. Its allocation is determined by the dominant use of the building or buildings included in the hereditament. Thus a factory with three-quarters of its floorspace used for production and one-quarter for offices will have the floorspace of both industry and offices counted as industrial floorspace. This may not be unreasonable for some purposes, particularly when the offices are ancillary to the manufacturing process, but it is a different matter when an office block on an industrial site has a head office function or when it is necessary to distinguish between industrial and office employment. The effect of classifying hereditaments according to dominant uses tends to give high estimates of industrial floorspace. To a much lesser extent some 'office' hereditaments will include industrial floorspace. The problem of gross floorspace (RCA) and net floorspace (EFA) has already been outlined at the beginning of this chapter. The combined effect of the dominant use approach and floorspace definitions can usefully be illustrated by comparing results at a borough and county level with those of a planning authority floorspace survey. The *GLC Land Use Survey 1966—Research Report No. 8* by Gebbett [QRL 34] gives total industrial floorspace totals on a RCA and apportioned mixed uses basis and the two sources are near enough in time to bear comparison. [QRL 34] gives a total of 274 million square feet and [QRL 60] 287 million square feet for Greater London but differences for individual boroughs are considerable.

5.1.4. There are difficulties in expressing certain types of industrial hereditaments in terms of floorspace and this results in the exclusion of some large undertakings such as steel works, oil refineries and cement works. These are therefore not included in [QRL 60] and in some areas must therefore be a serious deficiency.

5.1.5. *Changes in the Stock of Industrial Floorspace*

No. 1 in Series II [QRL 60], gives changes between April 1964 and March 1967, No. 2 [QRL 60] the changes between April 1967 and March 1968 and No. 3 [QRL 60] the changes between April 1967 and March 1969. The explanatory notes to No. 2 draw attention to doubts about the accuracy of the earlier statistics from which one infers that the series proper starts effectively with No. 2. The changes are on the same basis as the stock totals and are subject to the same limitations. At a local authority level they may be misleading though as regional indicators they appear to be rather better.

5.1.6. *Potential Changes in the Stock of Industrial Floorspace*

Annual and quarterly summaries of industrial floorspace statistics based on IDCs, have appeared in *Trade and Industry* [QRL 62] since 1969 and previously in the *Board of Trade Journal* (BOT). The objective of IDCs was to help promote a better distribution of industry. *Movement of Manufacturing Industry in the United Kingdom 1964–5* [B 22] by R. S. Howard, generally known as the Howard Report, reviews and interprets government policies designed to redistribute industry. From 1973 onwards, because of the reduction in the use of IDCs, the returns will no longer be published in *Trade and Industry* and unpublished figures will have to be obtained direct from the Department of Industry (DI).

5.1.7. Since 1947 an IDC has been needed as a prior condition from the DTI and previously the BOT to a planning application for proposed industrial developments over a certain size which would result in new industrial floorspace either from a change of use within an existing building or from new construction. The areas of the UK to which this has applied have varied as have the exemption limits for an IDC and IDCs were never required, for example, in Northern Ireland.

5.1.8. The statistics obtained from IDCs comprise floorspace information about permissions, refusals and completions with the basis of measurement RCA or gross floorspace. Until 1966 ancillary floorspace such as storage, office and canteens was excluded from approvals except in Scotland, Wales and Northern England. Since 1966 ancillary floorspace has been included in the total floorspace and so a certain amount of additional floorspace is concealed in the figures and may include, for example, a substantial amount of office floorspace. Unlike ODPs the IDCs returns do not cover relinquished floorspace, i.e. floorspace lost as a result of redevelopment. A considerable amount of industrial floorspace is also being replaced by warehousing floorspace and such changes are independent of IDC procedures.

5.1.9. One of the problems which has to be faced with [QRL 62] is that of double counting as there are a number of instances where more than one IDC is granted for a particular site. This has been partly dealt with for cases where initial refusals were followed by a permission during the same year or by January of the next year. Even if double counting is minimal the approvals and refusals are a long way from being a precise measure of demand and response to demand. In parts of the country some applications are abandoned after discussion and withdrawn before formal refusal. There are other projects where applications are not made because of knowledge of current regional policy on the location of industry.

5.1.10. The completions figures given by [QRL 62] are generally the total area of whole schemes when finally completed. Notifications from industrialists are sometimes not received until some time after the actual completion has taken place and for this reason completions statistics have not been published until two quarters later. Quarterly revisions have been made which incorporate amendments to the tables already published.

5.1.11. The granting of an IDC does not necessarily result in the granting of a planning permission and when it does it may still be for a smaller amount than that given by the IDC. The variability of the IDC exemption limits should also be borne in mind when considering a time series of the statistics.

5.1.12. In *Notes for Guidance in Interpreting Inland Revenue Floorspace Data for England and Wales* [B 50] the DOE outlines the reasons for differences between IDC [QRL 62] and Series II [QRL 60] totals. IDCs largely exclude buildings of 5000 square feet or less. IDCs only cover new construction and extensions and do not include change of use hereditaments as is the case for [QRL 60]. In general the IR [QRL 60] definition is wider than that of IDCs. Both lack floorspace data for properties such as steelworks where there are problems in obtaining meaningful floorspace measurements. The inclusion of ancillary floorspace in IDC totals is a further reason for the general rule that IR figures will be higher than those of the *Trade and Industry* [QRL 62] returns.

5.2. Stock of Office Floorspace

5.2.1. Series II, No. 4 [QRL 60] gives the stocks of office floorspace in England and Wales as at 1st April 1974 down to district level, together with a summary of regional changes from 1967 to 1974. The stock at April 1967 is given in No. 2 and changes from April 1967 to March 1969 are given in No. 3 [QRL 60]. Changes are given in No. 1 of [QRL 60] for the period 1964–7 as well as the stock as at 1st April 1964 but the notes in No. 2 make it clear that subsequent investigation has drawn attention to the figures for earlier years being so much lower than those for 1967–8 and preliminary results for later years so that users should for practical purposes regard the series as starting from 1st April 1967. Nos. 2 and 4 give useful notes and definitions but much more detailed information appears in the DOE unpublished *Notes for Guidance in Interpreting Inland Revenue Floorspace Data for England and Wales* [B 50].

5.2.2. Numbers of hereditaments are given in Series II with office floorspace divided into three categories of commercial, local government and central government in Nos. 2 and 3. The division into three categories is useful but should be treated with some caution. The allocation may depend on the purpose for which the office was built rather than the actual use. It can, in fact, happen that an office originally built on a speculative basis by a private developer and subsequently occupied by a local authority or government department may continue to be included in the statistics as a commercial office. In No. 4 there are only two categories—commercial and central government.

5.2.3. The use of net (EFA) floorspace instead of gross (RCA) is the most important difference between Series II floorspace and other sources such as ODPs and land-use surveys carried out by local authorities. Reference has already been made to the classification of hereditaments according to the dominant use. This results in substantial amounts of office floorspace associated with industrial sites, regardless of whether this has a head office function or is wholly or partly ancillary to the industry on the site, being classified as industrial floorspace. Conversely, but to a less significant degree, ancillary warehousing or industrial floorspace within a predominantly office hereditament will be included in the figures as office floorspace.

5.2.4. There are a number of important inclusions and exclusions applying to the IR statistics. General Post Offices have not been included as offices in Nos. 2 and 3 but Post Office hereditaments including administrative offices, Main Post Offices and telephone exchanges are included in No. 4 [QRL 60]. Banks are included as offices in 'office' areas but are counted as shops in 'shopping' areas. Offices of passenger and freight transport, gas, water and electricity boards are all excluded from the count of offices. The treatment of vacant offices is variable. If an office is newly completed and not yet occupied its inclusion depends on whether or not it happens to be in areas where the local authority uses its powers to rate empty property.

5.2.5. It is clear there are considerable problems in interpreting office floorspace figures derived from IR records. The DOE suggests [B 50] that the ratio of gross (RCA) to net (EFA) can be taken as 3:2 but evidence for this is limited to some thirty large buildings in the London area. The ratio must surely vary with the age and size of a building. The DOE intends to carry out further research into these relationships and this could provide more widely based and necessarily more complex conversion factors which could be applied to the IR data so that more precise estimates of gross floorspace might be obtained. However, the various inclusions and exclusions as well as the coding to dominant uses make it extremely difficult for planners to relate IR figures to other sources of office floorspace statistics. A striking illustration of the different totals of office floorspace that can be obtained because of the possible differences in definition is given by comparing [QRL 60] with the *GLC Land Use Survey (1966)* [QRL 34]. Series II, No. 2 gives 1967 figures which are reasonably close in time to the GLC figures for the same area but the total office floorspace recorded by the London boroughs on a gross (RCA) basis was virtually twice that in Series II on a net (EFA) basis.

5.2.6. *Changes in stock of office floorspace*

Changes in the stock between April 1967 and March 1969 in the stock of office floorspace are given in Series II, No. 3 [QRL 60]. Earlier changes in the series are not reliable (see Section 5.1.5).

5.2.7. *Potential changes in the stock of office floorspace*

Under the Control of Office and Industrial Development Act, 1965, Office Development Permits (ODPs) were required for the erection of a building for office purposes or for the change of use of a building to offices where the proposed floorspace exceeded 3000 square feet. This was intended as a means of securing a better distribution of employment and was required in advance of a planning application. ODPs have applied to certain prescribed areas in England but the areas affected have been steadily reduced so that by December 1970 only the South-east Region remained prescribed. Exemption limits have also changed for ODPs and in the GLC area, for example, they were raised in December 1970 from 3000 to 10,000 square feet. ODPs have never applied to Scotland and Northern Ireland. The basis of measurement is gross floorspace (RCA).

5.2.8. Quarterly floorspace returns from ODP data appear in *Trade and Industry* [QRL 62] and include statistics for the current and earlier quarters. A useful feature of the returns is the inclusion of relinquished floorspace, that is, floorspace which would be lost on demolition or change of use of existing offices if the ODPs were implemented. In the absence of national returns of office floorspace permissions ODPs give very useful indications of trends in permissions but apart from problems of comparability over a period which result from changes in prescribed areas and variations in exemption limits there are other problems in interpretation. Further details with a discussion of various aspects of office development are given in the annual report *Control of Office Development* [QRL 23] with comparative annual figures of floorspace in the 'pipeline'. This is given for three categories of complete and vacant, under construction and outstanding planning permissions and is derived from returns made by the local authorities concerned for all office permissions over 3000 square feet. The total floorspace of these returns will not correspond precisely to the permits previously granted for reasons which will be given in the following paragraph. The detailed lists provided for the DOE by the authorities are not published but some of the authorities may be prepared to provide research workers with copies identifying particular developments and giving details of floorspace and information about the progress of each development.

5.2.9. The total floorspace of ODPs given by [QRL 62] and [QRL 23] depends to some extent on the level of exemption limits but the analyses by size of development include some permits apparently below the exemption limit in force at the time. These are a minority of cases which arise in what is known as 'related development' where an ODP is required because the proposed offices and the previous office development on the same or on an adjacent site together exceed the exemption limit. However, even when account is taken of the varying exemption limits there is another change in the regulations which affects comparisons. From April 1969 it was no longer necessary, in general, to obtain an ODP within the curtilage of an industrial building for which an IDC had been issued. The figure included for the last full year (1968) for which ODPs were needed in these circumstances was as high as 18 per cent of the total area for which permits were issued so that the considerable increase in ODPs given in the South-East region which started at that time conceals in the returns some smaller but nevertheless appreciable reductions resulting from the exclusion of offices associated with large industrial developments.

5.2.10. This review is not directly concerned with quoting published statistics but some useful insight into ODP statistics can be obtained by a specific comparison between ODPs for the GLC area and planning permissions statistics compiled by the GLC from borough returns. The figures quoted here are from *Trade and Industry* [QRL 62], March 1974, and the *Annual Abstract of Greater London Statistics* [QRL 5]. The latter figures for 1966–72 are slightly amended from those originally published.

5.2.11. The trends in planning permissions reflect those of ODPs, when some allowance is made for the time-lag between the granting of ODPs and corresponding planning permissions. However, the general level of gross floorspace of ODPs is much higher

Table 1. *Office Floorspace*

| Year | ODPs | | GLC planning permissions | |
	Gross	Relinquished	Gross	Relinquished
1966	2929	1582	2701	715
1967	4522	1769	2690	1325
1968	8700	4569	3448	2216
1969	9945	3069	5124	1620
1970	16,031	5722	7447	2999
1971	18,879	5397	9338	4042
1972	17,601	5284	10,302	4099
1973	15,678	3411	8298	2373
1974	7138	838	8298	3994

Area: Greater London.   Units: thousands of square feet.
The basis of measurement for both sources is similar, i.e. RCA.

than that of planning permissions and there are a number of reasons why this should be so. Firstly, there is the problem of double counting. The ODPs [QRL 62] make no provision for revising earlier returns when an ODP is granted for a site where an earlier ODP had been granted, so that [QRL 62] tends to give high estimates of subsequent planning permissions. By contrast the GLC permissions [QRL 5] make allowance for the problem of multiple permissions [B 16] for the same site and do not include double counting. On the other hand, [QRL 5] contains permissions under 3000 square feet for all years whereas the ODP exemption limits (see Section 5.2.9) results in the exclusion not only of all permissions under 3000 square feet but in recent years also under 10,000 square feet. The significance of these smaller developments is not generally appreciated but unpublished data from [QRL 5] shown that in a conurbation they can account for as much as 15 per cent of the total permitted floorspace. On the other hand, there will be many ODP schemes abandoned before application for planning permission is made and this category will include a number of cases of double counting where an initial ODP not subsequently used was followed by a further application.

5.2.12. *Relinquished and net increase of office floorspace*

Gross floorspace returns such as those given by [QRL 62] give a measure of new floorspace relative to existing floorspace. Planners are, however, interested in the net increase in floorspace potential contained in ODPs or planning permissions. This net increase must be distinguished from the concept of net floorspace measurement (EFA). It is the difference between gross floorspace (RCA) and relinquished or existing floorspace. The relinquished floorspace is reported by the applicant for an ODP [QRL 62] and it would not be surprising if such figures were not sometimes overstated since this would give an apparent low net gain and hence increase the probability of the application being acceptable. This, however, does not appear to be borne out by Table 1 given in Section 5.2.11 which shows that the ODP [QRL 62] relinquished floorspace is relatively low when compared with that shown by planning permissions [QRL 5]. There are other considerations in comparing ODPs and planning permissions relinquished floorspace data. Offices are sometimes demolished and replaced by a different use. This happens a little more frequently than might be supposed particularly with the relocation or loss of industry when a substantial amount of associated office floorspace may be lost. Offices are also replaced sometimes in town centres by public buildings. These should be reflected in planning permissions data as pure losses (relinquished) floorspace but would clearly be excluded from ODP statistics.

5.2.13. *Office decentralisation*

The Location of Offices Bureau (LOB) was set up in 1963 by the Secretary of State for the Environment with the purpose of encouraging the decentralisation of employment from central London to suitable locations elsewhere. The LOB *Annual Report* [QRL 8] provides statistics since 1963 of office dispersal from central London. These are expressed in terms of numbers of firms, sizes of firms and numbers of jobs. The estimates of jobs are in part based on floorspace figures. Numbers of firms approaching the LOB are quoted as well as the numbers of firms who have actually moved within London and to other parts of the country. Reasons for decentralisation are also analysed although not all firms give a reason and some firms quote more than one reason. LOB have had problems in making detailed information available to researchers because much of the raw data have been held on confidential files. It has therefore set up a new system to overcome the problem of confidentiality and make the source more readily accessible. (See Addenda).

5.3. Stock of Shopping Floorspace

5.3.1. Series II, No. 4 [QRL 60] gives the stock of shopping floorspace in England and Wales down to district level as at 1st April 1974. The data were obtained from IR records and are measured on an EFA or net basis. Section 5.2.1 on office floorspace applies equally to shopping floorspace given by [QRL 60].

5.3.2. The IR definition of shops is a wide one and may include as many as 25 per cent to 30 per cent more hereditaments according to [B 50] than those covered as shops by the *Census of Distribution* [QRL 16]. For example, restaurants and cafés are classified as shops by IR but not by the Census. There are also a number of activities counted by IR as shops which might not be normally regarded as shops but which occupy what are called shop-type premises. Examples of such premises are banks in 'Shopping' areas, estate agents, insurance sub-offices, car salesrooms, betting shops and fish and chip shops. There is, however, one very important class of omission from Nos. 2 and 3 [QRL 60] known in the IR floorspace records as 'Shops with Premises', i.e. shops with living accommodation. This is because only total floorspace is recorded for such hereditaments and thus the floorspace for the shops is not separately recorded. The inclusion of such B 4 hereditaments, as this category is known, as shops would inflate the total shopping floorspace by the living accommodation floorspace. In terms of numbers of hereditaments the B 4 cases account for as much as 41.7 per cent of all hereditaments containing shopping uses. While these shops will individually tend to be small and their numbers are known from common experience to be declining, their exclusion severely limits the value of the data. [B 50] gives the percentage of [B 4] hereditaments by regions and quotes examples of extreme variations at the local authority level between Blackburn (58 per cent) and Crawley New Town (18 per cent). Estimates of average B 4 sizes are also given. In No. 4 [QRL 60] for 1974 a new category, shops with living accommodation, was introduced in which the floorspace shown was for shop area and excluded parts used for residential purposes. It should be noted that no information on vacant shops is included in [QRL 60].

5.3.3. Some limited floorspace information for 1966 on shopping is available from the *Census of Distribution* [QRL 16] now carried out by the Department of Industry and previously by the Department of Trade and Industry (DTI) and the BOT. The censuses give statistics of retail and service establishments in Great Britain. Full censuses took place in 1950, 1961 and 1971 and sample censuses in 1957 and 1966. Information is collected by questionnaires for the shop, known as the establishment, and the firm, known as the organisation. The chief difference between a full and sample census is that the former can provide detailed data for local authority areas, and for large towns, the central shopping areas and in certain cases the smaller shopping centres.

5.3.4. Floor space information was tabulated separately for the first time in the 1966 BOT *Census* [QRL 16]. Questions were asked about 'Total floorspace' and 'Selling space'. Total floorspace was defined as space on all floors normally used for selling, display, stockholding, offices, etc. It differed slightly from the IR definition of RCA by including outdoor space used for business on the premises. Living accommodation was excluded. 'Selling space' was the whole area used for selling to customers including the space to which customers have access such as counter space, window space, fitting rooms and space used by assistants behind counters. It excluded offices, storage, work rooms, cloakrooms and other amenities, rooms with the exclusion of lobbies, staircases, etc. Selling space bears some resemblance to the IR definition of net (EFA) floorspace. In the event the floorspace data published in Table 9 of Vol. 2.2 of the *1966 Census Report* [QRL 16] were limited to total floorspace although other retail variables such as turnover are given elsewhere in the report in terms of selling floorspace and it should be added that selling floorspace is generally considered as being much more useful than total floorspace for forecasting shopping demand.

5.3.5. In the notes on the 1966 floorspace tables [QRL 16] attention is drawn to the difference between the sampling procedures for floorspace information and those used for the collection of other establishment data. In consequence the shopping centre floorspace totals are not directly comparable with other tables in the census reports. However, it is stated that where the other tables have ratios involving floorspace, e.g. turnover per square foot of selling floorspace, the differences in procedures do not have a significant effect on the ratios.

5.3.6. Shopping centres, which feature extensively in [QRL 16], were defined for the 1961 Census by the BOT as those 'characterised by the presence of department stores or other large shops which attract shoppers from a wide area'. The delimitation of these centres, in terms of streets and parts of streets, was chiefly the responsibility of BOT staff. The limits of any centre were drawn where the shops gave way to non-retail uses. Where the break between the uses was indefinite, and the shops were interspersed with other units, the limit of the centre was drawn where the ratio of shops to all other properties fell below one in three. The BOT said their definitions produced some errors but suggested the statistics for a centre would not be significantly affected by the precise location of its boundaries. This may be generally true but there are examples such as the London borough of Harrow where in 1961 a number of local shopping parades, located outside the main centre, were included in the BOT Harrow Central Area. Other criticisms have been made of the definition of shopping centres such as the use of the 1961 centres in London as the sampling frame for 1966. The 1971 census arrangements met these criticisms by allowing the London boroughs to define their own centres, but the response to this offer was varied (see Section 7.1.13). Elsewhere the BOT carried out preliminary surveys to redefine centres on the general lines of the earlier censuses.

5.3.7. *Changes in Stock of Shopping Floorspace*

Series II, No. 3. [QRL 60] gives changes in the stock on a financial year basis for England and Wales down to the local authority level for 1967 to 1969. The figures are subject to the limitations in definitions of the source (see Section 5.1.5) particularly with regard to the exclusion of 'Shops with premises'.

5.4. Stock of Warehousing Floorspace

5.4.1. Warehousing is often known alternatively as commerce and is generally regarded by planners as the storage associated with wholesaling activities. The proposed National Land Use Classification [B 49], for example, includes warehouses, furniture repositories, cold storage, builders' yards, food storage and petroleum, oil and coal storage, etc. In some areas of the country there has been in recent years a marked reduction in industrial floorspace matched by a corresponding increase in warehousing floorspace. Series II [QRL 60] recognises the importance of warehousing by including warehousing totals of 'Warehouses, stores and workshops' on a net (EFA) basis.

5.4.2. The recording of warehousing always presents difficulties as, for example, when manufactured goods are stored on the site of the factory which made them. Confusion can arise if distinctions are not carefully made between the storage of raw materials and manufactured goods. Storage in shops will nearly always be for retail purposes but occasionally may be part of a wholesaling operation. The series II [QRL 60] practice of assigning all the floorspace in a hereditament to the predominant use means that such warehousing will be sometimes recorded as industry or shops. The Series II definitions have a further drawback. The unpublished notes [B 50] explain that stores and workshops are both on a very small scale and that premises covered by the Factory and Workshops Act, 1920 are included as industry in [QRL 60]. Even so it is suggested that activities of an industrial and research nature have been sometimes included as workshops. Finally it should be emphasised that in Nos. 2 and 3 of the Series II tables the category is described as 'Warehousing, etc.'. No. 4 [QRL 60] introduces a new category, warehouses—open land storage examples of which are builders yards and open storage land for cars. Open storage land wholly contained within an industrial undertaking or attached to a covered warehouse would not be included in this category.

5.4.3. *Change in stock of warehousing floorspace*

Series II, No. 3 [QRL 60] gives changes in the stock of warehousing in England and Wales on an annual basis down to local authority level for the same definitions as the stock (see Section 5.4.1).

5.5. Rateable Values

5.5.1. There are no comprehensive figures available on the sale prices of industrial and commercial properties. In this part of the market the property is more frequently rented and rateable values are therefore of greater significance than they may be for housing. In addition to the assessment each hereditament carries a description of the building and its use or uses. If there is a change in the use of the building a revaluation is made and similarly when alterations are made to the structure of the building.

5.5.2. *Rateable values (RVs) of industrial hereditaments*

Total rateable values at 1st April down to local authority level are given in *Rates and Rateable Values in England and Wales* [QRL 49]. The definition of an industrial hereditament is given in [QRL 49] as '. . . factories, mills and other properties of a similar character, but excludes mineral producing hereditaments and coal, water, power and transport undertakings'. This does not correspond to the industrial hereditaments included under the IR stock [QRL 60] of industrial floorspace because of the difficulties of expressing hereditaments such as steel works in terms of floorspace (see Section 5.1.4).

5.5.3. Information on industrial hereditaments for Scotland appears in *Rates and Rateable Values in Scotland* [QRL 50]. The hereditaments, or subjects as they are known in Scotland, are analysed for various types of areas including regions, cities and boroughs under three categories differing radically from [QRL 60]. One of these is Industrial and Freight Transport. *Local Authority Rate Statistics, Northern Ireland* [QRL 42] has as one of its main categories Industry and Freight.

5.5.4. *Rateable values of office hereditaments*

[QRL 49] gives for England and Wales offices as including banks in office areas. This corresponds to part of the definition of IR office floorspace and implies that the rateable values for office hereditaments can be compared with the IR office floorspace in [QRL 60] with the knowledge that the separately analysed industrial hereditaments will have an appreciable office content. No separate RVs of offices are given for Scotland and Ireland.

5.5.5. *Rateable values of shopping hereditaments*

The definition of shops in [QRL 49] included those assessed in England and Wales with living accommodation. In examining IR shopping floorspace data we have noted the exclusion of shops with premises, the B 4 category. This means there is no direct relationship between the published RVs for shops [QRL 49] and the floorspace of [QRL 60]. No separate figures are available for RVs of shops either in Scotland or Northern Ireland.

CHAPTER 6

PRODUCTION

In assessing the allocation of future resources account must be taken in development plans of the structural and locational components of the productivity of industry and agriculture. Comparisons may be made as in [B 45] between the productivity of major industrial groups in different regions. These considerations must also have regard to the requirements and performance of public utilities.

6.1. General

6.1.1. The six major divisions of industry within the framework of the SIC [B 52] are agriculture, mining and quarrying, manufacturing, construction, distribution, services and public administration, etc., but the source with the widest scope is the Census of Production. This has taken place at regular intervals since 1907 and in more recent years quinquennially in 1958, 1963 and 1968. The series until 1968 is listed in this review as *Census of Production* [QRL 20] and the new annual series introduced from 1970 onwards appears under *Business Monitor* [QRL 14].

6.1.2. *Census of Production Reports* [B 46] in the series *Guides to Official Sources* traces the development of the Census between 1907 and 1961. Browning [B 3] describes the procedures involved in preparing the 1963 and 1968 censuses, the collection of the data and their processing. The 1968 survey, the last of the quinquennial series, took the form of a 100 per cent census of all the SIC orders II–XVIII (1958 SIC). The employers were obliged to provide the required information. Data were collected for each establishment, the latter being defined as 'the smallest unit which can provide the information normally required'. The requests for information were not standard and the forms sent to the employers varied with the particular industry. The amount of detail collected from firms depended on their size and firms employing less than twenty-five persons had only to give a few important items of information.

6.1.3. The statistics available for the UK include the number of firms, employment, gross and net output. Definitions of gross and net output are given in *Trade and Industry* [QRL 62] of 23rd December 1971. For the 1968 Census of Production [QRL 20] results have gradually been published in separate reports for different industries and sections of industries. Lists of these are given in various issues of *Statistical News* [B 54].

6.1.4. The quinquennial Censuses of Production [QRL 20] have included results for Northern Ireland where quinquennial censuses have been carried out by the Ministry of Commerce on a basis comparable with that of the rest of the UK. For those years until 1968 in which detailed censuses had not been taken in Great Britain, the Ministry of Commerce has taken a less detailed census in Northern Ireland. Information has been collected on employment, wages and salaries, capital expenditure and output. Purchases and sales have not been so fully analysed by commodities as for the quinquennial censuses. Separate volumes of the 1968 *Report on the Census of Production* [QRL 20] have been published and will be followed by annual reports for 1969 and 1970.

6.1.5. The results of [QRL 20] are analysed down to the level of the standard regions and the GLC area. The absence of any further areal disaggregation limits the use of the statistics by local planning authorities. The problem of the time-lag before the publication of the results is as significant as for other government sources such as the population and distribution censuses.

6.1.6. In publishing the provisional results of the 1968 Census of Production, *Trade and Industry* [QRL 62] drew attention to factors affecting comparison between 1963 and 1968, including the revision of the 1968 Multi-unit businesses, i.e. businesses with premises in more than one location, tend increasingly to have difficulty in furnishing separate returns for individual units. The output of these units cannot always be assigned unambiguously to a single SIC and these combined returns occurred more frequently in 1970 than in earlier years. Browning and Fessey discuss the multi-unit problem in [B 4]. *Trade and Industry* [QRL 62] give comparisons for the UK for 1963, 1968 and 1970 of net employment and output.

6.1.7. Since the setting up of the Business Statistics Office (BSO) in 1969 a new centralised and integrated system of industrial statistics has replaced the large-scale quinquennial Census of Production and the short-term inquiries by various government departments. The general progress of the new approach is described by Fessey in *Statistical News*, No. 20 [B 13]. From 1970 onwards annual censuses are being held and summary statistics of total purchases and sales, stocks, capital expenditure, employment and wages are being collected. The details of manufacturers' sales are being obtained by quarterly inquiries and various supplementary inquiries, such as the purchases of goods and services, will be made at longer intervals. Results for individual industries for 1970 and 1971 have appeared in *Business Monitors* [QRL 14]. Provisional results for all industries for the 1971 Census were published in *Business Monitor C200* [QRL 14] and for the 1972 Census in *Business Monitor PA 1000* [QRL 14]. Summary results also appear in *Trade and Industry* [QRL 62]. The BSO held a post-census enquiry on the 1970 Census to determine the quality of the answers. This is described by Curtis [B 10].

6.1.8. The new annual Census of Production [QRL 14] and [QRL 62] provides a measure of net output and aggregated figures of sales, employment, etc. It covers establishments in Great Britain for orders II–XIX of the 1968 SIC. The Ministry of Commerce, Northern Ireland, provides data for all industries with the exception of mining and quarrying. These are incorporated in the tables to give UK totals. Census returns for [QRL 14] are required for all establishments with twenty-five or more employees. For small firms with an important contribution to output these returns applied to establishments with eleven or more employees.

6.1.9. *Index of Industrial Production.* The BSO prepares an index of Industrial Production which is published monthly in *Trade and Industry* [QRL 62]. The purpose and methods of compilation of the index appear in the *Measurement of Changes in Production* [B 47]. The index measures in a general way the monthly changes in the volume of industrial production of the UK. There are no regional disaggregations of the index but separate indices are produced for Scotland, Wales and Northern Ireland.

6.2. Agriculture

6.2.1. The companion review [B 8] by Coppock on Land Use considers in detail the annual censuses on the use of agricultural land in the UK. These began in 1866 and summaries of results appear in *A Century of Agricultural Statistics: Great Britain 1866–1966* [QRL 21]. The collection of data in the continuing annual census (which relates to the month of June) is the responsibility of the Ministry of Agriculture, Fisheries and Food (MAFF) in England and Wales, the Department of Agriculture and Fisheries for Scotland (DAFS) and the Department of Agriculture for Northern Ireland (DANI), the latter replacing the former Ministry of Agriculture for Northern Ireland (MANI) from 1st January 1974. There is a similar basis for the collection of data by the three government departments and all occupiers with holdings over 1 acre are enumerated. *Agricultural Statistics, England and Wales* [QRL 2] contains analyses, including some comparisons for a 10-year period, down to a county level of livestock, production of crops and agricultural holdings. Similar information appears in *Agricultural Statistics, Scotland* [QRL 3] and in the *Statistical Review of Farming* [QRL 57]. Nationally aggregated statistics are brought together in *Agricultural Statistics United Kingdom* [QRL 4]. Unpublished summaries from [QRL 4] are available for parishes and National Agriculture Advisory Service (NAAS) (now the Agriculture Development and Advisory Service) districts. There is in law an express waiver of confidentiality in favour of planning authorities.

6.2.2. An index of net agricultural output at constant prices is given in the *Annual Review of Agriculture* [QRL 10].

6.2.3. Another annual survey, known as the Farm Management Survey, is carried out in England and Wales, by university departments of agricultural economics. A small voluntary sample of 2500 farms is taken but the sample is not a random one and there is a bias towards large farms. The MAFF *Farm Incomes in England and Wales* [QRL 32] is based on the Farm Management Survey. Greater local detail may be obtained from the University departments (listed in [QRL 32]) carrying out the Farm Management Survey.

6.3. Mining and Quarrying

6.3.1. The main source of statistics of mining and quarrying is the *Census of Production* [QRL 20] and [QRL 14]. Under the Mines and Quarries Act, 1954 an annual census is taken of all workings. Details of national output collected by the Department of Energy are published in *Digest of United Kingdom Energy Statistics* [QRL 65].

6.3.2. Sand and gravel workings and the considerable land-use changes they entail are of special importance to planners. From returns made by local authorities the DOE publishes annually *Sand and Gravel Production* [QRL 54] for England, Wales and Scotland. This gives analyses by counties and by gravel regions.

6.4. Construction

6.4.1. A detailed review in this series entitled the *Statistics of Construction* is being written by M. C. Fleming. Another source of information on construction statistics is the earlier study (1967) commissioned by the MPBW which included an extensive *Directory of Construction Statistics* [B 40]. The main sources of production statistics for the construction industry are regular census and sample enquiries conducted by the DOE (details are given in the companion review by Fleming referred to above) supplemented by a quinquennial Census of *Production* [QRL 20] to 1968 and, since 1974 in the case of construction, annual censuses conducted by the BSO.

6.5. Public Utilities

6.5.1. *Gas*

Statistics of the gas industry are published in the *Annual Report and Accounts* [QRL 6] of the British Gas Corporation (formerly the Gas Council). This gives statistics for the Area Gas Boards in Great Britain. Gas Board statistics are also given in *United Kingdom Energy Statistics* [QRL 65] which includes details about gas undertakings in Northern Ireland. A detailed review in this series of the statistics of the Gas Industry is being prepared by H. Nabb.

6.5.2. *Electricity*

Annual sources of information are the Electricity Supply Council *Handbook of Electricity Supply Statistics* [QRL 35] and the Central Electricity Generating Board *Statistical Yearbook* [QRL 58]. Statistics for the UK are also given annually in *United Kingdom Energy Statistics* [QRL 65]. A detailed review in this series on the statistics of the Electricity Industry is being written by D. Nuttall.

6.5.3. *Water*

Water Statistics [QRL 66], compiled by the Society of County Treasurers, contains statistics of water supply in England, Wales and Scotland. It is not yet clear what form statistical returns will take with the creation of the new water authorities in 1974.

CHAPTER 7

DISTRIBUTION

7.1. Retail Trade

7.1.1. Data used in setting up shopping models and preparing plans for shopping include housing and population projections, consumer expenditure, floorspace surveys and a wide variety of information about the retail trade. A detailed earlier guide to official sources is *Distributive Trade Statistics* [B 41] published in 1970.

7.1.2. A general investigation into shopping developments with discussions of the use of statistics appear in *Future Pattern of Shopping* [B 43], the report of an inquiry sponsored by the National Economic Development Office (NEDO). Related problems are also studied in the companion volume *Urban Models in Shopping Studies* [B 57].

7.1.3. The *Census of Distribution* [QRL 16], carried out by the DI and formerly by the DTI and BOT, is the main source of information about the retail trade and some services. In discussing floorspace (see Section 5.3.3) reference has already been made to the Great Britain full censuses of 1950, 1961 and 1971 and the sample censuses of 1957 and 1966. The general method of obtaining data and the definition of shopping centres were briefly described. The first Census of Retail Distribution [QRL 17] in Northern Ireland took place in 1965. It was similar to the Great Britain censuses both in the topics covered and their presentation. The pre-census list of establishments was prepared by the Royal Ulster Constabulary (RUC) in mid-1965. The establishment comprised retail establishments, and the motor, hairdressing, laundering and shoe-repairing trades. As the RUC list did not give an exact description of the establishments, a single type of form was used. A higher level of response was achieved in Northern Ireland than in GB. Preliminary results of the 1971 Census in GB appeared in *Trade and Industry* [QRL 62]. A similar census planned for Northern Ireland in 1971 was cancelled.

7.1.4. The *Census of Distribution* [QRL 16] collects basic information about the retail trade including the address of the establishment, a description of the nature of the business and the products sold. The data are obtained for each establishment, that is, separate place of business or shop. In addition organisations or large retailers employing over twenty-five persons, co-operatives, multiples and independents were asked to give details of trading purchases, stock, book debts, capital expenditure and analyses of sales by commodity groups. The information obtained is confidential and the published reports are presented in such a form that it is not generally possible to identify individual establishments and their addresses so that where necessary figures are withheld or combined with others.

7.1.5. The period normally covered by the Census of Distribution is the calendar year but if this is not the business year of the organisation a return for the financial year is accepted. Thus an alternative to the calendar year for the 1966 Census was the financial year 6th April 1966 to 5th April 1967. Either approach implies, of course, that the actual data do not start to become available for processing until a year later than data obtained from population censuses for the same year.

7.1.6. At present the only results covering the whole country are for the 1950 and 1961 Censuses of Distribution and sampling procedures for 1966 were such that some towns were not included at all in the sample.

7.1.7. There have been differences of definition for multiples and independents for the various Censuses of Distribution. In 1950, 1957 and 1966 multiples were defined as having ten or more establishments whereas in 1961 a multiple comprised five or more establishments. Similar definitional variations apply to independents. However, where 1966 tables show comparisons with 1961, the 1961 figures have been reprocessed to make them consistent with the definitions for the earlier and later census years.

7.1.8. Central London was enumerated in full in 1966 and a sample of listed shops covered. Thirty-three of seventy-six other London shopping centres were enumerated in full and all shops covered. Elsewhere in London shops were selected systematically within a stratified sample of wards. Sixty large towns were covered by a sample of streets. Thirty-two special areas where there had been substantial development since 1961 were enumerated in full, and a sample of listed shops covered. The remainder of Great Britain comprised 1687 local authority areas and was represented by a stratified sample of whole areas averaging 10 per cent overall. There are always problems with such sampling frames which must be prepared several months ahead of the Census. In the ensuing period new shops will be opened and existing shops closed. The 1966 Census was intended to give reliable estimates for Great Britain with more limited results for the standard regions. The nature of the sample scheme means that in 1966 data were not provided for all towns and one frequently voiced criticism of [QRL 16] is that for many towns information currently available is over 10 years out of date. In 1966 the information for some towns and districts included in the sample does not appear in [QRL 16] but unpublished data are available on request from the DI.

7.1.9. *Retail turnover by establishment*

Turnover for different kinds of shops, or better still turnover per square foot, is one of the most important elements for planners forecasting shopping demand. Volume I of the 1966 *Census of Distribution* [QRL 16] gives various tables of turnover both for Great Britain and in some instances for the standard regions. Comparisons are made both for different forms of organisation and kinds of business. Appendix D of Volume 1 of the 1966 report gives notes on the revision of previous census figures for comparisons. The forms of organisation are co-operative societies, multiples (ten or more establishments) and independents (ten or fewer establishments). There are seven broad categories of retail business corresponding closely to the subdivisions used in the 1958 SIC which applied to both the 1961 and 1966 Censuses of Distribution. The categories are as follows:

1. Groceries and provisions dealers.
2. Other food retailers.
3. Confectioners, tobacconists, newsagents.
4. Clothing and footwear shops.
5. Household goods shops.
6. Other non-food retailers.
7. General stores.

Further subdivisions of these categories are used whereby data are given for twenty-three categories of intermediate businesses. At this level the analyses for 1957 and 1961 differed slightly from those of 1966. In 1966, for example, new categories were included for the installation and maintenance of consumer durables. The intermediate 'other food shops' (ice cream, health foods, etc.) was transferred from the broad category other food retailers' and included in 'groceries and provisional dealers'. Soft furnishing shops were also given a different category and radio and television hire shops, formerly a detailed kind of business in the intermediate category 'radio and electrical shops', were shown separately. Mobile shops in 1966 were restricted to those run by co-operative societies, large multiples or from other fixed shop premises. This meant that many market traders and some mobile shops included in 1961 were excluded in 1966. There were other mobile shops from 1961 which were included in the fixed shops from which they operated in 1966. Approximate estimates are given in [QRL 16] of the 1961 figures of these market traders but at a national level only so that comparison could be made between the two censuses.

7.1.10. *Retail turnover by organisation*

Volume 1 of the 1966 *Census of Distribution* [QRL 16] gives estimates for Great Britain of the shares of turnover for various commodities for the three forms of organisation, viz. co-operative societies, multiples and independents. Such tables are useful indicators of the changing structure of retailing. The introduction to [QRL 16] discusses the principles of classification of kinds of business into 'specialist' and 'composite'. The 'composite' headings provide for trades in which two or more commodity groups is frequent. The multiplicity of uses in shops is an increasingly important factor in the retail trades with supermarkets such as Tesco selling furniture and clothes. Conversely Marks and Spencers, classified as clothing shops, have an increasing proportion of food sales in their turnover. The character of the retail trade can change appreciably over a short period but their quantification of such changes through the quinquennial Census of Distribution tends to be several years after the event.

7.1.11. *Commodity analysis of turnover*

An analysis of the commodities sold by large retailers (defined as those with a turnover exceeding £1 million in 1966) appears in *Trade and Industry* [QRL 62] of 14th December

1972. The information was obtained from the Annual Enquiries into the Distributive and Service Trades for 1967 to 1970 conducted by the BSO and from the Census of Distribution. The large retailers covered by the figures accounted for over 40 per cent of the retail trade in 1966. The figures show changes in the value of sales of various commodities between 1966 and 1970 at a national level.

7.1.12. One of the chief drawbacks to the Census of Distribution is its relative infrequency. The statistics available at any time are nearly always several years out of date. *Distributive Trade Statistics* [B 41], for example, published in 1970 stated 'At the time of going to press neither of the volumes of the 1966 Census of Distribution has been published'. Moreover, even though Censuses have been taken roughly on a quinquennial basis full Censuses are only held decennially. This means that available statistics from this source for some towns and shopping centres are now over 10 years out of date. The non-availability of data for small areas because of confidentiality or the method of sampling is another problem. One of the difficulties for the BSO in processing the data is the initial non-response of some organisations and this delays the analysis as well as affecting the reliability of the results. In 1966, for example, the non-response was greatest among the small traders in the sample, of whom 20 per cent had not made a full return by the end of 1967; while most of the required returns were obtained during 1968 some estimation was needed for small credit traders and businesses in the laundry group.

7.1.13. The 1971 Census will present problems of comparison so far as shopping centres are concerned. We have seen in discussing shopping floorspace (see Section 5.3.6) that criticism was made of the definition of shopping centres in 1961 and 1966. The BSO has responded to this criticism by allowing London boroughs to define shopping centres for specific inclusion as such. The response to this offer has been varied with some boroughs defining as many as five centres and one none at all. The published results will thus be patchy and any second thoughts on the definition of centres will require the production of unpublished tabulations. An introductory article by Fessey to the 1971 Census 'How the 1971 Retail Census can help industry and retailer' appears in an article in *Trade and Industry* [B 12] of 25th November 1970.

7.2. Index of Retail Prices

7.2.1. In the development of shopping models and forecasts a means is needed by planners of comparing retail expenditure at different points of time at constant prices. This is provided by an index of retail prices. The General Index of Retail Prices in the United Kingdom is published monthly in the *Department of Employment Gazette* [QRL 25]. Its purpose is to measure the monthly change in the average level of prices of commodities and services purchased by the majority of households. It reflects prices as they affect a relatively homogeneous middle income group of the population. In the period 1957–60, 88 per cent of all Family Expenditure Survey (FES) (see Section 9.1.1) respondents were classified as index households. The index is based on the price movements of a large and representative 'basket' of goods and services. The percentage changes in the price levels of the various items are combined by the use of weights. A chain index was introduced in January 1962 with a reference base of 100 for the index and the weights brought up to date annually using the results of the *Family Expenditure Survey* [QRL 30]. The reference base was changed in January 1974 to 100 although [QRL 25] continued to give index figures for both 1961 and 1974 bases for a year before discontinuing the use of the earlier base. The monthly prices are collected from 200 local office areas by DE officers or by correspondence with suppliers. A full description of the index is given in *Method and Construction and Calculation of the Index of Retail Prices* [B 48].

7.3. Service Trades

7.3.1. The *Census of Distribution* [QRL 16] gives tables for three types of service:

1. Hairdressing and manicure (1958 SIC 888).
2. Boot and shoe repairing (1958 SIC 889).
3. Laundries, launderettes and dry cleaners (1958 SICs 885 and 886).

Simple estimates for Great Britain are given in the 1966 report [QRL 16] of the turnover of establishments for the three types of service with some further breakdown. Simple estimates for Great Britain of the share of different types of organisation in the turnover are also given. More detailed information was available for Northern Ireland in 1965 [QRL 17] for the following groups of services:

1. Motor and motor fuel businesses.
2. Catering.
3. Laundries and dry cleaners, hairdressing and repairers of clothing and footwear.

7.3.2. *Catering Trade*

The catering trade is not covered by the Census of Distribution. The DI publish short period statistics in *Trade and Industry* [QRL 62] of turnover, capital expenditure and stocks. A large-scale inquiry into the catering trades in Great Britain in respect of the year 1969 has been made by the BSO. In addition to providing new benchmarks for [QRL 62], information was collected for the first time on bedroom accommodation in licensed hotels and motels, licensed guesthouses and holiday camps. The results appear in *Catering Trades 1969* [QRL 15].

CHAPTER 8

EMPLOYMENT AND UNEMPLOYMENT

A structure plan must assess the impact of local employment opportunities on the development of the structure plan in its entirety. The necessary information ranges from totals for large areas, e.g. employment by industry for local authority areas, together with more detailed analyses which identify the main centres of employment within an area. From this information it is possible to establish areas of growth and decline and to identify potential centres of employment growth relating all of these to the main centres of residence and employment including shopping. Statistics of employment are described in detail in the Warwick University Industrial Relations Research Unit publication *British Employment Statistics* [B 28a].

8.1. Employment and Working Population

8.1.1. The Department of Employment (DE) (formerly the Ministry of Labour (MOL)) publishes data on an annual, quarterly and monthly basis on the numbers in employment in the UK. These statistics are published in the monthly *Department of Employment Gazette* [QRL 25] (formerly *Ministry of Labour Gazette*) but results for 1969 onwards have been brought together in the annual *British Labour Statistics Year Book* [QRL 13]. For earlier years reference can be made to *British Labour Statistics: Historical Abstract 1886–1968* [QRL 12].

8.1.2. Following the introduction of the comprehensive National Insurance Act in 1948 the DE used the National Insurance (NI) cards to make their annual and quarterly estimates. However, in 1971 this method was replaced by one based on an annual census of employment. The monthly estimates have always been made from returns from a sample of production industries. In June 1974 a new quarterly inquiry was instituted to collect information from those industries not covered by monthly returns.

8.1.3. *The NI card count*

The companion review No. 4 in this series on Social Security Statistics by Frank Whitehead [B 35] gives full details of the way in which statistics have been gathered from NI cards.

8.1.4. The most important of the DE NI card estimates of employees in employment were the annual June employment estimates, also known as the Employment Return II (ERII) which appeared in [QRL 25]. Local employment exchanges coded the cards of firms with five or more employees by sex, age and Minimum List Heading (MLH) of the SIC. Analyses made by local exchanges on this basis were then aggregated centrally by the DE into regional totals and these were published in [QRL 25].

8.1.5. The quarterly exchange of NI cards was used by the DE to obtain quarterly estimates of employees and working population. This series was started in 1965 but by using existing data an historical series was produced going back to 1950.

8.1.6. *Monthly estimates of employment*

These have always been derived from monthly returns by employers. For the months between the annual estimates the returns from a sample of establishments in the production industries are used as a basis for interpolating monthly estimates of the numbers of employees in employment. A new sample was introduced in June 1974 which reduced the number of returns from 20,000 to 14,000 establishments. All establishments which employ 250 or more employees are included together with samples of those having between 11 and 249 employees. Information is also obtained from the boards of the nationalised industries and, for the construction industry, from the Department of the Environment. More detail on the sample is given in [QRL 13]; see Appendix I of the 1974 Yearbook (the current issue at the time of writing).

8.1.7. *The census of employment*

Pilot trials for the new census were carried out in 1969 and 1970 and the first full census was carried out in 1971. In that year estimates were also made by the old method of a NI card count; see [QRL 25] August 1973.

8.1.8. The 1969 Finance Act contained a clause enabling the IR to pass on names and addresses of all PAYE schemes to the DE for use in issuing employment census forms. The census is conducted by means of an inquiry to each PAYE pay point. Under powers incorporated in Section I of the Statistics of Trade Act, 1974 the pay point has to provide for each local business address for which it holds pay records (census units) the name, full postal address, business description and employment details.

8.1.9. Three types of inquiry forms are used by the DE for collecting data which are subject to the Statistics of Trade Act, viz.

   (i) Pay points with pay records for a single establishment.
  (ii) Pay points with pay records for two or more establishments.
 (iii) Organisations and individuals not required by the Statistics of Trade Act to supply information but who are asked to provide information voluntarily.

A register of addresses in terms of census units is derived by passing information regarding establishments outside their area to the appropriate local office.

8.1.10. The pay records for groups of employees at a single address may be held at different paypoints, e.g. some staff may be paid locally while others, perhaps monthly paid, are paid from district offices. It can also happen that some staff, e.g. managerial, are paid from a head office. In such situations each group of staff forms a separate census unit which comprises all staff at one address whose pay records are held at the same pay point. Similarly where a firm finds it convenient to record separately the staff in each department or activity at a single address, each may be treated as a census unit. Unlike ERII [QRL 25] records the Census of Employment distinguishes between full-time and part-time employees. The data held for each census unit include numbers of full-time and part-time employees both subdivided by sex with the MLH heading of the SIC to which the unit has been classified. If one employee works for different employers he will be counted twice as the Census of Employment tends to count jobs rather than people.

8.1.11. The analyses derived from the census relate to employees in employment and in order to obtain estimates of the total number of employees, figures for the number of unemployed must be added. Employers and the self-employed are not included in the census. Estimates for these groups are therefore based on the Census of Population [QRL 18] and [QRL 19]. The total working population then comprises the total number of employees, employers and the self-employed together with all members of HM Forces.

8.1.12. Local authorities have been asked if they would like to receive detailed data from the Census of Employment on magnetic tape or whether they would prefer the provision of a central processing service. It became clear that outside London a central service was preferred. The DOE and DE are now carrying out a pilot survey to find out the types of analyses required.

8.1.13. From June 1974 a new quarterly inquiry was instituted. The results collected from those industries not covered by the monthly returns are combined with the quarter month figures for production industries. These figures are then used to give provisional quarterly estimates of employees in employment for all industries and services.

8.2. Economically Active Population

8.2.1. The Population Census [QRL 18] and [QRL 19] is a source of employment statistics giving not only more detailed information about the employment of individuals than DE sources but in such a form as to permit aggregations of the data more conveniently to areas of planning significance. The relative infrequency of the Censuses means, however, that such data are only available at best once every 5 years. In 1961 the Census was a full-scale one but questions on employment were limited to 10 per cent of the households, whereas in 1966 employment questions were asked of all the households included in the 10 per cent sample. In the 1971 full census some questions on economic activity were asked of all households whilst others were only asked of a 10 per cent sample. While the population is enumerated by place of residence questions are asked about names and businesses of employers and occupation in order to establish employment characteristics for workplace areas such as employment status, SIC and occupational classification.

8.2.2. *Economically active*

In the 1961, 1966 and 1971 Censuses the economically active consisted of:

(a) Persons in employment at any time during the week before the census. This included all who had a job including own account work, part-time work, etc. Persons temporarily away from work, e.g. holidays, sickness, industrial disputes, etc., were counted in employment if their job was waiting their return.

(b) Persons *out of employment*, registered or not registered, throughout the week before the Census who were seeking work or would have been but for sickness and injury, or who had found a job and were expecting to start work after Census day.

All persons 15 years of age or over not in employment or out of employment were classified as economically inactive.

8.2.3. The chief differences in 1961 between the working population in [QRL 25] and the Economically Active Population in [QRL 18] are analysed and discussed in the November 1965 *Department of Employment Gazette* [QRL 25]. A later discussion of these differences appears in Appendix A of [QRL 12]. Further details for 1966 appear in the foreword to [QRL 25] derived from post-enumeration surveys of the number of persons (e.g. some students, unregistered, unemployed, seasonal workers and irregular workers) likely to be included in the DE Annual Estimates [QRL 25] and excluded from the Census. It also gives estimates of persons (e.g. some employees working in the week before the Census) who were likely to be excluded from [QRL 18]. The differences between the estimates for males is explained fully; for females the position is less clear.

8.2.4. *Economically active by area of residence*

Employment figures in the *Department of Employment Gazette* [QRL 25] are built up from Census of Employment returns and are essentially in terms of workplace. In [QRL 18] enumeration of the economically active in GB is by place of residence. This means that data about the economically active can be tabulated with other information about households without additional coding to small areas such as individual or limited groupings of EDs. Additional questions are asked about the employer's address so that it is possible to code employment information by workplace. Thus employment information given in [QRL 18] and [QRL 19] has the dual aspect of residence and workplace unlike [QRL 25]. Questions are asked about the nature of the employer's business, the person's job and his employment status. These are used to code individuals by SIC (1958 SIC for the 1961 and 1966 Censuses; 1968 SIC for the 1971 Census). They are also classified by occupation (see *Classification of Occupations* [B 37]), status (e.g. self-employed, apprentice, etc.) and socio-economic group. In 1972 the DE issued a new occupational classification which differs in certain respects from its predecessor and it is not yet clear how this can be reconciled with the results of the 1971 Census. A background article explaining its principles, contents and uses appeared in the January 1972 issue of [QRL 25].

8.2.5. [QRL 18] give analyses for place of residence in GB of the economically active in terms of occupation, subdivided for males and females. The employment areas of residence included in 1971 were counties, county boroughs, local authority areas and conurbation centres.

8.2.6. *Economically active in employment by workplace*

The 1971 Census [QRL 18] analysed economically active persons in Great Britain subdivided by males and females in employment by areas of workplace for both industry and occupation. In addition to the published tables there are extensive unpublished tables for 1961 and 1966 [QRL 18] held by various planning authorities. OPCS have made at cost substantial additional coding to other workplace areas such as traffic zones on behalf of individual planning authorities or groups of planning authorities. Tabulations for these areas have been made not only directly by OPCS but also by planning authorities, subject to certain restrictions required by confidentiality.

8.2.7. The employment information from successive censuses represents the most detailed and comprehensive source of employment data. The principal drawback to its use is that all the employment tabulations do not become available until a considerable time after the actual Census so that the latest detailed information held by the planning authorities may be anything up to 7 years out of date on the assumption that censuses are quinquennial. In using the 1961 Census there is the question of bias and in 1966 the problem of underenumeration.

8.3. Unemployment

8.3.1. *Registered unemployment*

The local Employment Service Agency Offices and Youth Employment offices are the source of monthly employment statistics on the registered unemployed compiled by DE and appearing in the *Department of Employment Gazette* [QRL 25]. The monthly unemployment Press Notice is normally issued 10 days after the date on which the count takes place and gives provisional regional and national totals. These are superseded by the final and more detailed and accurate figures in [QRL 25].

8.3.2. The DE defines unemployment as 'The number of unemployed persons on the registers of Employment Service Agency Offices or Youth Employment offices who were out of a situation (or not at work) on the Monday in question'. Registered severely disabled persons who are unlikely to obtain work other than under special conditions are excluded. The count is made on a Monday in the middle of the month and analyses by industry are based on the SIC. The industry to which an unemployed person is assigned is that in which he was last employed for more than 3 days.

8.3.3. The unemployed are analysed by sex and age (over and under 18). The figures distinguish between those out of work (wholly unemployed) from those working short time or otherwise suspended from work who would shortly return to their former employment (temporarily stopped). Analyses are also given in *Department of Employment Gazette* [QRL 25] of duration of employment. Wholly unemployed and temporarily stopped are also analysed by industry, occupation and by region and by principal towns and development areas. Seasonal adjustments are made to allow for holidays, school terms, weather, etc. Descriptions of the methods used to estimate normal seasonal variations can be found in the September 1965, April 1970, February 1971 and August 1972 issues of the *Department of Employment Gazette* [QRL 25]. See also the study *Duration of Unemployment on the Register of Wholly Unemployed* by Fowler [B 15] and the article on unemployment in the UK by Thatcher [B 31].

8.3.4. The DE statistics [QRL 25] only relate to 'registered unemployed' and there are many people who are unemployed and do not register. Examples are married women who claim exemption, because of their husbands contributions, school leavers and recent immigrants. *Unemployment Statistics*, Cmnd. 5157 [B 55], discusses this problem. In some areas there may be overestimation caused by registration of some individuals at more than one exchange. [B 55] comments that in various reviews of the statistics some authors have concluded that the figures were high and others that they were low.

8.3.5. The breakdown to principal towns is of value to planners but the problem of non-coincidence of exchange areas with local authority and planning areas applies to unemployment statistics as it does to employment figures drawn from NI cards.

8.3.6. *Unregistered unemployed*

The DE unemployment estimates [QRL 25] are restricted to the registered unemployed and the only current source of Great Britain on the unregistered unemployed is the population census [QRL 18]. In 1966 questions were asked on 'Out of employment', that is, anyone who was not in employment at all in the week preceding the census. Persons who were not employed were asked which of the following categories they were in:

    (a) Registered at an employment exchange.
    (b) Seeking work but not registered.
    (c) Not seeking work because of temporary sickness or injury.
    (d) Waiting to take up a job after day of census.
    (e) Other reasons for not seeking work, e.g. housewife, permanent sickness, disablement, etc.

Unemployment Statistics [B 55] discusses the differences between the Census [QRL 18] and DE figures [QRL 25] giving two main reasons. Firstly, the census includes many who were sick, whereas the unemployment register is confined to those available for work. Secondly, those describing themselves as seeking work may range from those urgently needing work, to others not concerned in taking steps to obtain employment. The November 1966 *Department of Employment Gazette* [QRL 25] analyses differences between DE figures and the 1961 Census giving a table showing comparisons in Great Britain for age groups of both sexes.

8.4. Vacancies

8.4.1. *Outstanding vacancies*

Each month the *Department of Employment Gazette* [QRL 25] publishes statistics of vacancies in Great Britain notified by employers to Employment Service Agency Offices and Youth Employment offices which remain unfilled at the end of the month. Regional totals are analysed by industrial orders and for adults only on an occupational basis for each quarter. Separate totals are given for males and females and these are sub-divided into adults and young persons under 18 years of age. The statistics for vacancies remaining unfilled are also published with seasonal adjustments. The methods used are similar to those applied in the seasonally adjusted unemployed figures and are described in articles in the April 1970 and January 1972 issues of the *Department of Employment Gazette* [QRL 25].

8.4.2. [QRL 25] excludes all vacancies not notified to the DE offices so that the statistics are not claimed to measure the total demand of employers' immediate manpower requirements.

8.4.3. *Filled vacancies*

The *Department of Employment Gazette* [QRL 25] also gives statistics of placings made in GB by the DE for vacancies notified to them by employers. These are of limited value to planners as many employers will rely on other methods than the exchanges for recruiting staff. They may choose to recruit staff through advertisements in the press or to make use of private employment agencies which have been growing rapidly in recent years. Direct applications for work are also often received from persons seeking employment.

CHAPTER 9

INCOME AND EXPENDITURE

9.1. Income

Statistics of income are useful to planners in studying such topics as provision of shopping facilities, car parking and housing. A general discussion of the use of income statistics may be found in *Social Research Techniques for Planners* by T. L. Burton and G. E. Cherry [B 5]. A review on the sources of income statistics by Dr. T. Stark [B 30a] appears in this series in which all the sources mentioned below are described in considerable detail. There are a number of well-established annual continuous government surveys as well as occasional sources which provide income statistics. Some important points need to be borne in mind in using these sources. The income unit may be for an individual or for a household. The period of time to which the data refer can be a week, a month or a year. Not all sources of income for a unit, e.g. non-earned income, may be included. Finally the base of the data may be residential or workplace. A very useful review of the major sources with a bibliography is the *GLC Research Memorandum* No. 350, 'Survey of personal income in London' [B 25] by Redpath, Powell and Mrs. Kingaby. Much of the memorandum is a general discussion applicable to the whole country.

9.1.1. *Household income*

The Family Expenditure Survey (FES) has been in continuous operation since 1957 and the results, which include income as well as expenditure, appear annually in *Family Expenditure Survey* [QRL 30]. The Northern Ireland results are provided by a separate survey [QRL 31] carried out by the Department of Finance. A detailed description of operational procedures and survey organisation of the FES is given in *Family Expenditure Survey Handbook on the Sample, Fieldwork and Coding Procedures* [B 23]. Until recently the FES [QRL 30] was the only source of household income and as such is particularly useful for planners as it is thought that aggregated household incomes are most closely related to car ownership, trip generation, shopping expenditure, etc.

9.1.2. A further source of gross household income is the *General Household Survey* [QRL 33] conducted annually by the OPCS on behalf of the Central Statistical Office (CSO) which acts as co-ordinator of the interest of different departments. The first survey published in 1973 contains data for 1971 and the second survey published in 1975 contains 1972 data.

9.1.3. A further possible source of income statistics will be the results of the 1971

Census Income Follow-up Survey which was started by OPCS in 1972. Questions on income were asked of a 1 per cent sample of households selected at random from the 1971 Census of Population.

9.2. Earnings from Employment

9.2.1. The FES produces data on pay but, like those on income, they are subject to the limitations of sample size.

9.2.2. The main source of earnings data is the New Earnings Survey (NES) carried out by the DE for the first time in 1968 and annually in April since 1970. It provides data on the gross weekly and hourly earnings of employees in Great Britain in a given week. Originally this survey was based on a 1 per cent sample of NI card holders but from 1975 the survey is based on tax deduction cards. Summary results are published in sections in the *Department of Employment Gazette* [QRL 25] and more detailed analyses then appear in the annual report *New Earnings Survey* [QRL 46] (from 1974 published in six parts). Details for Northern Ireland are published in *Digest of Statistics, Northern Ireland* [QRL 27].

9.2.3. Since 1940 the DE has also carried out the Workers' Earnings (WE) Surveys. From 1970 these have been held in October only. The statistics are obtained from voluntary returns from a sample of 40,000 establishments in the UK employing 5 million workers—or nearly two-thirds of all manual workers in the industries covered. The results for average weekly earnings and hours are published in the *Department of Employment Gazette* [QRL 25] and *British Labour Statistics Year Book* [QRL 13].

9.2.4. The main disadvantage of the NES and the WE series is that the earnings figures apply to one period in the year and do not show annual earnings.

9.2.5. The Regional Statistics on Earnings (RSE) began in 1964–5 and are drawn from PAYE records by the Department of Health and Social Security (DHSS). Results are published in the *Abstract of Regional Statistics* [QRL 1] of gross annual earnings analysed by sex, age group and region.

9.3. Personal Income

9.3.1. The Inland Revenue carried out income surveys based on an annual systematic stratified sample of incomes reviewed for tax purposes. Up to 1970 results were published in the *Reports of the Commissioners of HM Inland Revenue* [QRL 52] but since and including 1970 the results have appeared in *Inland Revenue Statistics* [QRL 41]. Detailed results of the 1969–70 and 1970–1 surveys also appeared in *Survey of Personal Incomes* [QRL 61] (SPI). The SPI gives better information about the self-employed and the upper end of the income-distribution than FES.

9.4. Household Expenditure

9.4.1. *General household expenditure*

THE FES [QRL 30] is the chief source of personal, consumer expenditure with the household as the unit of data collection. Final results are published in the FES annual reports [QRL 30] and quarterly analyses are made in advance of [QRL 30] for the UK in the *Department of Employment Gazette* [QRL 25]. (See Stark's companion review for details of the FES.) The regional analyses, including the subdivision of the South-east into London and the remainder of the region, are made for 11 main groups of commodities and services and these are further divided into 101 categories. [QRL 30] specifies standard errors for all of these. The tabulations in [QRL 30] include cross-classifications of household expenditure by household income composition and age and occupation of the head of household. Regional distributions are also given of households with durable goods such as cars, washing machines, central heating, refrigerators, television sets and telephones.

9.4.2. There are a few items such as alcohol and tobacco for which it is known that some households understate expenditure. The most severe limitation on [QRL 30] for planners is that they cannot be used below regional or sub-regional level.

9.4.3. *Food consumption*

The National Food Survey is a sample survey carried out by the MAFF which gives more detailed information on one of the most important items of expenditure covered by the FES. It was started in 1940 to provide information for the government's war-time food policy and its main function now is to help analyse the demand for foodstuffs; the sample of 14,000 households is slightly larger than that of the FES but a report covers only one week and not two. Details are collected on prices, incomes and expenditure, and analyses of these are made by regions and urban areas with respect to the social class of the household, based on income definition and household composition. The main results appear in the annual report of the *National Food Survey Committee—Domestic Food Consumption and Expenditure* [QRL 44]. The methodology of the survey appears in Appendix A of the 1972 report. A three-stage stratified random sampling scheme is used for the whole of Great Britain. The successive stages are parliamentary constituencies, polling districts or combinations thereof and selected addresses within polling districts.

CHAPTER 10

TRANSPORT

Statistics in the field of transport are being covered in a group of reviews in this series. Road Passenger and Road Goods Transport are described in detailed reviews by the late D. L. Munby and A. H. Watson [B 29a, B 32a] published in Vol. VII of this series. Other forthcoming reviews will cover Civil Aviation and Ports and Inland Waterways as well as Sea Transport and Railways.

10.1. Motor Vehicles

10.1.1. Annual totals of motor vehicles currently licensed as well as new registrations of motor vehicles in the UK have been published in *Highway Statistics* [QRL 37]. As from 1976 all information previously published in *Highway Statistics* will appear in a new publication *Transport Statistics*. *Highway Statistics* also contained mid-year estimates of the percentages of households in Britain with cars for the years 1961 to 1972. Information on households owning cars can also be obtained from the results of the 1966 and 1971 *Census of Population* [QRL 18] and [QRL 19].

10.1.2. The National Travel Survey was started in order to set up a national data bank of household generated travel by all modes. It was preceded by a quarterly series of sample surveys on motoring between 1961 and 1964. The more comprehensive travel surveys themselves were carried out for 1964, 1965, 1966, 1972–3 and 1975–6 by the MOT (later DOE). The 1964 survey was published in two parts [QRL 45] but since then results have appeared as odd tables in such publications as *Passenger Transport in Great Britain* [QRL 47], *Highway Statistics* [QRL 37] and *Social Trends* [QRL 56] (see [B 29a] for details).

10.2. Road Traffic

10.2.1. Various road traffic censuses have been carried out since 1922 to measure the flow of traffic, by classes of vehicles, at a number of points on the main routes. Estimates of the volume of road traffic are obtained by monthly automatic counts at 200 (previously 50) junctions on trunk and classified roads. Results are published in *Highway Statistics* [QRL 37] and [B 30] and [B 32] give details of the census method. Three days a month manual counts are made at the 200 junctions to estimate numbers of different types of vehicle and these results also appear in *Highway Statistics* [QRL 37].

10.2.2. A general Traffic Census was carried out in 1954, 1961 and 1965 and results appeared in *Highway Statistics* [QRL 37]. In 1969 a new series of counts was started with counting spread over a 4-year cycle so as to provide a continuous flow of information and to spread the considerable amount of data processing. A new cycle of counts was started in 1974 in England and Wales after a 1-year interval whilst in Scotland a new cycle was begun in 1973. Some 6500 census points on 30,000 miles of motorways and A roads in Great Britain are being covered by roadside enumerators recording the numbers of vehicles in each of ten classes passing the census points. The main counts take place in August with supplementary counts at one quarter of each year's list of points taken in April to give a measure of seasonal variation. Additional data are available from the continuing monthly sample census. Details of the census and copies of the results of the 1969–73 census can be obtained from the DOE, SDD and Welsh Office.

10.2.3. The General Traffic Census and the monthly counts are useful guides to regional traffic flows but the results will tend to exaggerate flows in some areas because of the date of the main census. The absence of information about origins and destinations of the journeys involved limit the use that can be made of the statistics as does the relative infrequency of the Census.

10.2.4. Recent changes in the motorway network affect the estimates of traffic flows. The monthly sample census is used to give tentative estimates in [QRL 37] of the volume of traffic on the new sections. Attention is drawn to the problem of seasonal variations as the results are expressed as an equivalent annual rate although the estimates are based on data covering only part of a year.

10.3. Road Mileage

10.3.1. *Total mileage*

Highway Statistics [QRL 37] gives annual totals of mileage of roads in Great Britain for counties and county boroughs. The total mileages are divided into three categories of trunk, principal and other. *Basic Road Statistics* [QRL 11] gives road mileage figures for Northern Ireland analysed for trunk, class I, class II, class III and unclassified roads.

10.3.2. From 1st April 1967 substantial changes were made to the system of highway classification. Before that date the most important non-trunk roads were classified for purposes of Exchequer grants. Various grants were made to highway authorities for class I, II and III roads. Under the new system grants are payable for improvements on a single class of road known as principal roads which are roughly equivalent to the former class I roads.

10.3.3. *Motorway mileages*

The mileages of individual motorways in use in England compiled by the DOE appear in *Roads in England* [QRL 53]. Corresponding figures for Scotland compiled by the

SDD are published in the *Annual Report* [QRL 9] and for Wales by the Welsh Office in [QRL 28]. Separate lists of trunk road motorways and local authority motorways are given. The time reference is the end of the financial year.

10.3.4. *Motorways under construction*

The miles of motorway under construction are specified in [QRL 53,] [QRL 9] and [QRL 28].

10.3.5. *Potential motorways*

Details with mileages are given in [QRL 53], [QRL 9] and [QRL 28] of tenders invited, schemes made, draft schemes published and line (i.e. the centre line of a proposed motorway), not yet published for trunk road motorways. Similar details are given with respect to potential local authority motorways for schemes confirmed by the Minister and schemes made and submitted for confirmation by the Minister.

10.4. Road Transport

10.4.1. Large-scale surveys of transport of goods by road have been carried out in the years 1952, 1958, 1962 and 1967–8 by the MOT (later DOE). These have been followed by a continuing quarterly sample survey started in 1970. Articles on the 1952 and 1958 surveys appear in *The Outline of the Road Goods Transport Industry* [B 17] and *The Transport of Goods by Road* [B 18]. Results for the continuing survey appeared annually in *Highway Statistics* [QRL 37] and can now be found in *Transport Statistics* and a report *The Transport of Goods by Road 1970–72* [QRL 63] has been published on the first $2\frac{1}{2}$ years' operation of the survey.

10.4.2. Operators of public service road vehicles in Great Britain are required to make calendar year returns of numbers of passengers carried, vehicle miles and passenger receipts, to the DOE. Operators with more than twenty-four vehicles are also required to provide less detailed returns on a quarterly basis. The quarterly results are given in the *Monthly Digest of Statistics* [QRL 43] and the annual statistics have been published in *Passenger Transport in Great Britain* [QRL 47]. As from 1976 all information previously published in [QRL 47] will appear in *Transport Statistics*.

10.5. Rail

10.5.1. *Passenger transport*

Passenger Transport in Great Britain [QRL 47] includes statistics on rail travel derived from the British Rail Board (BRB) *Annual Report* [QRL 7] supplemented by information from the BRB, LTE and other rail undertakings. *Passenger Transport in Great Britain* [QRL 47] gives separate totals for these three sources for each year of the preceding decade of route mileages, numbers of passenger stations, passenger carriages, seating capacity, passenger journeys and passenger miles. The number of journeys are sub-divided for full fares, reduced fares and season tickets; return tickets are counted as two journeys and season ticket journeys estimated by BR since 1962 (because of the intro-duction of the 5-day working week) as 540 per annum as against the previous figure of 600 per annum. Through-booked journeys beginning with the LTE or other authorities are included in the figures. Statistics of passenger miles and journeys include counts of accompanied dogs, bicycles, etc. No estimates of their contribution are given and [QRL 47] remarks only that they are small in proportion to the total.

10.5.2. BRB holds a substantial amount of information on passenger journeys not normally published [B 45], for example, gives an interesting graphical representation of the number of BR passengers passing through main London termini in 1966 between the hours of 7 and 10 a.m. This is drawn from unpublished BR data.

10.5.3. *Freight*

General trends in freight receipts and traffic may be found in the BRB *Annual Report* [QRL 7]. The train and wagon loads are given for coal and coke, iron and steel and a miscellaneous category. Net ton miles are also specified.

10.6. Civil Air Transport

10.6.1. The consequences of the growth in the size and number of civil airports hardly needs to be stressed. Apart from environmental problems the impact of air cargo move-ments on land use over an extensive area are just as important as the growth of hotels consequent upon passenger movements. The recent growth of hotels near London air-port is well known. Not so obvious a phenomenon is the substantial demand for ware-housing (commercial) floorspace reflected in planning permissions in local authority areas containing and adjoining airports. See, for example, [QRL 5].

10.6.2. *Passengers by air*

The annual British Airports Authority (BAA) *Report* [QRL 51] contains statistics for all UK airports. The numbers of aircraft movements and passengers are given for individual airports with percentage changes with respect to the preceding calendar year. Breakdowns are given between international and domestic traffic. Further details are given for the BAA airports of Heathrow, Gatwick, Stansted and Prestwick though these are for the financial and not the calendar year.

10.6.3. *Cargo traffic*

The BAA annual *Report* [QRL 51] gives cargo statistics for all UK airports. Total cargo loads are shown for the calendar year with separate figures of international cargo and percentage changes with respect to the preceding year. Total values of imports and exports are quoted. Further tables on a financial year basis are given for the BAA airports of Heathrow, Gatwick, Stansted and Prestwick.

10.7. Ports

10.7.1. *The Annual Digest of Port Statistics* [QRL 26] is prepared each year by the National Ports Council. The statistics which refer to the calendar year are obtained from a number of sources including port authorities, government departments and non-governmental bodies. All the statistics refer to Great Britain and some include Northern Ireland. A considerable amount of information is given for individual ports and in a number of instances for standard regions. Attention is drawn to the port of Harwich which is included in East Anglia with the other ports of Ipswich and Felixstowe in the same estuary although Harwich is actually located in the South East Region. Some of the statistics are provisional and are subject to revision. The subjects covered include labour, goods traffic (commodity analyses and overseas trading areas), passenger traffic and shipping movements.

10.7.2. In the last decade there have been considerable developments in the use of container traffic and statistics have been published for the year 1965 onwards for Great Britain by the National Ports Council in *Container and Roll-on Port Statistics* [QRL 22]. (Since 1974 in *Annual Digest of Port Statistics*). Initially the statistics were derived from estimates made either by port authorities or by the Council, and later were based upon returns of actual traffic from port authorities introduced with effect from 1st January 1967 by the Council.

CHAPTER 11

DESIRABLE IMPROVEMENTS AND FUTURE DEVELOPMENTS

11.1. Land Use and Planning Decisions

11.1.1. In recent years there has been a marked intensification of DOE requirements in the field of planning statistics, viz. land-use and planning decisions. Three important DOE circulars have been issued in 1974–5 all of which aim at getting much more information from local authorities' records of planning permissions in England and Wales. These circulars are:

62/74 Industrial and Commercial Developments (see Section 11.3.2).
71/74 Statistics of Land Use Change (see Section 11.1.4 and companion review by Coppock [B 8]).

32/75 Statistics of Land with Outstanding Planning Permission (see Section 11.2.1). As yet there are no requirements for similar data in Scotland and Northern Ireland.

11.1.2. New planning authorities will find it difficult to meet the new and greatly increased DOE requirements and a number have expressed some concern. Their problems may be summarised as follows:

(i) Only a minority of authorities can draw upon well-established computer systems which facilitate the identification of all the relevant planning permissions.
(ii) The amount of work needed by some authorities to check and report on the progress of large numbers of individual permissions some of which may have been granted a number of years ago.
(iii) The adaptation of existing systems to the new National Land Use Classification [B 49].
(iv) The allocation of staff to new work in a period of economic stringency.

The DOE point of view is that it is seeking basic information which planning authorities should have been assembling in some form as a by-product of their normal administrative procedures. The information is seen by the DOE as essential to planning and in general terms the developments are to be welcomed by those who feel far too little is known about land-use changes and planning permissions. There will remain, however, the major reservation that perhaps too much is being attempted too quickly.

11.1.3. *Land-use changes*

Circular 71/74 in asking for annual land-use changes (74/5 optional, 75/6 obligatory), based on the National Land Use Classification [B 49] points out that there are a variety of sources which can be used to identify and measure land-use changes, examples of which are rating records and planning permissions. There may be considerable difficulty in providing reliable statistics promptly even at the grouped level needed by the DOE. Complete annual land-use surveys are not the answer and in any case the DOE is not at present trying to derive totals of existing uses. Planning authorities will need to integrate the requirements of this circular with those of 32/75 (outstanding permissions). Some planners have strongly questioned the value of these statistics and have suggested that it is by no means clear how they will be used to any real purpose by the DOE. (See Addenda).

11.1.4. *Planning applications*

In Section 3.2.1 comment was made on the change from the calendar year to the financial year as the basis of the returns [QRL 59] on the outcome of planning applications in England and Wales. The DOE, however, now proposes to ask planning authorities from 1976–7 onwards to supply greater detail when providing these returns. The categories of development will be broken down in two ways. Firstly, they will be allocated by the time taken from receipt of applications to the date of decision (under 2 months, 2 to 4 months, etc.) and secondly, simple classification into relative sizes of proposed developments. (See Addenda 11.2.1.)

11.1.5. *Expired planning permissions*

As a consequence of the Town Planning Act, 1968 a substantial number of planning permissions have expired in recent years. These will have to be identified as part of the requirements of Circular 32/75 and it would seem logical that in due course the DOE will ask for separate returns of expired permissions. Very little is known as yet about the significance of expired planning permissions.

11.2. Planning Permissions

11.2.1. Circular 32/75, Statistics of Land with Outstanding Planning Permissions, is chiefly concerned with permissions for housing developments in England and Wales and the circular itself implies that it is a continuation of the information required under Circular 102/72 (see Section 4.3.1) on housing land availability. Returns are being asked for initially to show the position at 1st July 1975 but it is suggested to the returning planning authorities that there will be a need for the returns to be periodically updated. The returns will take the form of lists of individual housing permissions for sites of 1 hectare or more (in metropolitan areas for sites greater than 0.4 hectare or 1 acre). The details for each site will include the address, number of dwellings, type of permission (full, outline or detailed), type of site (new housing site or redevelopment) and type of developer (private or public), the latter category including housing associations. The returns should include any site only once and care will be needed with multiple permissions for the same site. The details to be supplied are to refer only to the part of the site where the work is not complete if part of the development has already been implemented. The DOE original intention of asking for estimates of completions was not proceeded with. The DOE intends to publish the results of the survey in summary form as soon as possible and wishes to discuss with local authorities the publication of full details. (See Addenda).

11.2.2. The Circular 32/75 returns of outstanding planning permissions for housing are to be welcomed as the absence of any central sources of this sort has been one of the defects of housing statistics in the UK. A possible future development of this return would be the return of planning permissions as they are granted, say on an annual basis. This is already a standard procedure in some planning authorities. The DOE is, however, extremely optimistic in looking for a comprehensive statement of larger developments only 3 months (by the end of September 1975) after the date to which the return applies.

11.3. Industrial and Commercial Properties

11.3.1. As we have seen the floorspace data currently available are unsatisfactory in a number of respects. Series II [QRL 60] offers the widest coverage in England and Wales, giving figures of stock and change for industry, offices, shops and warehousing. Despite the definitional problems it remains the only central source and could be a useful indicator, certainly at least at the level of the region. However, as publication of the series trails on average about 5 years behind events it is at present little more than an historical series. If the resources available to process the data are so limited that the delays are likely to continue it might be better to concentrate on more recent years and abandon publication for earlier years. There is a clear need for similar floorspace statistics for Scotland and Northern Ireland.

11.3.2. The only other main source of office floorspace statistics were ODPs [QRL 23] and the other main source of industrial floorspace are IDCs. Changes in the regulations have limited the value of [QRL 23] and the discontinuance of IDCs in development and special areas have similarly led to a loss of information from [QRL 62]. It is this lack of proper coverage which has led to the DOE issuing Circular 62/74 on industrial and commercial developments. This requires information from planning authorities in England and Wales for all planning permissions involving industrial and commercial developments of over 10,000 square feet. The information will be for permissions granted after 1st April 1974 and in addition authorities in development areas no longer covered by IDC procedures are asked to provide what information they can for the interim period of July 1972 to March 1974. The returns take the form of copies of each planning application form related to every detailed permission covered by the circular although the DOE is prepared to accept alternatively lists of cases giving the equivalent information. Returns will be quarterly and the DOE may subsequently seek supplementary details from developers. As the application forms ask for information about existing as well as proposed uses the DOE will be in a position to obtain statistics of estimated change. Some caution will be needed in the interpretation of existing uses as reported by developers as well as careful liaison with local authorities operating their own monitoring systems in order to ensure that conflicting statistics are not being generated. The DOE, which has referred to this return as Statistics of Jobs in Prospect, has not yet said what form, if any, published statistics will take. It should be appreciated that, in any case, permissions over 10,000 square feet only account for varying proportions of the total floorspace granted for individual uses. In London unpublished figures [QRL 5] show, for example, that in 1972, 22 per cent of all office floorspace permitted derived from permissions of under 10,000 square feet and 27 per cent of all industrial floorspace permitted from permissions of under 10,000 square feet.

11.3.3. While Circular 32/75 is principally concerned with outstanding permissions for housing developments is also asks local authorities in England and Wales to provide similar information (see Section 11.2.1) for all industrial and commercial developments with outstanding total floorspace over 10,000 square feet. The circular requires only the dominant use of the permission to be specified and ignores such problems as main and ancillary uses which were discussed in Section 5.1.3. This will severely limit the value of the information which the DOE intends to publish.

11.3.4. One of the most notable deficiencies of the various sources of floorspace data is the lack of any statistics about vacant industrial and commercial properties. The only possible central source for this would be IR [QRL 60] but as we have seen (Section 5.1.2) there are problems in properly distinguishing between vacant and occupied properties.

11.4. Production

11.4.1. The outstanding parts of the 1968 *Census of Production* [QRL 20] giving comparable information for 1963 and area analyses will become available during 1974. Provisional results for the annual Censuses [QRL 14] will for the year 1973 onwards be published some 12 months after the end of the reference year.

11.4.2. The construction industry which was excluded from the new annual series [QRL 14] for the years 1970–3 will be included in 1974.

11.4.3. Membership of the European Economic Communities requires changes in the coverage and information in the annual Censuses. In the Censuses for 1973 to 1975 all establishments employing twenty or more (see Section 6.1.2 for earlier requirements) will be required to complete a questionnaire. There will be some slight changes in the content of the questionnaire and these are outlined in *Statistical News*, **20**, 36 [B 54].

11.5. Distribution

11.5.1. In the foreword to [B 43] Sir Bernard Miller stated that 'One clear result of our work, although sadly a negative one, has been to highlight the inadequacy of the data upon which any shop planning must be made'. The recommendation was made in

[B 43] that to obtain better data there should be closer collaboration between private enterprise and public authorities such as exists in Sweden and Denmark. The recommendation was favourably received by the government and on 1st April 1975 the Unit for Retail Planning Information was set up with the support of local and central government and the retail trade. The first quarterly newsletter [B 56] which was issued in the autumn of 1975 describes the initial objectives of the Unit.

11.5.2. The quinquennial series of Censuses of Distribution will be replaced by annual sample inquiries based upon the BSO's central register of business. The first inquiry will be held for retailing in 1977 in respect of the year 1976. Each annual inquiry will be concerned with basic retail information and be supplemented by special topic inquiries on a cyclical basis.

11.5.3. The DI is considering the compilation of a retail shop register which would hold for each shop basic data such as location, business activity, turnover, employment and, for some shops, selling space. This would make it possible to produce analyses of small areas such as shopping centres. For further details see No. 31 of [B 54]. The creation of such a register would need to be started soon if small area data are to be provided by the 1980s. The combination of annual inquiry with such a register would represent a greatly improved source of retail information.

11.5.4. The compilation of regional retail price indices has been considered by the Retail Prices Index Advisory Committee. The findings are published in *Proposals for Retail Price Indices for Regions*, Cmnd. 4749 [B 51]. The proposals have not yet been implemented, possibly because of the views of a minority of the committee that their publication would complicate wage negotiations and have an inflationary effect.

11.5.5. The BSO held a post-census inquiry in 1973 into the 1971 Census, similar to the post-census inquiry into the 1970 Census of Production. Difficulties were discussed with a sample of firms who took part in the 1971 Census. One of the objectives was to determine whether there are any special factors to be taken into account in interpreting the 1971 results.

11.5.6. The main results of the 1971 Census of Distribution are being published in thirteen separate parts in Business Monitors SD 10–SD 22, the first twelve of which appeared during 1975. Part I, SD 10, deals with Retail Outlets (Establishment Tables), Parts 2–11 (SD 10–SD 20) the Area Tables and Part 12 (SD 21) the Area Summary figures. The final volume, Part 13, was published in 1976 and gave the Retail Organisation Tables and Service Trades results. Every retail shop has been given an eight-figure National Grid reference code. The location of every shop has thus been identified within a 100-metre square and this will enable the BSO to provide specially aggregated figures of retail trade for any area defined in terms of complete 100-metre grid squares.

11.6. Employment

11.6.1. The DE has been asked by users that because employment records from the Census of Employment [QRL 25] are classified by SIC but not by occupational classification, individual records might be matched by local authorities with their land-use records to identify and code occupations. This would, for example, make it possible to estimate office and factory employment for a variety of areas. Inevitably, because of different dates of survey, there would be matching problems and, in addition, because of possible defects in the land use data, there would be some additional estimation. The LOB and some local authorities take the view that this could only be a temporary arrangement and that it would be desirable in the future to include occupational classifications as a normal part of the Census.

11.7. Income and Expenditure

11.7.1. SPI data [QRL 61] will continue to be coded on a regional and county basis but it will not be possible to go below the level of the new counties. For the counties estimates of income totals will still be available and the IR hopes to provide summary statistics of income distributions such as medians and quartiles. The IR will also be investigating the possibility of more detailed analyses for the larger counties. For some years it is hoped in future to obtain a larger sample than the usual 100,000 which will make more detailed analysis possible although it is unlikely that the sample will ever be as large again as 1,000,000.

11.8. Transport

11.8.1. The system of registration of motor vehicles at Local Taxation offices of some 180 county and borough councils in Great Britain was changed from 1st October 1974. Existing vehicle records are gradually being transferred to the Driving and Vehicle Licensing Centre at Swansea. Whereas in the past estimates were made for each Local Taxation office area, it is intended that in future postal codes will be used to allocate vehicles to new counties and more varied analyses by computer will be possible. The DOE will continue to have responsibility for the provision of statistics.

QUICK REFERENCE LIST

NOTES TO THE QUICK REFERENCE LIST

1. The QRL key to publications includes all those mentioned in the text arranged alphabetically by title.

2. For convenience, the QRL has been divided into sections following the major headings of the text. As a general rule the listing of the series follows the order in which they are mentioned and where one series is relevant under several headings it has been included where appropriate. However, there is no complete cross-referencing of series.

3. Area and Breakdown of Series
   The following abbreviations have been adopted:

LA	Local Authority
GLC	Greater London Council area
E & W	England and Wales
S	Scotland
GB	Great Britain
N/Ireland	Northern Ireland
UK	United Kingdom

4. A Note on Census Publications
   1. The tabulations included in the Quick Reference List refer to 1966 the last year for which complete results were available at the time the main part of this text was written. Two distinct references have been given, the first for Great Britain [QRL 18], where a sample Census was taken in 1966, and the second for Northern Ireland [QRL 19], where a full census was taken in 1966. Some reference has, however, been made to certain aspects of the full 1971 UK Census in various parts of the main text.
   2. The published County volumes of the Sample Census in Great Britain contain two levels of presentation (three in Scotland) which can be described in terms of the areas to which the tables refer:
   In England and Wales Scale A is the fullest scale and applies to:

(a) The administrative county as a whole with and without any associated county boroughs.
(b) Each county borough and new town.
(c) Each municipal borough and urban district expected to have more than 50,000, population on Census day.
(d) The aggregate, within the administrative county, of all municipal boroughs and urban districts combined and of all rural districts.

Scale B which is less detailed than Scale A and applies to:
  (a) Those municipal boroughs and urban districts expected to have between 15,000
      and 50,000 population on Census day.
  (b) All rural districts expected to have more than 15,000 population on Census day.
In Scotland Scale A applies to:
  (a) Each county of city.
  (b) Each county.
  (c) The county exclusive of large burgh(s).
  (d) Each large burgh expected to have more than 50,000 population on Census day.
Scale B applies to:
  (a) Each large burgh and small burgh expected to have a population of 15,000 or
      more but fewer than 50,000 on Census day.
  (b) Each district of county expected to have a population of 15,000 or more on
      Census day.
Scale C applies to:
  (a) Small burghs and districts of county with expected population of less than
      15,000 on Census day.

3. In the QRL reference will be made to the three scales of presentation adopted in
the County volumes but unpublished Census data is also generally available at Scale B
for all areas down to enumeration district and at Scale A for all local authorities in
Great Britain. Further details are available on application to the Office of Population
Census and Surveys, and the General Register Office, Scotland.

QUICK REFERENCE LIST—TABLE OF CONTENTS

171

QUICK REFERENCE LIST

Descriptive Title	Breakdown	Area	Frequency	Publication	Text Reference and Remarks
LAND USE AND PLANNING DECISIONS					
Land use					
Area, population, private households and dwellings	Scales A & B (plus scale C in Scotland)	GB	Decennial	County Reports [QRL 18]	3.1.2 to 3.1.4. A description of the scales A, B and C are given in *A Note to Census Publications* in the Notes to the Quick Reference List. Secondary source: [QRL 24]
Area, population, buildings for habitation, private households and valuation	County boroughs, counties, administrative areas and towns with 1000 or more population	N/Ireland	Decennial	General Report 1966 Census of Ireland [QRL 19]	3.1.2. See the comparion review *Land Use* [B 8] for full details of Land Use Sources in the UK
Allotments	GLC boroughs	GLC	Annual	[QRL 5]	3.1.5. DOE holds similar unpublished data for all local authorities in E & W
Planning decisions					
Numbers of permissions granted and refusals by class of development	E & W, totals of counties, county boroughs and London boroughs	E & W	Annual	[QRL 59]	3.2.1. Class of development has two main categories in E & W [QRL 59] and Scotland [QRL 10], viz. (i) building, engineering and other operations; (ii) change of use. These are subdivided in a fairly similar way in [QRL 59] and [QRL 9]. Secondary source: [QRL 24]
Numbers of permissions granted and refusals by class of development	Scotland	S	Annual	[QRL 9]	3.2.3. See above (3.2.1)
Numbers of permissions granted, conditional approvals and refusals	Northern Ireland	N/Ireland	Annual	[QRL 64]	3.2.3. New system introduced from 1st October 1973
Refusal rates by class of development	E & W, totals of counties, county boroughs and London boroughs	E & W	Annual	[QRL 59]	3.2.1
Numbers of permissions granted and refusals	E & W, economic planning regions, approved green belts and national parks	E & W	Annual	[QRL 59]	3.2.1

Subject	Area	Area code	Frequency	Source	Section
Numbers of types of advertisement decisions and discontinuance notices by type of advertisement	E & W	E & W	Annual	[QRL 36]	3.2.4
Numbers of advertisement decisions by type of authority and area	E & W, administrative counties, county boroughs, London boroughs, national parks and other areas	E & W	Annual	[QRL 36]	3.2.4
Planning appeals allowed and dismissed by class of development	E & W	E & W	Annual	[QRL 36]	3.2.4. Class of development as for decisions. Secondary source: [QRL 24]
Planning appeals in hand, received and withdrawn	E & W	E & W	Annua	[QRL 36]	3.2.4
Planning appeals decided by Secretaries of State and inspectors	E & W	E & W	Annual	[QRL 36]	3.2.4
Appeals against enforcement/ notices in hand, received, withdrawn, upheld and quashed	E & W	E & W	Annual	[QRL 36]	3.2.4
Established use certificate appeals in hand, received, withdrawn, decided	E & W	E & W	Annual	[QRL 36]	3.2.4
Certificate of appropriate development appeals	E & W	E & W	Annual	[QRL 36]	3.2.4
Mineral working and called-in Applications	E & W	E & W	Annual	[QRL 36]	3.2.4
Appeals relating to planning permissions, other planning appeals and advertisement appeals outstanding, received, sustained, dismissed, enforcement notices, types of decisions (land uses)	Scotland	S	Annual	[QRL 9]	3.2.4
Appeals received, withdrawn, allowed, carried forward to next year	Northern Ireland	N/Ireland	Annual	[QRL 64]	3.2.4. New system from 1st October 1973 onwards
Preservation of historic buildings/ listed buildings, works of alteration, intention to demolish and building preservation orders	E & W	E & W	Annual	[QRL 59]	3.2.5
Application for listed buildings consent for demolitions and alterations and extensions	E & W	E & W	Annual	[QRL 59]	3.2.5

Descriptive Title	Breakdown	Area	Frequency	Publication	Text Reference and Remarks
Planning decisions *contd.*					
Professional, technical and administrative expenses	Counties. Analysis of expenditure per 1000 population	E & W	Annual	[QRL 24]	3.2.6
Planning expenses for conservation and preservation of buildings, urban and industrial development, rural preservation and development, compensation under development control	,,	E & W	Annual	[QRL 24]	3.2.6
HOUSING					
Stock of dwellings					
Size, characteristics and tenure		GB	Decennial	[QRL 18]	4.1. See the companion review [B 11] for further details and sources
,,	,,	N/Ireland	Decennial	[QRL 19]	4.1. See the companion review [B 14] for further details and sources
,,	,,	GB	Quarterly	[QRL 38]	4.1. See [B 11] and footnotes to QRL list key
Changes in stock of dwellings					
New dwellings, constructions, completions, gains and losses, slum clearance, etc.		GB	Quarterly	[QRL 38]	4.2. See above remarks on stock of dwellings
Demolition, closure, improvements		N/Ireland	Quarterly	[QRL 40]	4.2. See [B 14]
Housing land availability					
Land stock in 1972 and 1973 in terms of dwellings units	Surrey, mid-Kent and West-Sussex		1972, & 1973	[QRL 39]	4.3.4
Allocations of land	,,		,,	[QRL 39]	4.3.4
Outstanding permissions (not started), under construction, completions	,,		,,	[QRL 39]	4.3.4
Allocated stock—proportion granted permissions	Surrey, Bucks, West Sussex, Kent		,,	[QRL 39]	4.3.4. Sites over three acres only except for Surrey with all sites included

INDUSTRIAL AND COMMERCIAL PROPERTIES

Industrial floorspace

Description	Coverage	Area	Period	Reference	Section / Remarks
Stock, and number of hereditaments by size groups	E & W and regions	E & W	1967 & 1974	[QRL 60]	5.1
	Regional subdivisions	E & W	1967	[QRL 60]	5.1
	Counties	E & W	1974	[QRL 60]	5.1
Stock, and numbers of hereditaments	E & W and Regions	E & W	1967 & 1974	[QRL 60]	5.1
	Regional subdivisions, counties and local authorities	E & W	1967		
Occupied industrial floorspace	Counties and districts	E & W	1974	[QRL 34]	5.1.3. Similar unpublished data is available for the former LCC area (1961) and the GLC area (1971)
	London boroughs, conurbation centre 500-m grid squares and other special areas	GLC	1966		
Vacant industrial floorspace	Conurbation centre	GLC	1966	[QRL 34]	5.1.3. With detail for all areas for 1971
Additions, reductions and net increases in stock of floorspace	E & W, regions and regional sub divisions	E & W	1967-9	[QRL 60]	5.1.5
Floorspace of new hereditaments by size group	E & W, regions	E & W	1967-9	[QRL 60]	5.1.5
Industrial development certificates of floorspace by size range (under 5000, 5000 and under 10,000, 10,000 and over 10,000 ft²)	E, W, S, England regions, development areas, intermediate areas. Under 10,000 ft² cases for two grouped areas only	GB	Quarterly	[QRL 62]	5.1.6. Statistics of approvals last published 27th April 1972 [QRL 62] for first quarter of 1972 with time series starting from 1967. Statistics for later quarters from Department of Industry, EcS4C, Room 815, Millbank Tower, London SW1P 4QU
Industrial development certificate refusals, numbers and floorspace by size range (under 5000, 5000 and under 10,000, 10,000 and over 10,000 ft²)	GB	GB	Annual	[QRL 62]	5.1.8. Last published 15th July 1971 [QRL 62] for data to the end of 1970. See preceding remarks on approvals

Office floorspace

Description	Coverage	Area	Period	Reference	Section / Remarks
Stock and number of hereditaments by type (commercial, local and central government)	E & W, regions and counties	E & W	1967 & 1974	[QRL 60]	5.2
	Regional subdivisions local authorities	E & W	1967		
	Districts	E & W	1974		

Office floorspace *contd.*

Descriptive Title	Breakdown	Area	Frequency	Publication	Text Reference and Remarks
Stock and number of hereditaments of commercial offices by size group	E & W, Regions Regional subdivisions Counties	E & W E & W E & W	1967 & 1974 1967 1974	[QRL 60]	5.2
Occupied office floorspace	London boroughs, conurbation centre, 500-m grid squares under other special areas	GLC	1966	[QRL 34]	5.2.5. Similar unpublished data is available for the former LCC area (1961) and the GLC area (1971)
Vacant office floorspace	Conurbation centre	GLC	1966	[QRL 34]	5.2.5. With details of vacant floorspace for all areas in 1971
Completed and vacant office floorspace	GLC and rest of Metropolitan region		1966	[QRL 23]	5.2.8
Additions, reductions, net increases to stock by type of office	E & W, regions and regional subdivisions	E & W	1967-9	[QRL 60]	5.2.6
New commercial office hereditaments by size groups	E & W, regions	E & W	1967-9	[QRL 60]	5.2.6
Numbers of Office Development Permits with gross and relinquished floorspace	Various planning regions in England with some sub-regional divisions	England	Annual and quarterly	[QRL 23] and [QRL 62]	5.2.7
Gross, relinquished and net aggregate area of permits in excess of 150,000 ft^2	GLC	GLC	Annual and quarterly	" "	5.2.7
Numbers of Office Development Permit refusals with gross floorspace	Various planning regions in England with some regional subdivisions	England	Annual and quarterly	[QRL 23] and [QRL 62]	5.2.7
Floorspace under construction resulting from Office Development Permits	GLC and rest of Metropolitan region	Metropolitan region	Annual and quarterly	[QLR 23] and [QRL 62]	5.2.8.
Outstanding planning permissions for Office Development Permit cases	"	" "	Annual and quarterly	[QRL 23] and [QRL 62]	5.2.8
Gross and relinquished floorspace of planning permissions for offices	GLC, London boroughs and conurbation centre	GLC	Annual	[QRL 5]	5.2.10. Available from 1st April 1965. Unpublished data held on completions, expiries (see 11.1.5) and outstanding permissions

Description	Area detail	Area	Period	Source	Section / Notes
Numbers of firms (and jobs) deciding to move from central London, numbers deciding not to move	Conurbation centre	GLC	Annual	[QRL 8]	5.2.13
Intended directions and distances of movement	"	GLC	Annual	[QRL 8]	5.2.13
Reasons (7) of firms for considering decentralisation	"	GLC	Annual	[QRL 8]	5.2.13
Numbers of firms and jobs considering decentralisation by SIC	"	GLC	Annual	[QRL 8]	5.2.13
Numbers of firms and jobs moving by direction and distance of moves	"	GLC	Annual	[QRL 8]	5.2.13
Numbers of firms deciding not to move by size range of jobs	Conurbation centre	GLC	Annual	[QRL 8]	5.2.13
Shopping floorspace					
Stock and numbers of hereditaments by size groups	E & W, regions / Regional subdivisions / Counties	E & W	1967 & 1974 / 1967 / 1974	[QRL 60]	5.3 N.B. Shops with living accommodation also given for 1974
Stock and numbers of hereditaments	E & W, Regions and Counties / Regional subdivisions and local authorities Districts	E & W	1967 & 1974 / 1967	[QRL 60]	5.3. "
Additions, reductions and net increases in floorspace	E & W, regions and regional subdivisions	E & W	1974 / 1967-9	[QRL 60]	5.3.
Floorspace of new hereditaments by size group	E & W, regions	E & W	1967-9	[QRL 60]	5.3.
Establishment by size of total floorspace by kind of business (intermediate retail and hairdressers)	Simple estimates for GB, Central London, GLC shopping centres with retail turnover in 1961 over £5 m. and under £5 m., provincial centres £20 m. and over, £10 m. to £20 m., under £10 m.	GB	Quinquennial	Vol. II [QRL 16]	5.3.3. Intermediate retail in 1966 gives data broken down into twenty three categories. All the estimates from [QRL 18] give aggregates of shopping centres
Turnover by form of organisation (intermediate retail and services)	"	GB	Quinquennial	[QRL 16]	5.3.3

Shopping floorspace contd.

Descriptive Title	Breakdown	Area	Frequency	Publication	Text Reference and Remarks
Turnover per square foot of total floorspace by size of total floorspace (intermediate retail and hairdressers)	"	GB	Quinquennial	[QRL 16]	5.3.4	"
Establishment by turnover per square foot of total floorspace (size of ratio) by kind of business (intermediate retail and hairdressers)	Simple estimate for GB	GB	Quinquennial	[QRL 16]	5.3.4	"
Establishments (intermediate retail) by size of selling floorspace, by turnover per ft² of selling floorspace, by turnover per ft² selling floorspace by size of shop		GB	Quinquennial	[QRL 16]	5.3.4	"
Ratios of selling floorspace to total floorspace by turnover size of shop by kind of business		GB	Quinquennial	[QRL 16]	5.3.4	"
Establishment and turnover by turnover size of shop by form of organisation for shopping centre types (intermediate retail and services)	Simple estimates for GB, Central London, GLC and provincial centres	GB	Quinquennial	[QRL 16]	5.3.4. Shopping centre types as defined above for GLC and provincial centres	"
Turnover and turnover per ft² of selling space by turnover size of shop (intermediate retail and hairdressers)	"	GB	Quinquennial	[QRL 16]	5.3.4	"
Ratio of selling space to total floorspace by turnover size of shop	Simple estimate for GB	GB	Quinquennial	[QRL 16]	5.3.4	"

Warehousing, etc., floorspace

Descriptive Title	Breakdown	Area	Frequency	Publication	Text Reference and Remarks
Stock and numbers of hereditaments	E & W, regions, counties	E & W	1967 and 1974	[QRL 60]	5.4
	Regional subdivisions and local authorities Districts		1967		
Stock and number of hereditaments by size group	E & W, regions and counties	E & W	1974 1974	[QRL 60]	5.4

Subject	Area detail	Country	Frequency	Reference	Notes
Additions, reductions, net increases to stock of floorspace	E & W, regions and regional subdivisions	E & W	1967-9	[QRL 60]	5.4
Rateable values					
Industrial hereditaments	E & W, Wales county boroughs, non-county boroughs, GLC inner and outer boroughs, urban districts and rural districts	E & W	Annual	[QRL 49]	5.5. Refers to factories, mills and other premises of a similar character, but excludes mineral-producing hereditaments, and coal, water and transport undertakings
Office hereditaments	"	E & W	Annual	[QRL 49]	5.5. Includes banks in office areas
Shops hereditaments	"	E & W	Annual	[QRL 49]	5.5. Includes shops assessed with living accommodation, banks in shopping areas and cafes
Industrial and freight-transport subjects, estimated population and area of land in authority area	S, counties and boroughs	S	Annual	[QRL 50]	5.5.3. Subjects include factories, workshops, docks, etc.
Commercial subjects, estimated population and area of land in authority area	"	S	Annual	[QRL 50]	5.5.3. These refer to premises normally found in commercial and business areas—shops, offices, banks, restaurants, storage and commercial warehouses, etc.
Industrial and freight hereditaments, estimated population, area of land (census)	NI, counties, towns urban and rural districts	N/Ireland	Annual	[QRL 42]	5.5.3
PRODUCTION					
General					
Establishments, employment, wages and salaries, gross and net output, sales and purchases by SIC orders III to XIX	Regions in E. and all conurbations	UK	Quinquennial (till 1968)	[QRL 20]	6.1. 1968 report gives comparisons with 1963. For later data see [QRL 14]. The 1973 report published in 1974 gives final 1970/71 results. 1972 results were at that time improved from provisional but not yet final. Final results of the 1973 Census, including analysis by size of establishment will appear in about 160 industry reports from the end of 1975 onwards. See also [QRL 62]
" for individual industries	Regions	E	"	[QRL 20]	
Net output within each industry (minimum list headings)	Regions (E), W, S & NI	UK	"	[QRL 20]	
Capital expenditure by industry groups	"	UK	"	[QRL 20]	

Descriptive Title	Breakdown	Area	Frequency	Publication	Text Reference and Remarks
General *contd.*					
Summary by industries and analysis of capital expenditure	S, W	UK	"	[QRL 20]	"
Index of industrial production	Manufacturing industries, construction, gas, electricity and water	UK	"	[QRL 20]	"
Agriculture					
Losses of agricultural land	1866–1966	E & W	Monthly	[QRL 62]	6.1.9
Changes and losses of agricultural land	1866–1966	S	Occasional	[QRL 21]	6.2.1
Numbers and size of agricultural holdings	1866–1966	E & W, S	Occasional	[QRL 21]	6.2.1
Acreages and percentages by types of crops	1866–1966	GB	Occasional	[QRL 21]	6.2.1
Area under crops and grass	E & W, S, NI	UK	Occasional	[QRL 21]	6.2.1
Livestock on agricultural holdings	E & W, S, NI	UK	Annual	[QRL 4]	6.2.1. See also [QRL 57] for separate NI information
Production of crops in eight categories	E & W, S, NI	UK	Annual	[QRL 4]	6.2.1
Number of agricultural holdings by size of holding	"	UK	Annual	[QRL 4]	6.2.1
Area under crops and grass and numbers of livestock on agricultural holdings	E & W counties, Isle of Man, Jersey and Guernsey	E & W	Annual	[QRL 2]	6.2.1
Numbers by type of holding of areas under crops and grass	"	E & W	Annual	[QRL 2]	6.2.1
Acreage analyses and number of holding without crops and grass	"	E & W	Annual	[QRL 2]	6.2.1
Index of net agricultural output at constant prices		UK	Annual	[QRL 10]	6.2.2
Cropping, stocking and labour of each type of farming and size of business	4 Regions	E & W	Annual	[QRL 32]	6.2.3. These regions (now based on county boundaries in force after 1st April 1974) are North, West, East, and Wales
Outputs, inputs, net income and average valuations per farm by each type of farming and size of business	4 Regions	E & W	Annual	[QRL 32]	"

Acreage of crops, grass and rough grazing, horticultural crops and net losses of agricultural land	Counties and regions	S	Annual	[QRL 3]	6.2.1
Yield per acre of cereal and root crops	"	S	Annual	[QRL 3]	6.2.1
Mining and quarrying					
Output and productivity of coal	National Coal Board Areas	GB	Annual	[QRL 65]	6.3.1. See also Census of Production [QRL 14] and [QRL 20]
Consumption of coal by countries	E, W, S & NI	UK	Annual	[QRL 65]	"
Sand and gravel production	E, W, S and gravel regions	GB	Annual	[QRL 54]	6.3.2. There are fifteen gravel regions in England. Marine dredging included in figures
Land won production	Gravel region and service area	GB	Annual	[QRL 54]	6.3.2 "
Landings of marine dredged production	E, S, W and gravel regions	GB	Annual	[QRL 54]	6.3.2
Sand gravel production	Counties	E	Annual	[QRL 54]	6.3.2
Construction					
Value or orders for public and private sector by type of development	E & W, regions, S, NI	UK	Annual	[QRL 1]	6.4. See also main source [QRL 36] and Census of Production [QRL 14] and [QRL 20]
Public investment in new construction	"	UK	Annual	[QRL 1]	"
Public utilities					
Gas					
Number of customer by type of user	Gas regions	GB	Annual	[QRL 6]	6.5.1
Gas sold and gas used	"	GB	Annual	[QRL 6]	6.5.1
Production and availability	"	GB	Annual	[QRL 65]	6.5.1. [QRL 65] gives boundaries, areas and mid-year populations of GB gas regions
Public supply by types of sales	"	UK	Annual	[QRL 65]	6.5.1
Electricity					
Public supply by types of sale	Electricity boards	UK	Annual	[QRL 64]	6.5.2. NI includes sales by the Electricity Board of NI and the two LA undertakings
Supplies to area boards, installed capacity and electricity supplied	Area boards	GB	Annual	[QRL 58]	6.5.2. More detailed information given also on power stations
Electricity supplied	Electricity regions	E & W	Annual	[QRL 35]	6.5.2

Descriptive Title	Breakdown	Area	Frequency	Publication	Text Reference and Remarks
Public utilities *contd.*					
Water					
Water supplied and distributed, income and expenditure per 1000 gallons	LAs, water boards, water companies, bulk supply boards, Scottish boards E, W and S	GB	Annual	[QRL 66]	6.5.3. Until reorganisation in 1974
DISTRIBUTION					
Retail Trade					
Establishments, turnover and persons engaged by form of organisation and kind of business	Regions	GB	Quinquennial	[QRL 16]	7.1.9
Electricity and gas showrooms: establishments and turnover	Regions	GB	Quinquennial	[QRL 16]	7.1.9
Self-service grocery shops: establishments and turnover by form of organisation	Regions	GB	Quinquennial	[QRL 16]	7.1.9
Turnover per ft² of total floorspace by kind of business	Shopping centre types	GB	Quinquennial	[QRL 16]	7.1.9 Shopping centre types are: (i) all centres aggregated (ii) Central London (iii) Greater London Shopping Centres in 1961 with turnover of £5 m. and over (iv) As (iii) with turnover less than £5 m. (v) Provincial shopping centres in 1961 with turnover in 1961 of £20 m. or over (vi) As (v) with turnover between £10 m. and £20 m. (vii) As (v) with turnover under £10 m.
Turnover per ft² of selling space by turnover size of shop by kind of business	Shopping centre types	GB	Quinquennial	[QRL 16]	7.1.9
Establishments, turnover, employment, wages and salaries	Local authorities and towns	N/Ireland	Decennial	[QRL 17]	7.1.9

Item	Breakdown	Area	Frequency	Reference	Section / Remarks
Establishments, turnover and capital expenditure	"	N/Ireland	Decennial	[QRL 17]	7.1.9
Retail Prices					
Index of retail prices	Groups and sub-groups	UK	Monthly	[QRL 29]	7.2.1. Groups are:—food, drink, tobacco, housing, fuel and light, durable household goods, clothing and footwear, transport and vehicles, miscellaneous, services and outside meals
Service Trades					
Turnover of establishments	Types of services	GB	Quinquennial	[QRL 16]	7.3.1
Turnover of different types of organisation		GB	Quinquennial	[QRL 16]	7.3.1
Establishments, turnover, employment, wages and salaries	Local authorities and towns	N/Ireland	Quinquennial	[QRL 17]	7.3.1
Establishments, turnover and capital expenditure	"	N/Ireland	Quinquennial	[QRL 17]	7.3.1
Catering Trade					
Organisations, turnover and analysis by kind of business	Regions	GB	1969	[QRL 15]	7.3.2. Estimates are given of non-response and non-registered traders for organisations and turnover
Establishments, turnover number of bedrooms by kind of business	Regions	GB	1969	[QRL 15]	7.3.2. Some additional information on licensed hotels, motels, licensed guest houses and camps at either local authority and/or county level is available from BSO

EMPLOYMENT AND UNEMPLOYMENT

Item	Breakdown	Area	Frequency	Reference	Section / Remarks
Employment and Working population					
Employees by sex	Regions	UK	Annual	[QRL 13], [QRL 25]	8.1. Employees are total of employed and unemployed. Statistics provided both on NI and Census of Employment basis
Employees in employment	Regions	UK	Annual	"	8.1. On two bases as above
Employees in employment (male and female) by industry order and MLH	Regions	UK	Annual	"	8.1 "
Male employees in employment	Regions	UK	Annual	"	8.1 "

Descriptive Title	Breakdown	Area	Frequency	Publication	Text Reference and Remarks
Employment *contd.*					
Employees in employment by industrial order		UK	Monthly	[QRL 13], [QRL 25]	8.1
Employees (in employment and unemployed)	Development areas	UK	Annual	"	8.1. Five development areas are South Western, Merseyside, Northern, Welsh and Scottish
Employees in employment	"	UK	Monthly	"	8.1. "
Employees in production industries		GB	Monthly	[QRL 25]	8.1.13
Persons in employment by area of workplace: occupation by sex	Scale A	GB	Decennial	[QRL 18]	8.1
Persons in employment by area of workplace: industry by sex	Scale A	GB	Decennial	[QRL 18]	8.1
Working population aged 15 and over by place of work, residence and sex	Administrative areas	N/Ireland	Decennial	[QRL 19]	8.1
Working population aged 15 and over by means of transport to work, residence and sex	Administrative areas	N/Ireland	Decennial	[QRL 19]	8.1
Working population aged 15 and over by place of work, residence and sex	"	N/Ireland	Decennial	[QRL 19]	8.1
Civil service employees by ministerial responsibilities	Civil departments	UK	Quarterly	[QRL 43]	8.1.6
Industrial and non-industrial civil service staff	Services	N/Ireland	Annual	[QRL 27]	8.1.6
Employment in public and private sectors	Central government, local authorities, public corporations and private sectors	GB	Annual	[QRL 29]	8.1.6. Public sector definitions are not identical with those of [QRL 13] and [QRL 25]
Economically active population					
Males, females and married females by age groups	E & W, S, regions and conurbations	GB	Decennial	Part I, Economic Activity Tables [QRL 18]	8.2

Description	Area	Country	Frequency	Source	Section
Industry by status and occupation by sex	"	GB	Decennial	Part II, Economic Activity Tables [QRL 18]	8.2
Socio-economic groups of economically active males	"	GB	Decennial	Part IV, Economic Activity Tables [QRL 18]	8.2
Economically active persons by area of residence: occupation and status by sex	Scale A	GB	Decennial	County leaflets [QRL 18]	8.2
Economically active males by area of residence and socio-economic group	Local authorities	GB	Decennial	"	8.2
Population aged 15 and over by industry, economic position and marital condition	County boroughs and counties	N/Ireland	Decennial	[QRL 19]	8.2
Unemployment					
Unemployed men and women and unemployment rates	Regions	UK	Monthly	[QRL 13], [QRL 25]	8.3
Unemployed men, women, boys and girls	Development areas and intermediate areas	UK	Monthly	"	8.3
Unemployed persons and unemployment rates	Local areas	UK	Quarterly	"	8.5. Based on Census of Employment Areas formed from those covered by local employment offices so that smallest possible groups could be aggregated to give meaningful figures. [QRL 13] gives lists of local offices
Unemployed men and women (and men separately) by industry order	Regions	UK	Quarterly	"	8.3
Unemployed men and women by occupation	Regions	UK	Quarterly	"	8.3
Vacancies					
Vacancies notified and remaining unfilled by industry order for men and women	Regions	UK	Biannual	[QRL 13], [QRL 25]	8.4

Descriptive Title	Breakdown	Area	Frequency	Publication	Text Reference and Remarks
Vacancies *contd.*					
Vacancies notified and remaining unfilled by occupation for men and women	Regions	UK	Quarterly	,,	8.4
Numbers placed in employment by local employment and youth employment offices	Regions	UK	Annual	,, ,,	8.4
Unemployed persons by age and duration of unemployment	Regions	UK	Biannual	,, ,,	8.4
INCOME AND EXPENDITURE					
Income					
Average total weekly household income and number of households	Regions	UK	Annual	[QRL 30]	9.1.2. Standard errors of household income are given for UK only. See [QRL 31] for separate NI report
Average total weekly with average weekly household income averaged under seven heads (two years combined)	Regions	UK	Annual	[QRL 30]	9.1.4. The FES gives averages of some results for two successive years taken together. [QRL 31] gives results for 3-year period in N. Ireland
Sources of household income as percentages of total household income	Regions	UK	Annual	[QRL 30]	9.1.2
Households by size, composition, number of workers and income	Regions	UK	Annual	[QRL 30]	9.1.2
Employment status, occupational grouping and age of head of household	Regions	UK	Annual	[QRL 30]	9.1.2
Sources of household income by groups of households by administrative areas	GLC, provincial conurbations, other urban and rural	UK	Annual	[QRL 30]	9.1.2. The administrative areas given are UK totals for these types of areas
Sources of household income as percentages of total household income	,,	UK	Annual	[QRL 30]	9.1.2 ,,
Percentage standard errors of income of households and numbers of recording households	UK	UK	Annual	[QRL 30]	9.1.2

Description	Region		Frequency	Reference	Notes
Households by type (a) by gross weekly household income and (b) by gross weekly income of head of household	GB		Annual	[QRL 33]	9.1.5
Households by size by gross weekly household income	GB		Annua	[QRL 33]	9.1.5
Percentages of households in gross yearly household income groups receiving income from each income source	GB		Annual	[QRL 33]	9.1.5
Earnings from employment					
Average gross weekly earnings of full-time manual and non-manual men and full-time manual and non-manual women with numbers and standard errors	Region and sub-regions	GB	Annual	[QRL 46]	9.2. Figures are not given for groups with under 50 persons in sample for earnings had a standard error of more than 4% Men—aged 21 and over, Women—aged 18 and over.
Distribution of gross weekly earnings of full-time men and full-time adult women	Regions	GB	Annual	[QRL 46]	9.2
Medians, quartiles and deciles of gross weekly earnings of full-time men and women	Regions	GB	Annual	[QRL 46]	9.2
Average gross weekly earnings of full-time manual and non-manual men and women by industry group	Regions	GB	Annual	[QRL 46]	9.2
Wages and salaries	Regions	UK	Annual	[QRL 30]	9.2.1
Average weekly earnings, hours worked and hourly earnings by SIC and sex (men 21 years and over, women 18 years and over)	UK, manual workers	UK	Annual	[QRL 25]	9.2.5. The principal sources of employment not covered are coal mining, railways, shipping, distributive trades, catering trades, entertainment, commerce, and banking and private domestics
Average gross annual earnings of persons in civil employment according to age/sex	Regions (place of residence)	UK	Annual	[QRL 1]	9.2.7. DHSS holds unpublished tabulations for sub-regions and finer breakdown of age and earnings groups

Descriptive Title	Breakdown	Area	Frequency	Publication	Text Reference and Remarks
Personal income					
Range of income by family circumstances (number of children)	E & W, S, NI, regions (excluding conurbations)	UK	Annual	[QRL 61]	9.3.1. [QRL 61] covers 1969-70 onwards. For earlier years up to 1965-6 see [QRL 52] and from 1967-8 *Inland Revenue Statistics* [QRL 41]
Range of employment income (main source) and numbers in employment	"	UK	Annual	[QRL 61]	More detailed information on income is given in [QRL 61]
Medians and quartiles of income distribution	"	UK	Annual	[QRL 61]	Separate "regional" totals given for merchant navy, public departments (civilians and forces)
Upper and lower quartiles of income distribution as percentage of median	"	UK	Annual	[QRL 61]	9.3.1
Percentage standard errors of total numbers in income ranges	E & W, S, NI	UK	Annual	[QRL 61]	9.3.1
Percentage standard errors of total numbers in ranges by family status	UK	UK	Annual	[QRL 61]	9.3.1
Incomes totals and number of cases	Counties in E, W, S and NI	UK	Annual	[QRL 61]	9.3.1
Ranges of total net income	"	UK	Annual	[QRL 61]	9.3.1
Household expenditure					
Expenditure on housing by type of tenure	Regions	UK	Annual	[QRL 30]	9.4.1
Expenditure on commodities and services	Regions	UK	Annual	[QRL 30]	9.4.1
Expenditure on commodities and services as a percentage of total household expenditure	Regions	UK	Annual	[QRL 30]	9.4.1
Numbers and percentages of households with certain durable goods	Regions	UK	Annual	[QRL 30]	9.4.1
Expenditure on housing by type of tenure	Administrative areas—GLC and totals of provincial conurbations and rural areas	UK	Annual	[QRL 30]	9.4.1
Expenditure on commodities and services	"	UK	Annual	[QRL 30]	9.4.1

Expenditure of household by household composition	"	UK	Annual	[QRL 30]	9.4.1
Percentage standard errors of expenditure and numbers of recording households	"	UK	Annual	[QRL 30]	9.4.1
Household expenditure per person per week on seasonal convenience and other foods with comparative indices of foods prices and the real value of food purchased	Regions and type of area: conurbations (London, provincial), other urban areas (larger towns), smaller towns), semi-rural areas and rural areas	GB	Annual	[QRL 44]	9.4.3

TRANSPORT

Motor vehicles

Time series from 1926 onwards of licensed vehicles	Private cars and private vans, motor cycles, public transport vehicles, agricultural tractors, crown and exempt vehicles, other vehicles	UK	Annual	[QRL 37]	10.1.1
Time series 1903, 1909, 1920 and annually from 1930 of licensed vehicles	"	GB	Annual	[QRL 37]	10.1.1. Censuses have taken place for all years since 1903 but [QRL 37] gives only selected years to 1920. More detailed breakdowns are given for each of last 10 years
Vehicles with current licenses	Regions, E, W, S & NI	UK		[QRL 1]	10.1.1
Private cars and private vans with numbers per 1000 population, motor cycles, three wheelers, public transport vehicles, goods vehicles, tractors and exempt vehicles	Regions, registration and licensing authorities	UK	Annual	[QRL 37]	10.1.2.
New registrations of all vehicles by type and size		UK & GB	Annual	[QRL 37]	10.1.2
New registrations of vehicles	Regions, E, W, S & NI	N/Ireland	Annual	[QRL 1] [QRL 27]	10.1.2 10.1.2
Current licences and new registration of vehicles					
Households by numbers of cars	Scale A	E & W	Decennial	[QRL 18]	10.1.3

Descriptive Title	Breakdown	Area	Frequency	Publication	Text Reference and Remarks
Motor vehicles *contd.*					
Cars by garaging arrangements and type of building	Scale A	E & W	Decennial	[QRL 18]	10.1.3
Households by number of cars and socio-economic group of chief economic supporter	Regions and conurbation	S	Decennial	[QRL 18]	10.1.3
Households with 2 or more cars; garaging arrangements for first and second cars	Regions and conurbation	S	Decennial	[QRL 18]	10.1.3
Households without cars by tenure	"	S	Decennial	[QRL 18]	10.1.3
Households by number of cars and composition of household	"	S	Decennial	[QRL 18]	10.1.3
Working population aged 15 and over by means of transport to work, residence and sex		N/Ireland	Decennial	[QRL 19]	10.1.2
Vehicle availability	Regions	GB	Occasional	[QRL 45]	10.1.4. See technical appendix of [QRL 45] for comments on geographical distribution of achieved sample
Vehicle availability by numbers of employed members of household, weekly mileage, household income, type of area	Regions	GB	Occasional	[QRL 45]	10.1.4 "
Vehicle occupancy	Regions	GB	Occasional	[QRL 45]	10.1.4 "
Percentages of households with regular use of a car by number of cars		GB	Annual	[QRL 37]	10.1.5. Estimates are given for the last 10 years
Road traffic					
Vehicle miles by type of vehicle		GB	Annual	[QRL 37]	10.2.1
Vehicle miles by class of road		GB	Annual	[QRL 37]	10.2.1
Volume of traffic		GB	Monthly	[QRL 37]	10.2.1
Volume of traffic on motorways, trunk roads and classified roads		GB	Monthly and daily	[QRL 37]	10.2.1
Thousands of vehicles per day by class of vehicle at selected points	Motorways	E	Annual	[QRL 37]	10.2.2
Annual vehicle miles on motorway system		GB	Annual	[QRL 37]	10.2.2

Road mileage

Trunk, principal and other roads	E, S, & W	GB	Annual	[QRL 37]	10.3.1
Dual carriageway roads	E, S, & W	GB	Annual	[QRL 37]	10.3.1
Trunk, principal and other roads	Counties, county boroughs, E, S, & W	GB	Annual	[QRL 37]	10.3.1
Trunk, class I, class II, class III and unclassified roads		N/Ireland	Annual	[QRL 11]	10.3.1

Motorways

Trunk motorways in use, under construction and in preparation pool	Motorways	E	Annual	[QRL 53]	10.3.3
Local authority motorways in use, under construction and in preparation pool	Motorways	E	Annual	[QRL 53]	10.3.3
Trunk (including motorways) roads	Administrative areas	W	Annual	[QRL 28]	10.3.3
Milage of motorways		S	Annual	[QRL 9]	10.3.3. From 1973-4 onwards see *Roads in Scotland*, HMSO, Edinburgh

Road transport

Estimated tonnage and ton milage goods vehicles		GB	Annual	[QRL 37]	10.4.1
Estimated length of haul		GB	1967-8	[QRL 37]	10.4.1
Characteristic of road goods fleet		GB	1967-8	[QRL 63]	10.4.1
Transport operations of roads goods vehicles		GB		[QRL 63]	10.4.1
Tons and ton miles performed by goods fleet			Quarterly 1970 onwards	[QRL 63]	10.4.1
Average length of haul, proportion of tons carried analysed by type of commodity			"	[QRL 63]	10.4.1

Railways

Route mileages for passenger traffic	British Rail, LTE and other railways	GB	Annual	[QRL 47]	10.5.1
Number of passenger stations, carriages and seating capacity	"	GB	Annual	[QRL 47]	10.5.1
Passenger journeys, miles and average lengths of journeys	"	GB	Annual	[QRL 47]	10.5.1
Passenger receipts by fare categories	British Rail, LTE and other railways	GB	Annual	[QRL 47]	10.5.1

Descriptive Title	Breakdown	Area	Frequency	Publication	Text Reference and Remarks
Railways *contd.*					
Total rail travel	British Rail and LTE	GB	Annual	[QRL 47]	10.5.1
Passenger receipts and traffic		GB	Annual	[QRL 7]	10.5.1
Civil air transport					
Aircraft movements	BAAB airports	GB	Quarterly and annually	[QRL 51]	10.6.2. BAAB airports are Heathrow, Gatwick, Stansted, Prestwick, Edinburgh, Aberdeen and Glasgow
Passenger movements	BAAB airports	GB	”		10.6.2. Comparisons are given with other UK airports
Cargo and mail	BAAB airports	GB	”		10.6.3　　”
Ports					
Commodity analysis, foreign and coastwise traffic	Ports	GB	Annual	[QRL 26], Vol. I	10.7.1
Goods traffic by type of service and unit	Ports and planning regions	GB	Annual	”	10.7.1
Passenger movements by sea between the UK and overseas areas	Ports by main areas of landing and embarking	GB	Annual	”	10.7.1. Vol. II of [QRL 26] gives commodity analysis, overseas trading and port finance
Loaded container and roll-on goods traffic	Ports and port groups	GB	Annual	[QRL 22]	10.7.2
Container and roll-on traffic inwards and outwards by type of service and unit		N/Ireland	Annual	[QRL 22]	10.7.2

QUICK REFERENCE LIST KEY TO PUBLICATIONS

Reference number	Organisation responsible	Title	Publisher	Frequency or date of publication	Remarks
[QRL 1]	Central Statistical Office	*Abstract of Regional Statistics*	HMSO, London	Annual to 1974	Appears as *Regional Statistics* from 1975
[QRL 2]	Ministry of Agriculture, Fisheries and Food	*Agricultural Statistics, England and Wales*	HMSO, London	Annual	
[QRL 3]	Department of Agriculture and Fisheries for Scotland	*Agricultural Statistics Scotland*	HMSO, Edinburgh	Annual	
[QRL 4]	Ministry of Agriculture, Fisheries and Food	*Agricultural Statistics, United Kingdom*	HMSO, London	Annual	
[QRL 5]	Greater London Council, Department of Planning and Transportation Intelligence Unit	*Annual Abstract of Greater London Statistics*	Greater London Council, the Information Centre, County Hall, London, SE1	Annual	
[QRL 6]	British Gas Corporation (formerly Gas Council)	*Annual Report and Accounts*	HMSO, London	Annual	
[QRL 7]	British Railways Board	*Annual Report and Accounts*	British Railways Board	Annual	Published until 1971 by HMSO, London
[QRL 8]	Location of Offices Bureau	*Annual Report*	Location of Offices Bureau	Annual	
[QRL 9]	Scottish Development Department	*Annual report of the Scottish Development Department*	HMSO, Edinburgh	Annual to 1972	Cmnd. 5274 Superseded by *Planning and Development* (Reports of the SDD and Scottish Economic Department)
[QRL 10]	Ministry of Agriculture, Fisheries and Food	*Annual Review of Agriculture*	HMSO, London	Annual	
[QRL 11]	British Road Federation	*Basic Road Statistics*	British Road Federation	Annual	
[QRL 12]	Department of Employment	*British Labour Statistics: Historical Abstract 1886-1968*	HMSO, London	1971	
[QRL 13]	Department of Employment	*British Labour Statistics Year Book*	HMSO, London	Annual	
[QRL 14]	Business Statistics Office	*Business Monitor*	HMSO, London	Occasional	Various issues covering Annual Census of Production from 1970 onwards

Reference number	Organisation responsible	Title	Publisher	Frequency or date of publication	Remarks
[QRL 15]	Business Statistics Office	Catering Trades 1969	HMSO, London	1972	
[QRL 16]	Business Statistics Office (formerly Board of Trade)	Census of Distribution	HMSO, London	Quinquennially	Various volumes
[QRL 17]	Ministry of Commerce	Census of Distribution and other Services, Northern Ireland 1965	HMSO, Belfast	1969	
[QRL 18]	General Register Office, London (now Office of of Population Censuses and Surveys), General Register Office, Edinburgh	Census of Population in Great Britain	HMSO, London	Quinquennially	Various volumes, details of which are given in HMSO sectional lists No. 56 (OPCS) and No. 50 (miscellaneous) for Scottish census publications
[QRL 19]	General Register Office, Northern Ireland	Census of Population, Northern Ireland	HMSO, Belfast	Decennial	
[QRL 20]	Department of Trade and Industry (formerly Board of Trade)	Report on the Census of Production	HMSO, London	Quinquennial to 1968	Various volumes. Annual series from 1970 onwards are published in *Business Monitors* [QRL 14]
[QRL 21]	Ministry of Agriculture, Fisheries and Food	A Century of Agricultural Statistics: Great Britain 1866-1966	HMSO, London	1968	
[QRL 22]	National Ports Council	Container and Roll-on Port Statistics, Great Britain Part (I)	National Ports Council	Annual to 1971	From 1972 information published in [QRL 26]
[QRL 23]	Department of the Environment	Control of Office Development	HMSO, London	Annual	
[QRL 24]	Society of County Treasurers	County Planning Statistics	County Planning Officer's Society, County Planning Office, 9, Guildhall Rd, Northampton		Copies may be obtained from County Treasurer, P.O. Box 38 Milner House, Rope Walk, Ipswich. (Aug. 75)
[QRL 25]	Department of Employment	Department of Employment Gazette	HMSO, London	Monthly	Formerly the *Employment and Productivity Gazette* and the *Min. of Lab. Gazette*
[QRL 26]	National Ports Council	Digest of Port Statistics	National Ports Council	Annual	Superseded by *Annual Digest of Port Statistics* Vol I and II from 1972
[QRL 27]	Ministry of Finance, Northern Ireland	Digest of Statistics, Northern Ireland	HMSO, Belfast	Biannual since March 1954	
[QRL 28]	Welsh Office	Digest of Welsh Statistics	HMSO, Cardiff	Annual	

[QRL 29]	Central Statistical Office	Economic Trends	HMSO, London	Monthly	
[QRL 30]	Department of Employment	Family Expenditure Survey	HMSO, London	Annual	
[QRL 31]	Ministry of Finance, Economic Section	Family Expediture Survey (Northern Ireland)	HMSO, Belfast	Annual from 1967	1968 and 1969 in one volume
[QRL 32]	Ministry of Agriculture, Fisheries and Food	Farm Incomes in England and Wales	HMSO, London	Annual	
[QRL 33]	Office of Population Censuses and Surveys	The General Household Survey	HMSO, London	Annual	(Introductory report-1970)
[QRL 34]	Greater London Council, L. F. Gebbett	GLC Land Use Survey 1966—Research Report No. 8	Greater London Council, The Information Centre, County Hall, London, SE1	1972	
[QRL 35]	Intelligence Section, Electricity Council	Handbook of Electricity Supply Statistics	Electricity Council, 30 Millbank, London, SW1P 4RD	Annual	
[QRL 36]	Department of the Environment (formerly Ministry of Housing and Local Government)	Handbook of Statistics (Local Government, Housing and Planning)	HMSO, London	Annual until 1971	Information obtainable in Miscellaneous Local Government and Planning Statistics 1972-75 and in Development Control Statistics 1976 onwards—available from Directorate of Statistics, DOE From 1976 information appears in Transport Statistics Great Britain
[QRL 37]	Department of the Environment	Highway Statistics	HMSO, London	Annual to 1975	
[QRL 38]	Department of the Environment	Housing and Construction Statistics, (formerly Housing Statistics)	HMSO, London	Quarterly	
[QRL 39]	Department of the Environment	Housing Land Availability in the South East	HMSO, London	1974	
[QRL 40]	Ministry of Development, Northern Ireland	Housing Return for Northern Ireland	HMSO, Belfast	Quarterly	
[QRL 41]	Inland Revenue	Inland Revenue Statistics	HMSO, London	Annual	
[QRL 42]	Ministry of Development, Northern Ireland	Local Authority Rate Statistics, Northern Ireland	HMSO, Belfast	Annual	
[QRL 43]	Central Statistical Office	Monthly Digest of Statistics	HMSO, London	Monthly	

Reference number	Organisation responsible	Title	Publisher	Frequency or date of publication	Remarks
[QRL 44]	Ministry of Agriculture, Fisheries and Food	*National Food Survey Committee— Domestic Food Consumption and Expenditure*	HMSO, London	1973	
[QRL 45]	Ministry of Transport	*National Travel Survey, Part II— Personal travel by public and private transport*	HMSO, London	1967	
[QRL 46]	Department of Employment	*New Earnings Survey*	HMSO, London	Annual	
[QRL 47]	Department of the Environment	*Passenger Transport in Great Britain*	HMSO, London	Annual to 1975	From 1976 information appears in *Transport Statistics Great Britain*
[QRL 48]	The Government Social Survey	*Private Motoring in England and Wales*	HMSO, London	1969	
[QRL 49]	Department of the Environment, Welsh Office	*Rates and Rateable Values in England and Wales*	HMSO, London	Annual	
[QRL 50]	Scottish Development Department	*Rates and Rateable Values in Scotland*	HMSO, Edinburgh	Annual	
[QRL 51]	The British Airports Authority	*Report and Accounts*	British Airports Authority	Annual	Also published separately as House of Commons Paper
[QRL 52]	Inland Revenue	*Report of the Commissioners of H.M.'s Inland Revenue*	HMSO, London	Annual	
[QRL 53]	Department of the Environment	*Roads in England*	HMSO, London	Annual	
[QRL 54]	Department of the Environment	*Sand and Gravel Production*	HMSO, London	Annual	
[QRL 55]	Scottish Statistical Office	*Scottish Abstract of Statistics*	HMSO, Edinburgh	Half-yearly	Replacing *Digest of Scottish Statistics* from 1971
[QRL 56]	Central Statistical Office	*Social Trends*	HMSO, London	Annual	
[QRL 57]	Department of Agriculture, Northern Ireland (formerly Ministry of Agriculture for Northern Ireland)	*Statistical Review of farming*	Department of Agriculture, Northern Ireland	Annual	
[QRL 58]	Central Electricity Generating Board	*Statistical Yearbook*	CEGB	Annual	Information Services, CEGB Sudbury House, 15 New- gate St., London, EC1A

[QRL 59]	Department of the Environment, Welsh Office	Statistics for Town and Country Planning, Series I, Planning Decisions	HMSO, London	Annual to 1975	Known until 1967 as Statistics of Decisions on Planning Applications. Replaced in 1976 by Development Control Statistics available from Directorate of Statistics, DOE
[QRL 60]	Department of the Environment	Statistics for Town and Country Planning, Series II Floorspace	HMSO, London	Occasional	N.B. No. 2 published 1972 No. 3 ,, 1974 No. 4 ,, 1976
[QRL 61]	Inland Revenue	Survey of Personal Incomes	HMSO, London	Annual	
[QRL 62]	Department of Industry	Trade and Industry (formerly Board of Trade Journal)	HMSO, London	Weekly	
[QRL 63]	Department of the Environment	The Transport of Goods by Road	HMSO, London	1974	1967-8 and 1970-2
[QRL 64]	Northern Ireland Information Service	Ulster Year Book	HMSO, Belfast	Annual	Information on planning applications provided by Department of Housing, local Government and Planning
[QRL 65]	Department of Trade and Industry (formerly Ministry of Power	United Kingdom Energy Statistics (formerly Annual Digest of Energy Statistics)	HMSO, London	Annual	From 1975 Digest of UK Energy Statistics
[QRL 66]	Chartered Institute of Public Finance and Accountancy	Water Statistics	Chartered Institute of Public Finance and Accountancy	Annual	Published by Institute of Municipal Treasurers for 1971-72 but copies for all years available from 1, Buckingham Place, London SW1 E6HS

BIBLIOGRAPHY

[B 1]   Berman, L. S. 'The Central Register of Businesses.' *Statistical News* (CSO), **4**, 5, Feb. 1969.

[B 2]   Blake, J. 'The development control crisis.' *Town and Country Planning*, April 1974.

[B 3]   Browning H. E. 'The Census of Production.' *Statistical News* (CSO), **5**, 1, May 1969.

[B 4]   Browning, H. E. and Fessey, M. C. 'The statistical unit in business enquiries.' *Statistical News* (CSO) **13**, 1, May 1971.

[B 5]   Burton, T. L. and Cherry, G. E. *Social Research Techniques for Planners*, University of Birmingham Centre for Urban and Regional Studies. Allen & Unwin, London, 1970.

[B 6]   Cherry, G. E. *The Evolution of British Town Planning*, Leonard Hill Books, Leighton Buzzard, 1974.

[B 7]   Cooke, R. and Peretz, J. 'The National and Local Government Statistical Liaison Committee.' *Statistical News* (CSO), **29**, 7, May 1975.

[B 8]   Coppock, T. E. 'Land use.' *Reviews of UK Statistical Sources*, Vol. VIII, No. 14. Pergamon Press, Oxford, 1978.

[B 9]   Cullingworth, J. B. *Town and Country Planning in Britain*. Allen & Unwin, London, 1970.

[B 10] Curtis, S. R. 'Post-census Survey on the Census of Production 1970.' *Statistical News* (CSO) **17**, 7, May 1972.

[B 11] Farthing, S. M. 'Housing in Great Britain.' *Reviews of UK Statistical Sources*, Vol. III, No. 5. Heinemann Educational Books, London, 1974.

[B 12] Fessey, M. C. 'How the 1972 Retail Census can help industry and retailer.' *Trade and Industry*, 25th Nov. 1970.

[B 13] Fessey, M. C. 'Progress of statistical work at the Business Statistics Office.' *Statistical News* (CSO), **20**, 12 Feb. 1973.

[B 14] Fleming, M. C. 'Housing in Northern Ireland.' *Reviews of UK Statistical Sources*, Vol. III, No. 6. Heinemann Educational Books, London, 1974.

[B 15] Fowler, R. F. *Duration of Unemployment on the Register of Wholly Unemployed*, Studies in Official Statistics Research Series No. 1 (CSO). HMSO, London, 1968.

[B 16] Gebbett, L. F. 'Analysis of planning decisions.' *GLC Intelligence Unit Quarterly Bulletin*, No. 20, Sept. 1972.

[B 17] Glover, K. F. 'The outline of the road goods transport industry. *Journal of the Royal Statistical Society*, Series A, Vol. 117, pp. 297-330, 1954.

[B 18] Glover, K. F. and Miller, D. N. *The Transport of Goods by Road*. HMSO, London 1960.

[B 19] Harris, R. and Scott, D. 'The role of monitoring and review in planning.' *The Planner*, Journal of the Royal Town Planning Institute, June 1974.

[B 20] Hart, Sir W. O. and Garner, J. F. *Introduction to the Law of Local Government and Administration* Butterworths, London, 1973.

[B 21] Hartley, C. 'The implications of suggested density controls in terms of housing land requirements.' Department of the Environment, 1973, unpublished.

[B 22] Howard, R. S. *Movement of Manufacturing Industry in the United Kingdom 1964-5*, Study by the Board of Trade. HMSO, London, 1968.

[B 23] Kemsley, W. F. F. *Family Expenditure Survey Handbook on the Sample, Fieldwork and Coding Procedures*. HMSO, London, 1966.

[B 24] Kent-Smith, D. B. and Pritchard, A. 'Development of statistical regions in the United Kingdom.' *Statistical News* (CSO), **27**, 1, Nov. 1974.

[B 25] Kingaby, S., Powell, M. G. and Redpath, R. U. 'Survey of personal income in London.' *GLC Research Memorandum* No. 350, June 1972.

[B 26] Lewes, F. M. M. and Parker, S. R. 'Leisure.' *Reviews of UK Statistical Sources*, Vol. IV, No. 7. Heinemann Educational Books, London, 1975.

[B 27] Lickorish, L. J. 'Tourism.' *Reviews of UK Statistical Sources*, Vol. IV, No. 8. Heinemann Educational Books, London, 1975.

[B 28] McLeod, K. and Watkin, E. 'Regional earnings and regional development.' *Centre of Environmental Studies*—Urban Working Paper 1, 1969.

[B 28a] Mackay, D. I. and Buxton, N. K. *British Employment Statistics*, Basil Blackwell, Oxford (forth-coming).

[B 29]   Mackenzie, R. H. 'The new planning law in Northern Ireland.' *Journal of Planning and Environmental Law*. Sweet & Maxwell, London, May 1974.

[B 29a] Munby, D. L. 'Road Passenger Transport.' *Reviews of UK Statistical Sources,* Vol. VII, No. 12. Pergamon Press, Oxford, 1978.

[B 30]   Scott, J. R. and Tanner, J. C. '50 Point Traffic Census—the first five years.' *Road Research Technical Paper* No. 63. HMSO, London, 1962.

[B 30a] Stark, T. 'Incomes.' *Reviews of UK Statistical Sources*, Vol. VI, No. 11. Pergamon Press, Oxford, 1978.

[B 31]   Thatcher, A. R. 'Statistics of unemployment in the UK.' *Department of Employment Gazette*. HMSO, London, May 1974.

[B 32]   Timbers, J. A. 'Traffic survey.' *Road Research Laboratory Report No. LR* **206**. Ministry of Transport, London, 1968.

[B 32a] Watson, A. H. 'Roads goods transport.' *Reviews of UK Statistical Sources*, Vol. VII, No. 13. Pergamon Press, Oxford, 1978.

[B 33]   Wheller, B. 'Definition of a dwelling.' *GLC Research Memorandum No.* **453**. GLC, London, 1975.

[B 34]   White, B. *Sourcebook of Planning Information*. Bingley, London, 1971.

[B 35]   Whitehead, F. 'Social security statistics.' *Reviews of UK Statistical Sources*, Vol. II, No. 4. Heinemann Educational Books, London, 1974.

[B 36]   British Urban and Regional Information Systems Association. *BURISA*. C/o PTRC Ltd., 167 Oxford Street, London, W1. [Bi-monthly issues of newsletter.]

[B 37]   Department of Employment. *Classification of Occupations*. HMSO, London, 1960, 1966, 1970, 1972.

[B 38]   Ministry of Housing and Local Government, Welsh Office, *Development Plans. A Manual on Form and Content*, HMSO, London, 1970.

[B 39]   Scottish Development Department. *Development Plans—A Scottish Interim Manual on Form and Content*, HMSO, Edinburgh, 1971.

[B 40]   Ministry of Public Building and Works. *Directory of Construction Statistics*. HMSO, London, 1968.

[B 41]   Statistics Sub-Committee, Distributive Trades Economic Development Council, *Distributive Trade Statistics—A Guide to Official Statistics*, National Economic Development Office, HMSO, London, 1970.

[B 42]   Department of the Environment. *The Future of Development Plans*. HMSO, London, 1972.

[B 43]   Economic Development Committee for the Distributive Trades, Shopping Capacity Sub-Committee, *Future Pattern of Shopping*, HMSO, London, 1971.

[B 44]   Department of the Environment. *The General Information System for Planning*. HMSO, London, 1972.

[B 45]   Greater London Council. *Greater London Development Plan—Report of Studies*. Greater London Council, 1968.

[B 46]   Inter-departmental Committee on Social and Economic Research. *Guides to Official Sources No.* **6**. *Census of Production Reports*. HMSO, London, 1961.

[B 47]   Central Statistical Office, *The Measurement of Charges in Production and other Output Measures*. HMSO, London, 1976.

[B 48]   Department of Employment and Productivity. *Method of Construction and Calculation of the Index of Retail Prices*. HMSO, London, 1967.

[B 49]   Department of the Environment. *National Land Use Classification*, HMSO, London 1975.

[B 50]   Department of the Environment. 'Notes for guidance in interpreting Inland Revenue floorspace data for England and Wales.' DOE, unpublished, 1972.

[B 51]   Retail Prices Index Advisory Committee. *Proposals for Retail Price Indices for Regions*, Cmnd. 4749. HMSO, London, 1971.

[B 52]   Central Statistical Office, *Standard Industrial Classification*. HMSO, London, 1948, 1958, 1968.

[B 53]   Standing Conference on London and South Eastern Regional Planning. Various monitoring papers. 28 Old Queen Street, London, SW1.

[B 54]   Central Statistical Office. *Statistical News*. HMSO, London. Quarterly.

[B 55]   Inter-departmental Working Party. *Unemployment Statistics*, Cmnd. 5157. HMSO, London, 1972.

[B 56]   *Unit for Retail Planning Information Newsletter*, 229 King's Road, Reading, RG1 4LS. Quarterly from Autumn 1975.

[B 57]   Economic Development Committee for the Distributive Trades, Shopping Capacity Sub-Committee, Models Working Party. *Urban Models in Shopping Studies*. NEDO, London, 1970.

APPENDIX OF FORMS

The forms included in this appendix are limited to a selection of those directly concerning the administration of planning procedures. No forms have thus been included for surveys and returns referred to in this review such as the Family Expenditure Survey and the General Household Survey since more detailed treatments of such surveys including specimen forms have been and will be given in other reviews in this series, e.g. see [B 11] for GHS—Household Schedule and Form P.2—Housing Returns to the DOE.

List of Forms

1. *Model planning application forms*

These forms were issued as Appendix 1 to the Joint Circular 23/72 from the DOE and 58/72 from the Welsh Office. Part of the *Notes for Applicants* are also reproduced here. In practice there has been some adaptation by individual authorities of these models but they may nevertheless be taken as reliable guides to the information provided by applicants. Part I, or its local variant, has to be completed by all applicants and similarly Part II additionally for those applications involving industry, offices, warehousing, storage and shops. The completed application forms and the resulting decisions are used in the provision of returns of planning applications for Series I [QRL 59], outstanding planning permissions required by Circular 32/75 (see 11.2.1) and information required on certain industrial developments by Circular 62/74.

2. *Application for an office development permit (ODP)*

The circumstances under which ODPs have been required are briefly described in Section 5.2.7 and the statistics derived from them are referred to in Section 5.2.8 onwards. The applications which were originally sent to the BOT are now sent to the DTI.

3. *Application for an industrial development certificate (IDC)*

Information on the submission of IDCs is given in Section 5.1.6 onwards and the statistics that they have provided are discussed in Section 5.1.7 onwards.

4. *Statement of planning applications (DC/1)*

Annual returns to the DOE by planning authorities in England and Wales of permissions and refusals resulting from planning applications. The results (see Section 3.2.1) are published in [QRL 59].

Please read the accompanying notes before completing any part of this form.

APPLICATION FOR PERMISSION TO DEVELOP LAND ETC.

Appendix 1 to Department of the Environment
Circular 23/72   (Welsh Office Circular **58/72**)

Town and Country Planning Act 1971

_____ completed copies of this form and plans

must be submitted to _____

For office use only
Ref.
Date received

PART 1—to be completed by or on behalf of all applicants as far as applicable to the particular development.

1. **Applicant** (in block capitals)	**Agent** (if any) to whom correspondence should be sent (in block capitals)
Name	Name ....
Address	Address ....
....	....
Tel. No.	Tel. No. ....

2. **Particulars of proposal for which permission or approval is sought**

(a)   Full address or location of the land to which this application relates and site area (if known)

(b)   Brief particulars of proposed development including the purpose(s) for which the land and/ or buildings are to be used

(c)   State whether applicant owns or controls any adjoining land and if so, give its location

(d)   State whether the proposal involves:—

    (i)   New building(s)

    (ii)   Alteration or extension

    (iii)   Change of use

    (iv)   Construction of a)   vehicular new access to a)   pedestrian highway)

    (v)   Alteration of an)   vehicular existing access)   pedestrian to a highway)

State Yes or No

If residential development, state number of dwelling units proposed and type if known, e.g. houses, bungalows, flats.

3. **Particulars of Application** (see note 3)

(a)   State whether this application is for:—

    (i)   Outline planning permission

    (ii)   Full planning permission

State Yes or No

If yes, delete any of the following which are not reserved for subsequent approval

1	siting	3	external appearance
2	design	4	means of access

    (iii)   Approval of reserved matters following the grant of outline permission

If yes, state the date and number of outline permission
Date
Number

    (iv)   Renewal of a temporary permission or permission for retention of building or continuance of use without complying with a condition subject to which planning permission has been granted

If yes, state the date and number of previous permission and identify the particular condition (see note 3d).
Date
Number
The condition

4. Particulars of Present and Previous Use of Buildings or Land

State

(i)   Present use of buildings/land   (i)

(ii)   If vacant, the last previous use   (ii)

5. Additional Information

(a)   Is the application for Industrial,   State   office, warehousing, storage or   Yes or No   If yes, complete Part 2 of this form

shopping purposes?

(See note 5)

(b)   Does the proposed development   State   involve the felling of any trees?   Yes or No   If yes, indicate positions on plan

(c)   (i)   How will surface water be disposed of?   (i)

       (ii)   How will foul sewage be dealt with?   (ii)

6. Plans

List of drawings and plans submitted with the application

Note: *The proposed means of enclosure, the materials and colour of the walls and roof, landscaping details etc should be clearly shown on the submitted plans, unless the application is in outline only*

I/We hereby apply for

*(a)   planning permission to carry out the development described in this application and the accompanying plans, and in accordance therewith.

OR   *(b)   planning permission to retain buildings or works already constructed or carried out, or a use of land already instituted as described on this application and the accompanying plans.

OR   *(c)   approval of details of such matters as were reserved in the outline permission specified herein and are described in this application and the accompanying plans.

*Delete whichever is not applicable.

Date..................................   Signed ....

On behalf of ....

(insert applicants name if signed by an agent)

Note *An appropriate certificate must accompany this application unless you are seeking approval to reserved matters—see Note* 10. *The following certificate will be appropriate if you are the owner or have a tenancy of all the land. Only one copy need be completed.*

Certificate under Section 27 of the Town and Country Planning Act 1971

Certificate A*   I hereby certify that:—

1. $\dfrac{\text{*I am}}{\text{The applicant is}}$ *the estate owner in respect of the fee simple / entitled to a tenancy   of every part of the land to which the accompanying application relates.

*2. None of the land to which the application relates constitutes or forms part of an agricultural holding; or

*2. $\dfrac{\text{*I have}}{\text{The applicant has}}$ given the requisite notice to every person other than $\dfrac{\text{*myself}}{\text{himself}}$ who, 20 days before the date of the application, was a tenant of any agricultural holding any part of which was comprised in the land to which the application relates, viz:—

Name of Tenant	Address	Date of service of notice

Signed ....

*On behalf of ....

Date ....

*Delete where inappropriate

PLANNING APPLICATION FORM. PART 2

Application No.
(For Official Use Only)

Additional Information required in respect of Applications for Industrial, Office, Warehousing, Storage or Shops

(Those questions relevant to the proposed development to be answered)

1. In the case of industrial development, give a description of the processes to be carried on and of the end products, and the type of plant or machinery to be installed.	
2. If the proposal forms a stage of a larger scheme for which planning permission is not at present sought, please give what information you can about the ultimate development.	
3. Is the proposal related to an existing use on or near the site ? If so, please explain the relationship.	State Yes or No
4. Is this a proposal to replace existing premises in this area or elsewhere which have become obsolete, inadequate or otherwise unsatisfactory ? If so, please give details including gross floor area of such premises and state your intentions in respect of those premises.	State Yes or No

5.

		Existing (if any)	Proposed new floor space
(a)	What is the total floor space of all buildings to which the application relates ?	(a) m²/sq. ft.	m²/sq. ft.
(b)	What is the amount of industrial floor space included in the above figure ?	(b) m²/sq. ft.	m²/sq. ft.
(c)	What is the amount of office floor space ?	(c) m²/sq. ft.	m²/sq. ft.
(d)	What is the amount of floor space for retail trading ?	(d) m²/sq. ft.	m²/sq. ft.
(e)	What is the amount of floor space for storage ?	(e) m²/sq. ft.	m²/sq. ft.
(f)	What is the amount of floor space for warehousing ?	(f) m²/sq. ft.	m²/sq. ft.

6. (i)	How many (a) office (b) industrial and (c) other staff will be employed on the site as a result of the development proposed ?	(a) Office	(b) Industrial	(c) Other staff
(ii)	If you have existing premises on the site, how many of the employees will be new staff ?	(i) (ii)		
(iii)	If you propose to transfer staff from other premises, please give details of the numbers involved and of the premises affected.			

7. In the case of industrial development is the application accompanied by an industrial development certificate ? If "No" state why a certificate is not required.	State Yes or No
8. What provisions have been made for the parking, loading and unloading of vehicles within the curtilage of the site ? (Please show the location of such provision on the plans and distinguish between parking for operational needs and other purposes)	
9. What is the estimated vehicular traffic flow to the site during a normal working day ? (Please include all vehicles except those used by individual employees driving to work).	
10. What is the nature volume and proposed means of disposal of any trade effluents or trade refuse ?	
11. Will the proposed use involve the use or storage of any of the materials of type and quantity mentioned in note 12 ? If "Yes" state materials and approximate quantities.	State Yes or No

SPECIMEN

Application for Planning Permission or Approval of Reserved Matters

NOTES FOR APPLICANTS

1. These notes are provided to help you with your planning application. It may also be helpful to you to call at to discuss your proposals before you complete the application.

2. If you are in doubt whether your project requires planning permission because it may not involve development or it may be permitted by the General Development Order, you may apply to the local planning authority to determine the issue under section 53 of the Town and Country Planning Act 1971. This may be done by letter which should give details of the present or last use of the land/building and of the proposed new use including the processes to be carried out and any machinery to be employed. You may at the same time as you seek such a determination apply for planning permission.

3. This form is for the under-mentioned kinds of application and if the information required does not fit the circumstances of your case you should seek further advice from the Council.

    a. **Outline planning application:** If you wish to know whether planning permission will be given for the erection of buildings on a site before you have detailed drawings prepared, you should make an application for outline permission. It will help the authority if you give as much information as possible. If you show in reply to question 3 in the application form certain matters as reserved for subsequent approval but send the authority plans showing tentative ideas of how the development might be carried out, those plans will not form part of the application, and any permission granted may require you to obtain approval of these matters. If you show any matters as not reserved for approval you must include in your application plans showing adequate details.

    b. **Approval of reserved matters.** Where outline permission has already been granted, you may make application on this form for approval of the reserved matters. Please state in your answer to question 2(b) for which reserved matters you are now seeking approval. Approval of details should not be sought if current proposals would not be within the outline permission or would conflict with conditions imposed; in those circumstances you should apply for planning permission. The outline permission will lapse if details of reserved matters have not been submitted to the authority within the period stipulated in the permission or, where no period was stipulated in the permission, as laid down in section 42 of the 1971 Act.

    c. **Full planning application.** This is needed if you wish to make a change in the use of land or buildings, or carry out works or operations including the erection of buildings where you do not wish to follow the outline procedure above. It will also apply where development has been carried out without permission and application is being made to regularise the position; in this kind of case you should, in reply to question 2(b) make it clear that you wish to retain the existing buildings or continue existing uses.

    d. **Renewal of temporary permission or relief from conditional permission.** If you wish to apply for permission to retain works or to continue a use without complying with a condition subject to which the original permission was granted (including any requirement that works should be removed or that the use should cease by a specified date), you should say so in reply to question 2(b) and give the date of the original permission and identify the particular condition in reply to question 3(iv).

4. **Renewal of time-limited permission** (Section 41 or 42 of the 1971 Act). Where the application is made before the appropriate time limit expires provision is made for a simplified application. It is not necessary for this form to be completed; the application may be by letter giving sufficient detail of the previous planning permission to enable the authority to identify it; such application must be accompanied by the appropriate certificate under section 27 of the Act.

5. **Industrial Development.** If you are seeking planning permission (outline or detailed) for the erection of more than   square feet (square metres) of industrial floor space, including ancillary space such as staff rooms, storage etc, your application cannot be considered unless you attach a copy of an Industrial Development Certificate issued by the Department of Trade and Industry. A certificate is also needed where an application relates to a change of use affecting a corresponding floor area. Industrial floor space is measured internally.

6. **Minerals.** The form does not include questions dealing with the special matters on which information is needed in the case of a mineral application. On request the council will say what information they need in such a case.

DRAWINGS AND PLANS

7. **Site plans.** Each application (except for approval of reserved matters) should be accompanied by a plan or sketch of not less than 1/2500 scale, showing the site to which it refers and its boundary. This requirement will not be insisted on if the site has a numbered address in a regular sequence of numbers in a clearly defined road. The application site should be edged or shaded in red and any other adjoining land owned or controlled by the applicant edged or shaded blue.

8. **Other drawings.** Except in the case of outline applications where additional drawings are not normally needed, these should normally be to a scale of not less than 1/100 if in metric or ¼" to a foot if imperial measure is used. They should show the existing features of the site including any trees, and be in sufficient detail to give a clear picture of any new building. They must indicate clearly the location of the proposed development within the site and the amount of floor space to be used for different purposes. Where existing and new works are shown on the same drawing, new work should be distinctively coloured. The materials to be used in the external finish of walls and roofs and their colour should be indicated on the drawings. The means of access to the site, and the type of wall, fence or other means of enclosing the site should be shown. Applications for change of use of part of a premises must be accompanied by floor plans showing the extent of the existing and proposed uses unless the areas are readily identifiable by description.

9. Plans and drawings are open to inspection by the public. Applicants are not, however, required to disclose any proposed security arrangements.

O.D.P. No. _____

APPLICATION FOR AN OFFICE DEVELOPMENT PERMIT

Under the Control of Office and Industrial Development Act 1965

INSTRUCTIONS

A. After completion, two copies of this form should be sent to the Board of Trade Regional Office at the address shown at the foot of page 4.

B. Not all the questions apply to each applicant and only those which appear relevant should be answered. Any answers for which there is insufficient space on the form should be given on separate sheets of paper marked with the number of the question(s).

C. "Office floor space" means gross floor space in an office or in the office part of a building and includes ancillary space used wholly or mainly in connection with the office space, e.g. canteens, halls, staircases, lavatories, etc.

D. All areas are to be ascertained by external measurement (i.e. to the outside of external walls) in square feet. If one or more of the walls enclosing the space to be measured is a party wall, measurement should be to the centre of the wall.

E. "Office workers" means those engaged in office work which includes the purposes of administration, clerical work, handling money, telephone and telegraph operating and the operation of computers. "Clerical work" includes writing, book-keeping, sorting papers, filing, typing, duplicating, punching cards or tapes, machine calculating, drawing and the editorial preparation of matter for publication.

F. The Board of Trade Regional Office will give advice on any point of difficulty.

THE APPLICANT

1. Name and address of applicant

2. Nature of business

3. Name and address of applicant's parent company or group, if any

---

THE PROJECT

4. Address of the proposed development

5. Name of local planning authority

6. Date(s) of planning application, and of permission if obtained (Please attach a copy of each)

    Application: _____

    Permission: _____

7. If the offices are part of a wider development scheme, give details (stating whether an industrial development certificate has been applied for)

8. Office floor space for which planning permission has been obtained (since 4th November, 1964, in the metropolitan region, since 13th August, 1965, in the Birmingham conurbation or since 20th July, 1966, in the remainder of the South East, East Anglia, East Midlands and West Midlands Economic Planning Regions) for any other development:

    (a) in respect of the same building   _____ sq. ft.

    (b) in respect of an adjacent or contiguous building for the purposes of the scheme now under consideration or for the purposes of the same undertaking   _____ sq. ft.

OD/1

THE PROJECT (continued)

9.   Will the proposed offices be for the applicant's sole use?   Yes/No
     If not, give details of all intended occupiers:-

Name	Address	Nature of business in proposed office	Area of office floor space (sq. ft.) in new offices

                                                                      Sq. ft.

10. Area of office floor space   (a) New building/Rebuilding
     for which a permit is required

                                  (b) Alteration/Extension

                                  (c) Change of use

                                  (d) Continuing use as offices

11. Areas of ancillary space   Canteen
     (other than circulation and
     lavatories) included in 10   Garage

                                    Storage

Please answer questions 12-17 as appropriate

New building/Rebuilding, Alteration/Extension

12. Present use of site of proposed development

13. Floor space to be created for each purpose
     not appropriate to 10 above (e.g., shop,
     warehouse, residential etc.)

For Alteration/Extension only

14. Present area and use of all floor space
     in the building, excluding area in 10(b)

Change of Use

15. Present use of floor space in 10(c)

16. Present area and use of all other
     floor space in the building

Continuing Use as Offices

17. In all cases where space is shown in 10(d)
     state:-

         (a) use prior to office use

         (b) expiry date of planning permission

         (c) extension needed

EMPLOYMENT

18. Number of office workers (i.e. managerial, executive, professional, technical, clerical, and others) to be employed when the development is in full use:

	Male		Female		Total
	Under age 18	18 years and over	Under age 18	18 years and over	
Now employed at site of development					
To be transferred from other offices					
To be recruited					
Total employment when development in full use (viz. _____ 196 _____)					

Applicants total non-office employment at site of the development   _____

19. Give the address(s) of the office(s) from which workers will be transferred

20. For a development intended for occupation by more than one organisation, give available details of the numbers to be employed by each user

EXISTING PREMISES

21. Address(es) and area(s) of existing premises occupied by applicant:

Address	Square feet					
	Offices	Industrial	Canteen	Storage		Other
				Office	Industrial	

22. If the existing offices are to continue in office use:

    (a) who will occupy the offices?

    (b) how many office workers will be employed there?

23. If the existing offices are not to continue in office use state:

    (a) amount of office floor space to be demolished

    (b) amount of office floor space to be transferred to other uses (and state uses)

    (c) number of office workers at present employed in (a) and (b)

NEED FOR NEW OFFICES

24. State the purpose:

    (a) for which the new offices are required, e.g.
head office, works office, branch office, or department.

    (b) of the rest of the development, if any

25. Why are the existing offices considered
inadequate?

26. What steps have been taken to find alternative
accommodation under construction or already built?
What accommodation has been found and why is it
considered unsuitable?

27. Why cannot the activities to be carried on in the
proposed development be undertaken outside the
area of control?

GENERAL SUMMARY

28. Other information in support of this application:

Signature _____   *Date* _____

Name in
BLOCK LETTERS _____   *Status* _____

For official use only

Stamp of issuing office   Received by   M.O.L. Ex. Area

                                                 S.I.C. (M.L.H.)

                                                 L.A. Area

IDC/1A No. ....

**APPLICATION FOR AN INDUSTRIAL DEVELOPMENT CERTIFICATE
FOR THE ERECTION OR EXTENSION OF A BUILDING**

*This application (no copies required) should be sent to the issuing office of the
Department of Trade and Industry whose address is shown overleaf and who will be
glad to advise on any point of difficulty.*

For applications for the change of use of a building, please complete form IDC/1B

1. (a) Name of firm* ....

    (b) Address of Registered Office ....

    ....

    (c) Nature of business ....

    *If the firm is one of a group of companies, or a subsidiary, please give name of
Group or Parent Company

    ....

2. Location of Project

(a) Name of planning authority to whom
it is intended to make application
for planning permission

(b) Name of local authority in whose
area site is located

(c) Exact location of proposed development
i.e. postal address or reference to
prominent features, e.g. road junction

3.	Floor space (in sq. ft.) of:	Production*	Ancillary			Total
			Storage	Offices	Other	
(a)	Proposed development					
(b)	Existing buildings ✝					
(c)	Building now under construction or for which approval has already been given ✝					
(d)	Buildings to be demolished (if any) ✝					

* *Any ancillary space which is not separate from the floor space used for the
industrial process(es) should be included under production.*

✝ *On the same site as the proposed development*

4. Purpose for which the
new building is required,
giving particulars

5.   Any buildings erected on the site
or for which planning permission
has been granted, and/or changes
of use for which planning permission
has been granted, since an i.d.c.
was last issued, or since 1st April,
1960, whichever is the later date

6.   If as a result of the proposed development you
would vacate any premises you at present occupy
please state location, size and (if known) probable
future use of the building(s) to be vacated.

7.   Employment

Please give total number of workers
(administrative, technical and clerical
staff and operatives)

	Men and Boys	Women and Girls	Total
(a) Now employed at this location			
(b) Expected to be employed when any buildings now under construction or already approved for construction are completed			
(c) Expected to be employed when the proposed development is in full use			

(d)   When is proposed development likely
to be in full use?*   .... 19 ...

(e)   If workers are to be transferred
from other works, please give their
numbers and the locations of the works
from which they are being transferred

** If this date is more than four years from the time of application, please state at
(c) how many you expect to employ within this period and how many subsequently.*

Date .... Signature ....

Status of Signatory .... Telephone No. ....
(Signatory should be a director
or partner of the firm.)

FOR OFFICIAL USE ONLY

Stamp of Issuing Office	Received by	
Department of Trade and Industry LONDON & SOUTH EASTERN REGIONAL OFFICE Cromwell House, Dean Stanley Street, Millbank, London, SWIP 3HY		L.O. .... Category .... S.I.C. .... Type .... GF/PF ....

Statement of planning applications decided during the year 1/4/75 to 31/3/76

in the area of ....District Council

London Borough Council

INCLUDING planning applications in approved Green Belts or National Parks (3)

DC/1

(repeat)

Class of development (5) and (6)	Permissions granted (2) (7)	Refusals	Total decisions
A Building, engineering and other operations (8)			
1 Residential (a) Redevelopment (9)			
(b) New development within the boundary of any approved or submitted Town Map......			
(c) New development outside the boundary of any approved or submitted Town Map			
2 Industrial			
3 Offices			
4 Shops and restaurants			
5 Petrol stations (with or without repair facilities) and repair garages			
6 Domestic garages and lock-up garages (including those for commercial vehicles)			
7 Mineral working			
8 (a) Storage/Warehousing			
(b) Betting offices			
(c) Educational buildings			
(d) Health, welfare and social services			
(e) Amusement/Recreation			
(f) Public utility works			
(g) Agricultural buildings (other than dwellings)			
(h) All other classes of building and other operations			
B Changes of use (including incidental building operations) (5)			
9 To residential caravan sites (7) (including sites for single caravans) without time limit			
for limited period only			
10 To Holiday caravan sites (7) (including sites for single caravans) without time limit			
for limited period only			
11 To Car Sales			
12 To Car parks			
13 Change of use to office			
14 Change of use to shop			
15 Change of use to industry			
16 (a) Change of use to storage/warehousing			
(b) Change of use to betting office			
(c) Change of use to education			
(d) Change of use to health, welfare and social services			
(e) Change of use to amusement/recreation			
(f) Change of use to agricultural buildings (other than dwellings)			
(g) All other changes of use of land and of buildings			
TOTALS			

1 N/L
2 N/L
3 N/L
4 N/L

Note: The small numerals in brackets refer to the numbered notes overleaf.

See notes 3 & 4 and delete whichever statement is not applicable.   *The figures relating to any part of an approved Green Belt or of a National Park for which the council is the planning authority have been returned on the appropriate form and not included in this return.*   *No part of an approved Green Belt or a National Park lies within the council's administrative area for the purposes of planning control.*

Signature ....

Designation ....

Authority ....

Notes

1   This return relates only to planning applications which have been decided by a local planning authority (ie, District or County Council, Joint Board or other National Park authority) during 1975/6. **Separate returns for Green Belt and National Parks areas are no longer required** and decisions relating to these areas should be included in this return (see note 3 below).

2   The return is intended to provide information about *the number of applications* which local planning authorities have had to determine. Where there have been successive applications for the development of the same site all of them should be included in the figure given. An outline application, and any subsequent requests for approval to detailed plans should, for the purposes of this return, be counted as separate applications and included in the figures.

3   Where planning control in a National Park is exercised by a Joint Board or National Park authority the returns may be made by the Park or District authorities, whichever is the more convenient. Joint Planning Boards or Park authorities making returns should send in a separate form (QC/1) for each District area within the Park.

4   It will be seen that the classes of development listed fall into two main groups—first, building, engineering and other operations, and secondly changes of use. Where a proposal has elements which fall into more than one class, the application should be classified according to the major interest, if there is one. For example, a new block of ships with a flat above each shop should be included in "Shops and restaurants" (4). Similarly a change of use of part of a house to shop, even though it involves some building operations, should be classed as "Change of use to shop" (14). A comprehensive proposal including development of various types but having no predominant feature should be included in "All other classes of building and other operations" (8(h)). No application should be included in more than one class.

5   For practical reasons the number of classes for which separate figures are to be given has been severely limited. Proposals which do not quite fit any of the listed classes should be included in whichever of the miscellaneous items is relevant (8(h) or 16(g)). For example, holiday chalet sites should not be included with "Holiday caravan sites" (10), nor should car breakers' yards and dumps be included with "Car parks" (12).

6   Applications which received permission for a limited period or subject to other conditions should be included in the figures for "Permissions granted", except for classes 9 and 10, where a distinction should be made between consents given with and without time limit.

7   "Building operations" (in the sub-heading for the first eight classes) include not only the erection of new buildings, but also extensions and alterations, provided these are not merely incidental to a change of use (Note 5).

8   For the purpose of this return "Redevelopment" (1(a)) means the provision of new housing on land which has previously been built upon or used for any purpose other than agriculture of forestry.

SUBJECT INDEX TO TOWN AND COUNTRY PLANNING STATISTICS